Criminology Explains Police Violence

Criminology Explains
Police Violence

Philip Matthew Stinson, Sr.

UNIVERSITY OF CALIFORNIA PRESS

University of California Press
Oakland, California

© 2020 by Philip Matthew Stinson, Sr.

Cataloging-in-Publication Data is on file at the Library of Congress.

ISBN 978-0-520-30008-8 (cloth : alk. paper)
ISBN 978-0-520-30009-5 (pbk. : alk. paper)
ISBN 978-0-520-97163-9 (ebook)

29 28 27 26 25 24 23 22 21 20
10 9 8 7 6 5 4 3 2 1

CONTENTS

ACKNOWLEDGMENTS

This book is dedicated to my son, Matthew, who has taught me the importance of never giving up. I would like to thank the following people who encouraged me to write this book or offered guidance and words of encouragement along the way: Randall Wallace, Maura Roessner, John Liederbach, Susan Brown, Michael Buerger, Adam Watkins, Derek Mason, Andy Kozal, Jeffrey Cohen, Robert Brooks, Will Oliver, Jeffrey Ian Ross, David Jackson, Steve Demuth, Bill Balzer, James Ciesla, Virginia Dubasik, Ron Scherer, Dan Lee, Yolanda Trimble, Madison Wetzell, and Sabrina Robleh. This book would not have been possible without the support of the Wallace Action Fund at Tides Foundation.

I would also like to thank each of the student research assistants who worked with me in the Police Integrity Research Group at Bowling Green State University over the past decade: Christy Adams, Sana Ali, Warifa Azeez, Jenna Bartholomew, Marta Bettinelli, Joelle Bridges, Gregory Burger, Zachary Calogeras, Evin Carmack, Paige Crawford, Vincent Crews, Natalie DiChiro, Monica Eaton, Charles Eberle, Douglas Fay, Rachel Fettinger, Madeline Fisher, Quinn Foley, Jacob Frankhouser, Maria Gardella, Madison Guinther, Austin Hadamuscin, Joanna Hanson, Justin Hernandez, Breanne Hitchen, Isaac Houser, Dominique Howard, James Howell, Ryan Hunter, Stacey Jacovetti, Nicholas Jellison, Lyla Johnson, Jessica Kirkpatrick, Tanya Korte, Conor Krofft, Theresa Lanese, Mariah Lax, Megan Lewis, Krista Long, Morgan Major, Monica Matticoli, Katelyn Moran, Kathleen Murray, Raven Ory, Jordan Parker, Tiffany Pleska, Andrew Pope, Jessica Rentner, Julia Rhoad, Ashley Roberts, Matthew Roberts, Dennis Roehrig, Andrew Rudnik, Bethany Sager, Adam Sierra, Lexie Sigsworth, Scott Stevenson,

Mackenzie Stewart, Jacob Stose, Callie Stull, Christin Swanepoel, Megan Swinehart, Taylor Szalkowski, Preston Tartt, Erin Thomson, Natalie Todak, Kevan Toney, Marissa Ulmer, Baylee Valerius, Troy Wendel, Chloe Wentzlof, Georgianna Whitely, Mallorie Wilson, Emma Wirtz, Natalie Wise, and Alton Woods.

Introduction

POLICE VIOLENCE

Some cops are bad. Some cops are even criminals. The power of having a gun and a badge leads some police officers to think they can commit crimes because they are above the law, exempt from law enforcement, and able to get away with it. After all, who polices the police?

A serial rapist attacked numerous woman over a period of several years from 2002 to 2005 in Bloomington, Illinois. A masked intruder would tie up his victims and cover their heads with a pillowcase, sometimes first using duct tape to cover his victim's mouth before sexually assaulting a woman. The rapist told one of his victims that he had been stalking her and knew everything about her. He knew what car her fiancé drove, what her sister looked like, and he even knew her work schedule. Afterward, he would force his victims into the bathroom for a long soak in the bathtub to wash away any forensic evidence. He knew exactly what he was doing. Then one night around 1:00 a.m. in June 2006, a twenty-nine-year-old woman named Jonelle Galuska awoke to her startled dog and immediately called the police. Galuska had felt for some time that she was being watched by someone, maybe even stalked. She just sensed it. Bloomington police officer Dave Zeamer was first to arrive and saw a man, dressed in all-black clothing, standing outside next to the side of Galuska's house. Officer Zeamer immediately recognized the person. It was Bloomington police sergeant Jeff Pelo. Pelo's explanation did not make any sense; he claimed that he was scouting out the area looking for a new place for his mother-in-law. Detectives later realized that Pelo had run the license plate numbers of several of his victims in a law enforcement database. Several of his victims identified Pelo as their rapist. Pelo selected his rape victims carefully by using the training, resources, power, and status of being a police officer. He thought he could get away with it. Even without

DNA or other forensic evidence at his trial, a jury convicted Pelo on dozens of sexual assault, armed home invasion, burglary, and stalking charges. Ultimately, a judge sentenced Pelo to 375 years in prison. Jeff Pelo—a seventeen-year police veteran—was a serial rapist.[1]

Jeff Pelo is not the only police officer to misuse a law enforcement database. During the years 2005–12, at least 142 police officers across the United States were charged with a crime for illegally accessing a law enforcement database.[2] Drug corruption or an officer's misguided pursuit of women is often at the root of these cases. Numerous cases involve a police officer enmeshed in the illegal drug trade who provided information from a law enforcement database to a drug dealer. In other cases an officer was paid to provide confidential law enforcement information to private investigators. Often the officers arrested for misusing a law enforcement database did so to obtain personal information, such as the home address of a woman they had come into contact with on the job as a police officer. Presumably, the information was then used to contact or stalk the woman. Some officers used license plate numbers to find out the identity of the new boyfriend of an ex-wife or ex-girlfriend. Prior to the 1980s the only way for a police officer to access vehicle and driver license information was to request that a police teletype operator or dispatcher conduct a computer search. The ubiquity of mobile computers in police cruisers has made it tempting for some officers to illegally obtain information from law enforcement databases. The procedures in place to prevent misuse of the database systems are passive because no human interaction is needed for a police officer to search a law enforcement database. I suspect that the problem at many police departments is much larger than the 142 known cases of an officer being arrested for criminal misuse of a law enforcement database would suggest. The secret nature of the police subculture provides ample opportunities for officers to misuse law enforcement resources.

THE PROBLEM OF POLICE VIOLENCE

Nobody starts their career as a police officer thinking they will end up a criminal. No rookie police officer wants to become a bad cop. Successful applicants for jobs as sworn law enforcement officers all look good on paper. They might have attended college for a few years or earned a college degree. They might be a military veteran. They are all in good physical shape and typically have no known criminal history and no known drug problems. Their neighbors, friends, college professors, former employers, and roommates all indicate to background investigators that they are good people who have the personality suitable to be a police officer. They even have good credit scores. Most law enforcement agencies require applicants for a police officer position to have all the above characteristics and to pass pre-employment psychological and polygraph examinations. Yet, there is something about the job of a police officer that leads some officers to become criminals.

The job of a police officer is unlike any other job. It is a job that comes with incredible power to control other people. Officers cannot simply "turn off" their jobs when they go home at the end of a shift. Police officers on the street work without close supervision. They always carry their badge and gun even when they are off duty. Police officers do not tolerate others well and they like to be in charge. They are used to telling people what to do and expect that people will follow their directions. Eventually most police officers conclude that it is an us-versus-them world. There are police officers and there are assholes. Officers think that everyone who is not a police officer is probably an asshole. This reality of the police subculture shapes everything a police officer does. It leads many officers to conclude that they are above the law and can do whatever they want to do. Sometimes this includes police officers engaging in criminal activity. For some officers, things unravel only when their crimes become public.

Chronic Offenders

Some police officers manage to keep their jobs even after being arrested multiple times. Occasionally officers are arrested numerous times within a short period of time in which their personal lives unravel. Other officers are arrested numerous times over the course of many years during their careers.

Lt. Kenneth Parrish of the Prince George's County Police Department in Maryland was arrested for driving under the influence of alcohol on four occasions in 2008. In February of that year, Parrish was arrested while allegedly driving a police cruiser off duty while drunk. Then in July he was arrested for driving under the influence, driving with a suspended license, and reckless driving, and again in September he was arrested for driving under the influence and failing to stop after a motor vehicle accident. The arresting officer in the July incident had to deploy a Taser and use pepper spray to get Parrish handcuffed. Parrish ended the year with a fourth drunk driving arrest in December 2008, where his blood alcohol content was three times the legal limit and he admitted to drinking a half pint of vodka earlier in the morning. After the December arrest, acting police chief Roberto Hylton was quoted in the *Washington Post* saying that Parrish "had taken a downward spiral" after a difficult year in which his marriage ended and his mother died.[3] The chief also noted that Parrish had been treated for alcohol dependence through the county's employee assistance program. Parrish was convicted of driving under the influence for only the last arrest. In July 2009, he was sentenced to one year of supervised probation. Although most of Parrish's arrests do not involve acts of police violence, his multiple drunk driving arrests within a short time are typical of sworn law enforcement officers who get repeatedly arrested when their personal lives are unraveling.

Another officer, John Lewis of the Schenectady Police Department in New York, was arrested nine times between April 2008 and May 2010. It should have been clear to anyone that Lewis's life was spiraling out of control as he was arrested for violating an order of protection, stalking, drunk driving, criminal mischief, witness tampering, and other offenses during those three years. Lewis was terminated from the police department just before he was arrested on a federal firearms offense in 2010. After his death in 2014 at the age of forty-four, his attorney Michael Horan said, "It's tragic that his personal life and career took such a terrible turn. He made some bad choices but was a good cop in many ways."[4] All indications are that Kenneth Parrish and John Lewis were good cops, but they unraveled personally and professionally after each having served about twenty years as a police officer, when their problems led to their multiple arrests.

Rarely, an officer is arrested for crimes over many years during his or her law enforcement career, often for seemingly unrelated offenses. These are bad cops who game the system to keep their jobs for a long time after being flagged as problem officers. Jeff Brunswick, who joined the Cincinnati Police Department in Ohio in 1980, was one such officer.[5] He was fired in 1990 after a supervisor accused him of operating his car in a reckless manner and then lying about it. The allegation was that Brunswick had used his police cruiser to bump a fleeing suspect. He was also accused of firing bottle rockets into a parking lot in northern Kentucky while he was drunk. The Civil Service Commission upheld Brunswick's termination, but a court later reversed that decision and ordered that he be reinstated as a Cincinnati police officer. He was promoted to sergeant in 1997.

Brunswick was arrested in May 2005 and charged with misdemeanor assault after a woman accused him of punching her in the face and choking her. The criminal case was dismissed following mediation between Brunswick and the woman. Then, at age fifty-one in August 2008, Brunswick was charged with menacing and stalking a twenty-seven-year-old female police officer under his supervision. He was acquitted at a jury trial in the Hamilton County Municipal Court. In February 2011, Brunswick got into a bar fight and punched another off-duty police officer in the face. He pleaded guilty to a minor misdemeanor charge of disorderly conduct and was sentenced to one day in jail. A minor misdemeanor in Ohio is the equivalent of a violation, infraction, or summary offense in other states. Brunswick continued to work as a police sergeant in Cincinnati until he was indicted two years later in May 2013 on two counts of obstruction of justice and four counts of unauthorized use of property. It was Brunswick's fourth arrest while employed as a police officer. The indictment stemmed from allegations that Brunswick had accessed a law enforcement database to assist two men in Chesterfield, Virginia, who were wanted for armed robbery in South Carolina. While on suspension after the indictment, Brunswick was charged with promoting prostitution following an incident at a Cincinnati-area hotel where he had sex with a prostitute and then paid for her hotel room so that she could service other men.[6] Sergeant Brunswick retired from the Cincinnati Police Department at age fifty-seven with thirty-three years of service, and later he was sentenced to three years of probation after pleading guilty to promoting prostitution and offenses related to unauthorized use of a police computer.

Cops Think That Everyone Is an Asshole

Police officers often view the world as an us-versus-them place, even when off duty, and are used to people doing exactly what a police officer tells them to do. This sometimes leads to odd encounters at public events. Every year at least a few off-duty police officers around the country are arrested at sporting events and concerts, often at outdoor venues. Sometimes the arrest is for public intoxication during a concert or drunk driving when leaving a concert. Other times off-duty officers are arrested for incidents that arise from the officers' intolerance for assholes. Lt. Robert Walker and Sgt. Kenneth Ciesla, both of the Hudson Police Department in Ohio, were convicted in 2005 for beating a man whose picnic basket accidentally bumped their car as they left a James Taylor concert at the Blossom Music Center.[7] Two Pittsburgh, Pennsylvania, police detectives, Patrick Moffatt and Joseph Simunovic, were arrested in 2007 for aggravated assault in the parking lot of the Post-Gazette Pavilion outside a Toby Keith concert they were attending.[8] Nicholas Maurer, a police officer in Fremont, California, was convicted of assault after getting mad at an off-duty firefighter whose wife pointed out to Maurer that he was leaning against the door of a train on the way to a Kenny Chesney concert in 2008 at AT&T Park.[9] An off-duty Altoona police officer in Pennsylvania, Matthew Plummer, was charged with aggravated assault in 2013 for punching a man who exposed his buttocks following a Kid Rock concert at First Niagara Pavilion. Plummer pleaded guilty to a reduced charge of disorderly conduct, was fined $1,000, and kept his job with the Altoona Police Department.[10]

Ohio Highway Patrol trooper Jason Fantone was arrested and charged with disorderly conduct for throwing peanuts at deputy sheriffs in January 2011 while attending a Cleveland Browns football game against the Pittsburgh Steelers at Cleveland Browns Stadium.[11] Trooper Fantone was also charged with vandalism for damaging the latch on the steel door of the holding cell where he was taken after being arrested and removed from the stadium.[12] He entered a court diversion program that allowed for his record to be expunged after a period of good behavior. Fantone was fired from the Ohio Highway Patrol following his January 2011 arrest but was reinstated a year later when an arbitrator overturned his dismissal.[13] Trooper Fantone was arrested again in July 2013 for operating a vehicle while impaired when he was found sleeping in his vehicle outside a Buffalo Wild Wings restaurant. He had been asked to leave the restaurant after being served two beers and falling asleep on the bar. He later pleaded guilty to a reduced charge of being in physical control of a vehicle while intoxicated and was sentenced to thirty days in jail with all but three days suspended, placed on probation for six months, and required to attend an alcohol treatment program; his driver's license was also suspended for six months except for driving to work or medical appointments.[14] Fantone was terminated from the Ohio Highway Patrol in September 2013.

It is not uncommon in these scenarios for the officer being arrested to let it be known to the arresting officers that he or she, too, is a police officer. In one such 2007 incident, Officer Kenneth Magielski of the Boynton Beach Police Department in Florida was arrested while off duty for disorderly intoxication at a minor league baseball game in Port St. Lucie. An off-duty firefighter told a deputy sheriff that Magielski was upset that his child was not allowed to participate in on-the-field youth activities. When deputies asked Magielski to leave the ballpark, he said, "I am a fucking cop, you do not know who you're messing with. . . . I can't believe they gave you two assholes a uniform."[15] Other times an off-duty officer's dislike for someone the officer perceives as being an asshole results in the officer's arrest at his or her child's sporting event. In one such incident during 2007, Sgt. William Stradley of the Marcus Hook Police Department in Pennsylvania was cited for stalking and harassment after he punched a referee at a youth association wrestling match.[16] Stradley apparently took issue with a penalty imposed against his son by the referee for an illegal wrestling move and unnecessary roughness. Howard Lewis, a Charlotte-Mecklenburg, North Carolina, police officer, was charged with assaulting his daughter's coach during a softball game in 2009.[17] Two years earlier Lewis had been involved in another incident at a youth basketball game and told to leave.

Revenge as Police Violence

Some police officers who think they are above the law engage in acts of revenge that result in criminal charges. Rogue officers have the power of the gun and badge, as well as an arsenal of law enforcement tools and resources not available to the general public, which are occasionally used for the improper purpose of exacting revenge on someone. The ability to mess with somebody for sport is too tempting for some bad cops because they know they can get away with it and are routinely exempt from law enforcement consequences. Police officers who commit crimes of revenge think they are above the law and can do whatever they want. Their actions often suggest they are out of control with rage. Cases in which a police officer is arrested for a crime that constitutes an act of revenge generally involve an officer using either (a) his or her police authority to violently beat someone or (b) the resources of law enforcement to embarrass someone, even having someone falsely arrested as the ultimate act of retaliation. Several police officers in New Jersey were convicted in 2016 of conspiracy for retaliating against another officer as an act of revenge. Officers Michael Dotro, Victor Aravena, Brian Favretto, and Sgt. William Gesell of the Edison Police Department conspired in 2012 against a North Brunswick police officer who had arrested one of Dotro's relatives for drunk driving after being shown a police union card. Although no retaliation occurred, the four Edison officers conducted surveillance and illegally accessed a law enforcement database to find personal information on the North Brunswick officer. Meanwhile, Dotro was convicted and sentenced to twenty years in prison for attempted murder and aggravated arson after firebombing his captain's home in the middle of the night.[18] Prosecutors alleged that Dotro was retaliating against the police captain for ordering him to undergo a psychological evaluation following the eleventh excessive force complaint filed against Dotro.

Even high-ranking officers have been arrested for crimes of revenge. Suffolk County police chief James Burke in New York pleaded guilty and was sentenced in late 2016 to forty-six months in federal prison for criminal deprivation of civil rights for assaulting and threatening to kill a handcuffed and shackled suspect, Christopher Loeb, at a police station. Loeb was a twenty-six-year-old heroin addict in 2012 when he broke into the police chief's department-issued SUV and stole a duffle bag containing the chief's gun belt, ammunition, cigars, sex toys, and adult pornography. Chief Burke allegedly pressured police officers who witnessed his attack on Loeb to conceal the event through an elaborate cover-up. Officers later testified in federal court that Burke went berserk in the interrogation room when Loeb called the chief a "pervert" and that the beating ended only when a detective said, "Boss, that's enough, that's enough."[19] Apparently, Loeb mistakenly believed that the pornography he stole from the police chief's vehicle was child pornography.

Off-Duty Officers Who Misuse Their Guns

In 1980 James Fyfe found that the reasons were not readily articulable for many off-duty acts of bizarre violence involving police officers and their firearms.[20] He noted that a growing body of literature had concluded that intense psychological pressures on police officers and their families might explain such bizarre violence. Research shows that 6.6 percent ($n = 316$) of the off-duty police officers arrested during the years 2005–12 were involved in gun incidents of bizarre violence.[21] One such case in 2005 involved William Doyle, a lieutenant with the New York Police Department. Doyle became enraged at his forty-seventh birthday party when his wife arrived with a cake, but not the ice-cream cake that he wanted. According to the police report, Doyle doused the cake with a glass of wine and then held a masonry hammer to his wife's head, saying, "I could kill you right now and open up your head." He then held his department-issued handgun to the back of his wife's head and screamed, "I will kill you!" Before leaving to work the midnight shift later that evening, Doyle grabbed his handgun again and threatened his wife while pointing the gun at her chest, saying, "Don't fuck with me. . . . I'll end this now."[22] Menacing charges were dismissed a few months later when Doyle's wife refused to cooperate with prosecutors.[23]

Officer-involved domestic violence is a form of police violence often over-looked because victims feel they have nowhere to go when the abuser is a member of the local police department. Presumably one concern a victim might have in calling 9–1-1 is that the abuser might not only get arrested but also lose his or her job as a result of the arrest.[24] Persons convicted of a qualifying misdemeanor crime of domestic violence are prohibited from possessing firearms or ammunition pursuant to the Lautenberg Amendment to the federal Gun Control Act.[25] There is no exception from this statutory provision for active-duty military personnel or sworn law enforcement officers. The US Supreme Court later clarified that a qualifying crime of domestic violence includes any offense committed by a person who has a specified domestic relationship with the victim, whether or not the misdemeanor statute itself designates the domestic relationship as an element of the crime.[26]

Officer-involved domestic violence emerged from the shadows in 2003 when Tacoma, Washington, police chief David Brame shot and killed his estranged wife, Crystal Judson, and then himself in front of their two children in a parking lot outside a shopping mall. Brame had been accused of repeatedly threatening and strangling his wife during the months preceding the murder-suicide, and a subsequent investigation revealed details of long-term domestic abuse by the police chief.[27] The murder of Crystal Judson galvanized a movement to increase public awareness of domestic violence within police families and demands for accountability. My research has identified more than 1,250 arrest cases from across the country during the years 2005–13 in which an officer was arrested for a crime arising out of an officer-involved domestic violence incident.

Predatory Police Sexual Violence

A few cops are sexual predators.[28] They believe they can get away with their crimes because they are police officers. These predator officers carefully select their victims based on a calculation that the victim will not be believed if she or he files a complaint. Many victims are girls and women living on the fringes of society; they are often addicts, sex workers, homeless, or maybe have extensive criminal records themselves.

The police sexual violence that has arguably received the most media attention in recent years involved twenty-seven-year-old Oklahoma City police officer Daniel Holtzclaw.[29] He was in his third year with the police department when charged with numerous on-duty sex crimes in August 2014, including rape, rape by instrumentation, forcible sodomy, sexual battery, and indecent exposure. Investigators soon realized that Holtzclaw was a sexual predator who had attacked more than a dozen black women he encountered on the streets and during traffic stops while on patrol in some of the city's poorest neighborhoods. Holtzclaw targeted mostly older women of color he thought were unlikely to contact the police or be believed if they did. Some were the most vulnerable women in the community, including victims Holtzclaw thought were sex workers, criminals, or women with drug addiction or alcohol problems. One of his victims was a grandmother who thought Holtzclaw was going to kill her if she did not comply with his demands. His youngest victim was a seventeen-year-old who testified at trial that Holtzclaw pulled up next to her in his patrol car while she was walking home. He proceeded to rape the girl on the front porch of her family's home, telling her that he had to conduct a search. Holtzclaw was convicted on eighteen of thirty-six charges at a jury trial, including four counts of forcible rape, and in early 2016 he was sentenced to 263 years in prison.

There are also bad cops who victimize children and adolescents they come into contact with while working as a police officer. Robert Pavlovich always liked young girls.[30] In 1995 Pavlovich, then a police officer in Manheim Township, Pennsylvania, was acquitted at a jury trial on charges of indecently assaulting a teenage girl. He was fired from the Manheim Police Department but soon found work as a police officer about fifty miles northwest in Duncannon, Pennsylvania. Pavlovich left the Duncannon Police Department after borough officials received two similar complaints alleging sexual misconduct involving underage girls. In 2000 he again found work as a police officer, this time in Marysville, a borough along the Susquehanna River about fifteen miles southeast of Duncannon. Seven years later the Pennsylvania State Police filed criminal charges against Pavlovich alleging that he had used his position of authority as a Marysville police officer to coerce and solicit sex from fourteen girls, some as young as twelve. Pavlovich was convicted at a jury trial on charges including involuntary deviate sexual intercourse, indecent assault, bribery in official matters, and corruption of minors. He was sentenced to serve ten to twenty-six years in prison and as of July 2019 was incarcerated at the State Correctional Institution in Albion, Pennsylvania.

Dozens of police officers across the country have been arrested since 2005 for sex crimes against teenage girls who participate in law enforcement

Explorers programs. Samuel Walker and Dawn Irlbeck, writing in 2003, first recognized the sexual exploitation of teenage girls in police department–sponsored Explorers programs as a pattern of police sexual abuse.[31] The Explorers programs are career-oriented scouting programs for teenagers, sometimes as young as thirteen, who are interested in learning about police work. One of the main activities for individual youths participating in Explorer programs is to go on ride-alongs with an on-duty patrol officer. Some police departments and sheriff's offices limit the number of ride-alongs an Explorer can go on with the same officer, and there have been instances where police supervisors do not allow teenage girls to ride with officers who have developed a reputation for pursuing sexual relationships with teenage girls.

Easy Targets

Bad cops who prey on vulnerable victims is a problem not limited to cases of police sexual misconduct. Dozens of on-duty sworn law enforcement officers across the country were arrested in 2005–16 for stealing money from Hispanic motorists during traffic stops. A Tennessee case offers facts similar to most of such shakedown arrest cases. Two Chattanooga police officers, Frank Goodwyn and O'Dell Draper, were each sentenced in 2006 to eighteen months in federal prison after pleading guilty to one count each of conspiracy to violate civil rights pursuant to 18 U.S.C. § 241. According to court records filed by the US attorney for the Eastern District of Tennessee, "Hispanic individuals were targeted because they would often be illegal residents concerned about possible deportation, might have large amounts of money on them, i.e., they would have no bank account, speak little or no English and would, therefore, be unlikely to complain about the officers' conduct."[32]

The Officer Shuffle

Even when police officers are arrested, they sometimes do not lose their jobs and often are not convicted of any crime. Many officers convicted of misdemeanors are not terminated from their jobs, especially in states that have collective bargaining in the public sector. However, in right-to-work states, where often there is no property right to continued public employment, it is common for police officers who are arrested for any offense to be immediately terminated. Some officers who are terminated after being arrested end up working as police officers in other jurisdictions, sometimes even in other states, where their new employers are somehow unaware of their prior law enforcement experience or criminal history.

Zusha Elinson, a reporter at the *Wall Street Journal*, called me in early 2015 and wanted to know if I would be willing to share some of my data on arrested officers. I had known Zusha for several years and the research question he proposed intrigued me. How many officers who have been convicted of a crime and/or terminated from their employment after being arrested are still police officers today, either at the same law enforcement agency or another one? This was not an easy question to answer. A team of reporters, including Zusha Elinson, Louise Radnofsky, Gary Fields, and John Emshwiller, endeavored to obtain lists of certified and decertified police officers from each state across the country. The plan was to compare that list of 832,275 names against my list of 3,458 officers who had been arrested from 2005 to 2011 and then either convicted or fired. The project took almost two years to complete. Almost 10 percent, 332 of the officers, remained in law enforcement. Some of these officers had been convicted for injuring or killing someone through recklessness or negligence or for drunk driving offenses. Others had been convicted of assaults, weapons offenses, stealing, or lying.[33]

One officer whose name appeared on lists from two states was Claudia Wright. She was fired in 2010 from the Daytona Beach Police Department in Florida when arrested for uttering a forged instrument and criminal use of personal identification information after she allegedly forged her grandmother's signature on loan applications to buy a car. Wright surrendered her state certification as a police officer in a plea deal with prosecutors to dismiss the criminal charges against her. Nevertheless, we found Wright in 2016 employed as a deputy sheriff in Richmond, Virginia.

We found that other officers were still employed at the same police department where they had worked when they had been arrested years earlier for crimes of violence. Gary Steele of the Detroit Police Department was suspended from his job after being arrested in 2008 following a fight with his girlfriend. Steele was charged with several felonies, including assault with attempt to murder, for allegedly hitting his girlfriend with a bat, pinning her down, firing three shots near her head, and putting the gun into her mouth while screaming that he would kill her.[34] A year later Steele was back on the job as a Detroit police officer, having pleaded no contest to a misdemeanor charge of reckless discharge of a firearm. Steele was in the news a decade later when a social media video showed the officer making racist comments about a young woman he had pulled over in a traffic stop during a snowstorm in January 2019. Steele was fired from the Detroit Police Department a month later, but only after the video went viral and garnered national media attention.[35]

The Extent of the Problem

The specific offense, and whether it was committed while on or off duty, tends to impact on whether an officer is ultimately convicted in court after being arrested. Courts are very reluctant to convict officers of any violence-related crime that is committed while an officer is on duty, especially crimes involving firearms. Officers are more likely to be convicted of an on-duty crime if the crime is drug- or alcohol-related. When officers are charged with a crime committed off duty, they are unlikely to be convicted if the underlying incident was committed by an officer in his or her official capacity acting as a police officer. Courts have examined numerous factors in considering whether an off-duty police officer's crimes were committed in his or her official capacity, such as whether officers identified themselves as a police officer, were wearing their police uniform, displayed their department-issued firearm, displayed a badge, conducted an off-duty search, made an off-duty arrest, or intervened in an existing dispute pursuant to a policy of their employing law enforcement agency.[36]

It has never been easy to gauge the incidence and prevalence of police misconduct because it is hard to measure. The police often do not do a good job of policing their own ranks. Most police misconduct goes unreported, and the public is never aware of the extent of the misconduct, crime, and corruption committed by state and local police officers. Less than 2 percent of all police officers are arrested for committing a crime at some point during their careers. A much higher percentage of police officers presumably wash out early in their careers or are allowed to resign later in their careers in lieu of being arrested for some crime they have committed.

Some scholars conclude that police crime is a form of occupational deviance and leave it at that. However, it is more than that. A sense of entitlement comes with the badge and gun. Police officers simply do whatever they want to do, and they are rarely held accountable even if their actions are criminal in nature. The irony, of course, is that most people have a high regard for the police and think of police officers as the good guys. The presumption is that most police officers are indeed the good guys. Others argue that crime committed by police officers is perpetrated by just a few bad apples. The reality is that we simply do not know how bad the problem of police crime is at nonfederal law enforcement agencies across the United States.

EXPLAINING POLICE VIOLENCE

Police violence includes any amount of force used by a nonfederal sworn law enforcement officer that cannot be accounted for under the auspices of lawful necessity in the line of duty.[37] Police officers are legally justified in using that amount of force necessary to effectuate an arrest. It is often difficult to determine when excessive force was used because the police generally own the narrative when reviewing the facts of a violent street encounter. Police perjury—"testilying," as the police call it—is rampant in some jurisdictions and has long been recognized as a problem by judges, prosecutors, and defense attorneys.[38] When I was a young police officer in the mid-1980s, some officers I knew referred to the practice of writing an incident report or arrest report as "creative report writing," and the running joke among those officers when asked by a supervisor why they had arrested someone was, "I don't know yet. I'll think of something and let you know when I get down to the booking room." This practice proliferates in the US criminal justice system where, in many jurisdictions, more than 95 percent of criminal cases end in a plea bargain without any trial. Officers who lie have no fear of getting caught because they know there is almost no chance of a case going to trial, where they would be cross-examined by a defense lawyer.

Rarely are citizen versions of an incident involving police violence taken seriously by investigators, although the ubiquitous nature of smartphone, bodycam, dashcam, and security or surveillance video recordings are having an impact; these occasionally provide an alternative narrative to the police version of events in the aftermath of police shooting incidents and other violent street encounters. Rarely are acts of police violence treated as criminal behavior by sworn law enforcement officers because everyone recognizes that policing often involves violence. Police officers encounter violent people in the normal course of their day-to-day patrol activities. In numerous cases since 2014, video recordings have provided an alternative narrative to the official police reports filed by officers following a police shooting. These are cases where the statements and testimony of officers are factually inconsistent with the video evidence. Nevertheless, rarely do prosecutors, judges, and juries hold officers accountable in those rare instances where a police officer is charged with murder or manslaughter as a result of an on-duty fatal shooting. Complicating matters is the reality that police officers are generally exempt from law enforcement, meaning that police officers do not like to arrest other police officers.[39]

The Difficulty in Prosecuting Police Officers

Sometimes crimes committed by sworn officers come to the attention of an officer's employing law enforcement agency during the course of internal disciplinary investigations. In *Garrity v. New Jersey*, the US Supreme Court held that a police officer is required to answer questions truthfully in internal disciplinary investigations where the officer would be subject to involuntary termination for failing to answer the questions, but that any statements made in that context cannot then be used in criminal proceedings against the officer.[40] The court's rationale was that any statements made by a police officer are coerced if obtained under the threat of being fired for refusing to cooperate during an administrative disciplinary investigation, by reason of the fact that an officer who refused to answer such questions could lose his or her position as a police officer. Such statements would be considered to have been obtained by coercion and made under legal duress in violation of the Fifth and Fourteenth Amendments to the US Constitution, because an officer would have to choose between self-incrimination or job forfeiture. The police officers in *Garrity* were questioned by state investigators about allegations of fixing traffic tickets. Before being questioned, each officer was "warned (1) that anything he said might be used against him in any state criminal proceeding; (2) that he had the privilege to refuse to answer if the disclosure would tend to incriminate him; but (3) that if he refused to answer he would be subject to removal from office."[41]

Many investigations into allegations of police violence are stymied because police administrators and investigators must decide whether to gather information by questioning an officer in a disciplinary investigation or to forgo any such questioning and instead proceed with a criminal investigation against the officer. If investigators decide to proceed with a criminal investigation, the officer under investigation is entitled to the constitutional right against self-incrimination afforded under *Miranda v. Arizona*.[42] Most police officers are very familiar with their *Garrity* rights, and I have long presumed that each year hundreds of police officers across the United States are involuntarily terminated from their jobs with state and local law enforcement agencies and escape any criminal prosecution or public disclosure of their misconduct and crimes. Many of them find employment with other local law enforcement agencies.[43] Prosecutors, however, seem less familiar with the *Garrity* rights of sworn law enforcement officers. I call it the *Garrity* problem. It occurs when prosecutors fail to build their criminal case against a police officer with evidence *other than* statements obtained from that officer during an administrative disciplinary investigation. See the introduction's policy box, "The *Garrity* Problem," for an example of this situation.

Researching Police Crime

I study police crime, including the violence-related criminal arrests of non-federal sworn law enforcement officers. Since 2005 I have collected and analyzed data on cases involving officers across the United States who were arrested for committing one or more crimes. My research team adds approximately 1,100 cases each year to our project database, and we follow each officer's case through media reports and, when available to us, court records. Several years later we code each case on more than 270 quantitative variables, and then the coded data are added to our master data set for statistical analyses. As of 2019, the master data set includes 10,287 criminal arrest cases from the years 2005–14, involving 8,495 individual nonfederal sworn law enforcement officers, each of whom were charged with one or more crimes.[44] The arrested officers were employed by 3,429 state, local, and special law enforcement agencies located in 1,486 counties and independent cities in all fifty states and the District of Columbia. Approximately 47 percent of the arrest cases in the data set involve acts of violence-related police crime. Admittedly, most acts of police violence do not result in the officer being arrested as a result of his or her behavior. My research, however, represents the largest database and data set of police violence ever undertaken, and it serves as the empirical backdrop for this book.

There have been few applications of criminological theory to the study of police violence or even, more generally, police misconduct.[45] Indeed, much of my own scholarship on police crime has avoided the application of criminological theory and theory testing. That is because police crime is different than the crime committed by other people and it is hard to empirically measure crimes by police. Sworn law enforcement officers are legally allowed to use reasonable force to maintain order and public safety and to take suspects into custody. The policing work environment provides an opportunity

THE *GARRITY* PROBLEM

DeKalb County, Georgia, police officer Torrey Thompson was on-duty at 3:15 a.m. on September 12, 2006, when he and other police officers were dispatched to a report of a motor vehicle being stolen from an apartment complex parking lot.[a] When the officers arrived, they quickly determined that the car, a Chevrolet Monte Carlo, had not been stolen but instead had been involved in a hit-and-run car accident a short time earlier that morning. Thompson and the other officers canvassed the apartment complex looking for the individuals whom witnesses had observed exiting the Monte Carlo following the hit-and-run. One witness told officers that Lorenzo Matthews, who lived in the complex, had been the driver of the Monte Carlo. Officers recognized Matthews's name and knew that he often carried a gun and was wanted for questioning regarding a recent shooting at a nearby apartment complex, as well as for assaulting a police officer in another recent incident.

While officers were knocking on doors looking for Matthews, he confronted Officer Thompson on a porch. Matthews pointed at Thompson with an object in his hand. Witnesses claimed the object was a cell phone, but Thompson and another officer thought the object looked like a gun (although no gun was found during a later exhaustive search of the scene). Another officer, Knock, ordered Matthews to stop and drop the object, but Matthews ran down a staircase as Knock fired his service gun at Matthews four times. Matthews then ran directly in the direction of Thompson, and Thompson fired two rounds at Matthews. Matthews then ran into a wooded area adjacent to the apartment complex, with Thompson chasing after him on foot. Thompson realized that the woods would provide Matthews with a tactical advantage and the ability to easily hide from officers, so Thompson fired at Matthews as he ran. As Matthews approached the woods line, Thompson fired another shot just before Matthews jumped over a fence and out of sight. Matthew's body was found on the other side of the fence a short time later by a canine officer searching the woods. It was later determined that he had sustained eight gunshot wounds, two of which were fatal injuries.

A police sergeant on the scene directed the officers involved in the shooting to separate themselves and wait in their respective patrol cruisers until internal affairs investigators (and detectives from the

a. State v. Thompson, 702 S.E.2d. 198 (Ga. 2010).

Major Crimes Unit) arrived to take their statements. Officer Thompson gave a statement to one major crimes detective and participated in two walk-throughs of the area with a sergeant from internal affairs. Although he was not told that he was required to answer questions, Thompson later said that he cooperated with investigators because he felt compelled to do so or risk losing his job. Thompson was charged with several offenses, including felony murder and voluntary manslaughter. The officer's attorney filed a motion to suppress the statements he had given to investigators after the shooting, arguing that the criminal prosecution of Thompson violated his constitutional rights pursuant to *Garrity v. New Jersey*. The trial court found that Thompson subjectively believed he would get fired if he did not answer questions from investigators after the shooting and that his subjective belief was objectively reasonable. The Supreme Court of Georgia upheld the ruling of the trial court, which held that Officer Thompson's statements were inadmissible in the criminal proceedings against him. Six months later, the District Attorney's Office in DeKalb County dropped all charges against Thompson when they realized they could not prove the mens rea (criminal intent) needed to get a conviction.[b]

b. Rankin, "Ex-officer Avoids Murder Charge."

structure for rogue officers to engage in various types of police crimes, including those involving acts of police violence, without guardians capable of providing deterrence. Officers are not closely supervised during their daily work hours. Victims of police abuse rarely come forward, and when they do file complaints against officers their accounts are often not believed. Bad cops are often able to hide their crimes because the police own the narrative when they submit false reports of street encounters in which they have abused citizens. As a result, it is difficult to measure crime by sworn law enforcement officers because there are no official data available to researchers for inferential statistical analyses.

Purpose and Organization

This book provides a concise and targeted overview of criminological theory as applied to police violence. My goal is to bring to life the relationships between theory, research, and policy. Applying different (and sometimes wildly divergent and conflicting) explanatory models to police violence highlights the similarities and differences among criminological theories and allows linkages across explanatory levels and across time and geography. Explaining police violence from criminological theory perspectives is a unique challenge because sworn law enforcement officers are generally exempt from law enforcement, violence is often considered a normal part of policing, and theory is often lacking from police misconduct research. This book draws extensively from my own research on police crime across the United States to provide real-life context for different types of police violence, including areas such as police brutality and excessive force, street justice, police sexual violence, off-duty bizarre gun violence, and officer-involved domestic violence. Focusing on police violence in the United States is justified because policing in this country is decentralized (with approximately 700,000 sworn officers employed by more than 18,000 nonfederal state, local, and special law enforcement agencies), resulting in difficulties in controlling the phenomenon.

There are three primary audiences for *Criminology Explains Police Violence*. The first includes professors of criminology and related academic disciplines who may adopt the book as a supplemental text in criminological theory classes or as a primary text in special-topic classes in policing, police violence, police culture, and related elective courses. The second consists of graduate students and researchers who need a concise review of the literature on criminological theory as applied to the subject of police violence. The third consists of general readers who have become familiar with my work or want to learn more about police violence and, more generally, police crime and police misconduct.

This book follows the format of the Criminology Explains series, and the chapters are designed to be read in conjunction with corresponding chapters in criminology theory textbooks. This book serves as a useful overview of police violence as a substantive type of crime and deviance. Chapter 1 offers an overview to help understand the subject of police violence, describing the nature and extent of the phenomenon, measurement issues and challenges, and how police violence has been socially constructed. The chapter ends with a brief discussion of the social-ecological model that is a constant theme in the volumes of the Criminology Explains series. Chapters 2 through 7 are similarly organized. Chapter 2 applies victimization, lifestyle, and deterrence theories to the phenomenon of police violence. Chapter 3 considers individual-level (micro) theories. Chapter 4 discusses social structure (macro) theories, and chapter 5 covers social process theories. Chapter 6 explores various critical theories. Lastly, chapter 7 addresses several integrationist theories. Criminology textbooks typically offer a detailed and comprehensive discussion of a wide variety of criminological theories and crimes, but they do not always have a "through line" that enables the reader to make connections across the theories and chapters. This book focuses all the relevant theories on one problem—police violence—and provides such a through line, allowing for greater synthesis and thus deeper and longer-lasting retention of learning. Applying different explanatory models to the same problem highlights the similarities and differences among the criminological theories and facilitates linkages across explanatory levels and across time and geography.

CRITICAL THINKING QUESTIONS

1. Alan Dershowitz refers to police perjury as "testilying." How does testilying relate to police violence?

2. Some police officers are arrested for committing violent crimes while off duty. Should these incidents be considered police violence?

3. How is officer-involved domestic violence different from other forms of domestic violence?

4. How might the *Garrity* problem make it difficult to collect data and study the phenomenon of police violence?

———

ONE

Understanding Police Violence

Policing scholars have long argued over the conceptualization of police violence. William Westley argued that police violence includes any amount of force used by a nonfederal sworn law enforcement officer that cannot be accounted for under the auspices of lawful necessity in the line of duty.[1] Lawrence Sherman, however, conceptualized police violence as the "justified and unjustified use of any physical force (including deadly force) against citizens."[2] This book focuses on police violence that involves unjustified physical force, including violence-related police crime through intimidation, coercion, or threats of violence. Most acts of police violence never come to the attention of prosecutors or the general public.[3] Acts of police violence are often hidden crimes that are not counted or labeled as crime because everyone recognizes that policing is violent. Police officers encounter violence as a normal part of their patrol duties in street encounters with citizens and rarely is police violence recognized as law-breaking behavior. It is often explained in the legalese of officers being justified in using force and in using that amount of force necessary to effectuate arrests or some other lawful police activity. Victims of police violence are often left with no recourse because their complaints are viewed as untrustworthy and often lack corroboration. And law enforcement *is exempt from law enforcement* because police officers do not like to arrest other police officers.[4]

Police are allowed to use that amount of force that is reasonably and proportionately necessary to effectuate an arrest or otherwise protect public safety.[5] Since the 1960s policing scholars have examined factors that influence police use of force, and quantitative studies have focused on predictors such as individual, organizational, community, and situational variables. The studies have found that situational factors largely influence the decision of a police officer to use coercive force.[6] Police officers resort to violence in street encounters with physically aggressive persons and in situations where someone resists police efforts to control a situation. The research on officer decisions to use deadly force primarily focuses on situational risk faced by a police officer in a scenario when the officer must decide to shoot or not shoot a person. Other research has found that situational factors are also the primary determinants of police use of nondeadly force.[7] Determinations of whether a police officer's use of nondeadly force was legally justified, excessive, or even criminal are largely subjective and discretionary, made on a case-by-case basis by investigators and prosecutors. A police officer who uses excessive levels of force may be criminally prosecuted for his or her actions, but most police violence never comes to the attention of prosecutors, and researchers have struggled to determine the extent and nature of police violence. This chapter identifies various methodologies that have been invoked to measure police violence and, more generally, police misconduct, police corruption, and police crime.

The study of police violence has been hampered by conceptual confusion and lack of consistent definitions for related terms. *Police misconduct* involves those behaviors by sworn law enforcement officers that violate the administrative policies of an officer's employing law enforcement agency (e.g., police department, sheriff's office, etc.) and can result in internal administrative or disciplinary sanctions against an officer.[8] *Police corruption* consists of organized occupational deviant acts committed in violation of recognized norms within the law enforcement community. Some acts of police corruption are unethical because the behavior violates departmental policy or is for an improper purpose, while other acts of police corruption are crimes for which an officer could be prosecuted. Both police misconduct and police corruption fall within the realm of *police deviance* as abuse of authority or occupational misconduct. *Police crime* involves the criminal behavior of sworn law enforcement officers who, by virtue of their employment, are empowered with the general power of arrest pursuant to statutory authority.[9] In the broadest conceptualization, *police violence* includes any use of physical force (including, but not limited to, the application of deadly force), whether justified or unjustified, against any person, by a sworn law enforcement officer acting pursuant to his or her police authority or power.[10] Not all acts of police violence are crimes, although because this is a criminological theory book the focus herein is largely on unjustified police violence. Since 2014, media attention to numerous fatal shootings by police officers across the United States has

There were many reported shootings in the 1970s and 1980s of unarmed black men and boys by police officers across the United States and allegations that police officers involved in the shootings were often motivated by racial discrimination. State laws at that time often allowed police officers to use deadly force to stop anyone fleeing from a police officer. Two seminal opinions from the US Supreme Court changed the law on when sworn law enforcement officers are legally justified in using deadly force. In *Tennessee v. Garner* the court held that the US Constitution prohibits the use of deadly force by a police officer to prevent the escape of a person suspected of committing a felony unless (a) use of such force is necessary to prevent the escape and (b) the police officer has probable cause to believe that the suspected felon poses a significant threat of serious bodily injury or death to the police officer or someone else.[a] The appellant was the father of a fifteen-year-old boy, Edward Garner, who was shot in the back of the head and killed by a police officer in Memphis, Tennessee. Cleamtee Garner alleged in his civil rights lawsuit pursuant to 42 U.S.C. § 1983 that the police acted under the color of state law to violate his son's federally protected rights under the Fourteenth Amendment to the Constitution. At that time of the Garner shooting, Tennessee law allowed a police officer to use all means necessary to effectuate the arrest of a fleeing suspect so long as the officer first provided notice of his or her intent to arrest the person.

The Supreme Court clarified in *Graham v. Connor* that the standard for when a police officer is legally justified in using deadly force is one of objective reasonableness.[b] That is, the question of whether an officer was justified in using deadly force is determined from the point of view of a reasonable police officer with the facts known to the officer at the time he or she makes the decision to use deadly force. A police officer is justified in using deadly force if that officer has a reasonable apprehension of an imminent threat of serious bodily injury or death against the officer or another person. Thus, if a police officer's subjective belief of an imminent threat is objectively unreasonable, then the officer's use of deadly force would not be legally justified and the officer could be criminally charged with murder or manslaughter, depending on the circumstances of the shooting incident.

a. Tennessee v. Garner, 471 U.S. 1 (1985).
b. Graham v. Connor, 490 U.S. 386 (1989).

Since the 2014 shooting death of Michael Brown by a police officer in Ferguson, Missouri, greater attention has been paid to fatal police shootings by the media, policy makers, and concerned citizens. We now know that approximately 900 to 1,000 people are killed each year by on-duty police officers across the United States, and on average only seven officers each year are charged with murder or manslaughter as a result of an on-duty shooting. Most of the officers involved in fatal on-duty shootings are not charged with any crime because investigators and prosecutors determine that the officer's use of deadly force was legally justified pursuant to *Tennessee v. Garner* and *Graham v. Connor*. Even so, many fatal on-duty shootings by police officers across the United States are unnecessary, inappropriate, and in violation of agency policies. Some states, including California, have considered changing use-of-force law to limit use of deadly force by law enforcement officers to only when it is necessary to defend against imminent death or serious bodily injury.[c]

c. Wilson, "California Considers Nation's Strictest Police Use-of-Force Standard."

resulted in scrutiny on law enforcement practices and the use of deadly force by the police. See this chapter's policy box, "When Can Police Use Deadly Force?" for an overview of the legal standard for when a sworn law enforcement officer is justified in using deadly force.

MEASURING POLICE VIOLENCE

Closely related to the process of conceptualizing police violence is the process of measurement. Hubert Blalock defined measurement as "the process of attaching numbers to objects" and noted that measurement has long been a neglected area in social science research.[11] As in all the sciences, the purpose of measurement in the social sciences, including criminology, is "to quantify, count, or assign meaningful scores to variations in some phenomenon, using valid and reliable methods."[12] Measurement is performed through the specification of operational definitions for the procedures used in measurement.[13] Much of the criminological research on the police has been hampered by inadequate measurement methodologies, including failure to invoke operational definitions in the research design.[14] Scholars have long struggled with the measurement of police violence because there are no official data collected or available for research analyses.[15] Additionally, crimes committed by sworn law enforcement officers often go unreported because police officers do not like to arrest other police officers.[16] Researchers have resorted to a variety of measurement methodologies to study police behaviors such as police violence, including quasi-experimental designs, surveys, sociological field observation studies, investigations by independent commissions and watchdog organizations, reviews of agency records, and content analysis of media reports. Investigative reporting by news media organizations has also contributed to the body of knowledge on various types of police misconduct.

Official Data Are Lacking

Government efforts to collect, analyze, and disseminate information such as statistical data on the incidence and prevalence of police violence acts have been almost nonexistent. Official government efforts to collect data on police violence have been largely the result of political crime-control rhetoric to stem moral panics and public outrage after specific incidents of police violence have been captured by citizens in video recordings, fueling national news headlines. One such failed effort occurred after the 1991 beating of Rodney King by Los Angeles police officers; federal legislation was enacted that requires the US Department of Justice to collect data on the use of excessive force by police officers and requires the US attorney general to "publish an annual summary of the data acquired under this section."[17] No such annual summary of police use of excessive force has ever been published in the more than two decades since the law first mandated it.[18] FBI director James Comey went so far as to say in 2016 that "Americans actually have no idea" about police violence because the federal government had not bothered to collect the data.[19] In 2015, the US Department of Justice announced two new projects for collecting data on police violence. The Bureau of Justice Statistics plans to count arrest-related deaths, but by early 2018 the project had stalled. Similarly, the FBI plans to track the number of people killed by police across the United States, but by early 2018 only 1,600 of the 18,000 state and local law enforcement agencies across the country had agreed to submit data for the project, and initial data collection had not yet commenced.[20]

Investigations by Independent Commissions
and Organizations

Numerous times in the past century independent commissions were established by state governors or large-city mayors to investigate allegations of police corruption after public outcry over a police scandal.[21] Additionally, roughly every twenty years for more than a century independent commissions were established to investigate widespread allegations of police corruption in the New York Police Department, including the Lexow Commission in 1895, the Curran Commission in 1913, the Seabury Commission in 1932, the Gross Commission in 1954, the Knapp Commission in 1973, and the Mollen Commission in 1994.[22] Typically these commissions have been established by an executive order granting the commission the legal authority to hire investigators and other staff, to grant immunity to cooperating witnesses, and the subpoena power to compel production of documents and require testimony under oath under threat of being held in contempt.

Most of these New York City commissions dealt with police corruption scandals not involving police violence. The Knapp Commission, for example, identified two types of corruption-involved police officers in the New York Police Department in the early 1970s: "grass-eaters" and "meat-eaters."[23] It defined grass-eaters as police officers who engage in petty acts of corruption such as accepting small cash gratuities, and it found that the majority of police officers who engage in corrupt activities fall into this type. The Knapp Commission also identified a small percentage of New York police officers who were meat-eaters. The meat-eaters spent much of their workdays aggressively seeking out situations to exploit for their own financial gain, including narcotics and gambling activities for profits in the thousands of dollars. In addition to distinguishing between the petty corruption of grass-eaters and the more serious form of meat-eater police corruption, the Knapp Commission identified five factors that influenced the nature and extent of an officer's corrupt activities, including (1) the character of the officer, (2) the branch of the police department where an officer was assigned, (3) the geographic area within New York City where an officer was assigned, (4) the officer's assignment (e.g., foot patrol or vehicle patrol), and (5) the officer's rank within the police department.

Two decades later, the Mollen Commission found systemic changes in the nature of police corruption within the New York Police Department. No longer was there a proliferation of grass-eater corruption involving petty acts of corruption. By the 1990s the situation was reversed, and the Mollen Commission determined that the more serious form of meat-eater corruption was prevalent, "primarily characterized by serious criminal activity" fueled by a dramatic rise in cocaine trafficking that created new opportunities for corruption throughout the New York Police Department.[24]

The Mollen Commission found that much of the drug-related police corruption in New York City in the 1990s involved officers using their police powers to actively assist, facilitate, and strengthen the illegal drug trade throughout the city. Numerous sources alleged that street drug dealers often paid corrupt police officers to work hand in hand with them to facilitate their drug-related criminal enterprises and activities. The Mollen Commission developed an erosion theory of police corruption: much police corruption seemed to be the result of constant exposure to opportunities for drug-related corruption in crime-ridden police precincts that worked to change the behaviors and attitudes of some police officers across the city. The commissioners hypothesized that the constant exposure to opportunities for drug-related corruption also worked as erosion on other police officers, who developed a tolerance for widespread police corruption throughout the department. While some corrupt officers in the New York Police Department were motivated by greed and profit, others were drug users themselves. Some corrupt officers cultivated relationships with drug dealers who lived in the precincts where the officers worked, and soon these officers were selling illegal drugs while they were on duty and even when off duty. Other corrupt police officers acquired illegal drugs while on duty and then sold the drugs while off duty in their own neighborhoods and towns, often outside New York City. Some corrupt off-duty police officers of the New York Police Department even robbed drug dealers they had previously encountered while on the job. The findings of the Mollen Commission represented the first official acknowledgment that some police crime occurs while officers are off duty.

The link between police corruption and police violence was one that the Mollen Commission could not ignore, but the commissioners found it difficult to quantify police brutality. It recognized that official records regarding incidents of police brutality were virtually nonexistent in the New York Police Department. The commissioners concluded that the motivations for police brutality were varied and complex. Some threats and police violence were directly related to corruption in the police department, but the Mollen Commission found that in other instances acts of police violence and brutality were administered as "an officer's brand of vigilante justice; and some, it appears, for no apparent reason at all."[25] The commission determined that corruption-prone police officers were more than five times as likely to have five or more citizen complaints alleging excessive force filed against them than were officers in a random sample. The commissioners offered no causal relationship but suggested that academic researchers should study the link between police corruption and police violence. The Mollen Commission also found that police brutality often occurs unrelated to corruption as part of the culture of policing. Acts of police violence occurred in the New York Police Department by officers who wanted to show power or compel respect from people in the community and who sometimes acted out of frustration or anger.

One officer testifying before the commission, Bernard Cawley, made it clear that sometimes innocent bystanders were violently victimized by police officers during street encounters:

QUESTION: Did you beat people up who you arrested?

ANSWER: No. We'd just beat people up in general. If they're on the street, hanging around drug locations. It was a show of force.

QUESTION: Why were these beatings done?

ANSWER: To show who was in charge. We were in charge. The police.[26]

Cawley admitted to hundreds of acts of brutality during his time as a police officer but was the subject of only one citizen complaint for excessive force, and no other officers ever reported him. He was part of the us-versus-them police subculture where police violence was the norm, and he was widely known by fellow police officers as "the Mechanic" because during street encounters with citizens he frequently "tuned people up" with beatings.[27] The Mollen Commission found that police violence of this sort was widespread and almost universally tolerated by patrol officers and police supervisors alike. Gratuitous police violence was seen as a form of street justice in which unnecessary force was a means to the end of maintaining order in crime-ridden New York City neighborhoods. Supervisors routinely turned a blind eye—when confronted with an arresting officer's story of what had transpired—after obviously beaten suspects were arrested on bogus resisting-arrest charges. The police typically own the narratives in these situations and rarely is a citizen's complaint of excessive force or police brutality taken seriously.

Other independent commissions have made significant findings on police misconduct and in identifying those sworn law enforcement officers at risk for engaging in acts of police violence and other behaviors that violate citizens' civil rights. In 1981 the US Commission on Civil Rights issued a report documenting its investigation of police practices in the Houston Police Department in Texas and the Philadelphia Police Department in Pennsylvania.[28] It found that a very small number of police officers in Houston were chronic offenders who had accumulated a high number of citizen complaints. One Houston police officer was the subject of twelve citizen complaints in a two-year period, including five excessive force complaints and one complaint stemming from a fatal police shooting, and yet there was no indication that the pattern of misconduct was even noticed within the Houston Police Department. In Philadelphia, the commission also found that a very small number of problem officers accounted for the majority of citizen complaints and determined that police supervisors routinely ignored obvious early warning signs of violence-prone police officers. Similarly, in its report investigating the 1991 beating of Rodney King by Los Angeles police officers, the Christopher Commission identified forty-four police officers with extremely high rates of citizen complaints in the Los Angeles Police Department.[29] The commission found that 10 percent of Los Angeles police officers accounted for 27.5 percent of all excessive force complaints filed in the years 1986–90, including forty-four officers who were each the subjects of six or more excessive force complaints, sixteen officers who were the subjects of eight or more complaints each, and one officer who was the subject of sixteen excessive force complaints.

The staff investigators of Human Rights Watch (an international human rights advocacy organization) extensively researched issues relating to accountability for police brutality in fourteen US cities in the mid-1990s, including Atlanta, Boston, Chicago, Detroit, Indianapolis, Los Angeles, Minneapolis, New Orleans, New York, Philadelphia, Portland (Oregon), Providence, San Francisco, and Washington, DC. Much of the data collected by Human Rights Watch were through telephone interviews with prosecutors in each jurisdiction. The investigators found that prosecutors systematically failed to charge abusive police officers with crimes committed in their official capacity and to collect adequate data on the prosecution of sworn law enforcement officers, making it impossible to measure the nature and extent of police violence in large urban jurisdictions across the United States.[30]

Most of the prosecutor's offices advised that criminal prosecutions of police officers for crimes involving police brutality were rare, and the prosecutors typically denied keeping lists or records counting the number of police officers who had been prosecuted. There were a few exceptions. The Hennepin County Attorney's Office in Minneapolis reported that its prosecutors had a reputation for aggressively pursuing criminal prosecution of police officers and acknowledged that the office maintained an informal list of all police defendants prosecuted. In the District of Columbia, where federal prosecutors from the US Attorney's Office handle all criminal prosecutions in both the local trial court (Superior Court of the District of Columbia) and the federal trial court (US District Court for the District of Columbia), Human Rights Watch determined from press reports that twenty-nine police officers were prosecuted for assaultive behavior between 1990 and 1998. Tucker Carlson and others have blamed the large number of police officers arrested in the District of Columbia on a systematic failure within DC's Metropolitan Police Department during 1989 and 1990, in which no background checks were conducted on applicants for police officer positions.[31]

Media Reports of Police Violence

Investigative journalism reports have uncovered patterns of police corruption and brutality. These are often published as special reports in newspapers and have raised public awareness, served as catalyst for reforms within police departments, and at times led to the appointment of independent commissions.[32] Although investigative journalism is not subject to the rigors of institutional review board approval and academic peer review required of scholarly research, media reports have significant policy implications and are often cited by scholars as evidence of systemic police misconduct.

The problem of no official data being available on police violence in the United States became obvious to many in August 2014, after the shooting death of Michael Brown by police officer Darren Wilson in Ferguson, Missouri. Members of the press were clamoring to find out how often police officers were arrested for murder or manslaughter resulting from on-duty shootings. I received a phone call from a reporter at *Talking Points Memo*, Dylan Scott, who wanted to know if I had any data on police shootings. It was a question I had not previously pondered because I had not specifically researched police shootings. But it turned out that I did have the data to answer the question. I was able to query my data set of coded cases based on a variable coded in each case: whether an officer's arrest involved an incident where the officer had pulled, pointed, held, or fired a gun. That led to a narrowing of cases by selecting variables in the data set, such as officer's duty status at time of the crime and whether an arrested officer was charged with murder or manslaughter. Within minutes, I had an answer: at least thirty-one nonfederal sworn law enforcement officers were arrested for murder or manslaughter resulting from an on-duty shooting from 2005 to 2011.[33]

Several months later David Fallis, an editor at the *Washington Post*, called me and asked if I would be willing to share my data for a joint research project with the newspaper. I explained that my fully coded data covered 2005–11 and that we would have to query my database in other ways to find relevant cases from 2012 forward. Fallis and I agreed to work together and he sent one of his investigative reporters, Kimberly Kindy, to meet with me at my office in Ohio. Kindy and I spent several days pouring over records from my database, and she drilled me with questions about my data collection methods, including on how I structured and used Google Alerts to constantly query the Google News search engine for articles using automated search terms designed to find articles reporting the arrests of police officers across the country. A few months later the *Washington Post* published our findings, in which we reported that from the beginning of 2005 through early April 2015, fifty-four police officers across the country had been charged with murder or manslaughter resulting from an on-duty shooting.[34] My data collection methodology using Google Alerts also became the basis for the *Washington Post* to design their own data collection system and a database that counts all on-duty fatal police shootings across the country.[35] As a result, we now know that on-duty police officers across the United States shoot and kill between 900 and 1,000 people each year. Only a handful of those officers are ever charged with a crime.

Social Science Research of Police Misconduct

In the 1960s researchers interested in police behaviors used observational research studies to examine discretionary aspects of police work not manifest in official records such as arrest reports. Early field studies were largely ethnographic qualitative studies, with researchers "walking around" with police officers to observe encounters with citizens.[36] Sociological field studies of police patrol work became more quantitative with Albert Reiss's development of Systematic Social Observation (SSO) methods, which included selection of a problem to study, preliminary field observation, definition of the universe to be studied, design of sampling elements, development of an instrument to systematically collect and record field observations, training of research observers and pretesting of the data collection instrument to reduce measurement error, and conducting the field observations and quantitative data analysis.[37]

Reiss employed thirty-six students as field researchers who spent seven weeks in the summer of 1966 riding on patrol with police officers in Boston, Chicago, and Washington, DC. Although the purpose of the research was to study police behaviors, Reiss and his researchers misled the police officers who willingly allowed the researchers to accompany them on patrol, telling them "that the research was not concerned with police behavior but only with citizen behavior toward the police and the kinds of problems citizens make for the police."[38] Reiss found that 20 percent of observed police officers engaged in on-duty crimes (other than assaults and syndicated crime) such as thefts of money and goods by accepting bribes or taking property from burglarized businesses. Reiss concluded that most observed police crime provided supplemental income for the officers who engaged in the criminal behavior through "exchange relationships."[39] Reiss's field researchers recorded only forty-four incidents (out of 3,826 encounters) where police officers were observed using force in a citizen encounter. Thirty-seven of those forty-four incidents were coded by observers as having involved excessive force by police.[40] No other field observation studies have endeavored to determine the prevalence of police committing crimes, although field researchers working in Stephen Mastrofski and colleagues' study of police behaviors in Indianapolis and St. Petersburg, Florida, "observed many instances of police behavior that could have been cause for disciplinary action."[41]

The most extensive study of police behavior using agency records is James Fyfe and Robert Kane's study of career-ending misconduct by 1,543 police officers fired from the New York Police Department during the years 1975–96 compared with a randomly selected stratified sample of New York City police officers who served honorably during the same period.[42] Using the personnel files and disciplinary records of each officer, Fyfe and Kane concluded that the police officers most likely to end their careers through involuntary separations were officers who lacked any college education, had prior delinquency or criminal records when they were hired, did not advance through the ranks with any promotions, were assigned to work in busy patrol beats, and had accumulated numerous complaints during their time as police officers.

Fyfe and Kane further found no bright-line distinction between the on-duty and off-duty misconduct of police officers. They identified several factors that made it difficult to determine when off-duty criminal conduct of officers was related to their positions as sworn law enforcement officers. Police officers have special knowledge and the powers and authority that come with a badge and gun. Some access to criminal opportunities and contraband that an officer gains while on duty may facilitate the off-duty criminal activities of a bad cop. Many law enforcement agencies, including the New York Police Department, grant full law enforcement authority throughout the state to off-duty police officers and require that off-duty officers always carry their service weapons. Since 2004, federal law has permitted police officers to carry concealed weapons across state lines.[43]

As Fyfe and Kane noted, the combination of officers having full police authority and carrying guns while off duty has resulted in countless off-duty police violence incidents and civil liability concerns at state and local law enforcement agencies across the United States. Only about 8 percent of the New York City police officers in their study who were involuntarily terminated from their jobs ended their careers as a result of on-duty abuse of authority disciplinary charges. Fyfe and Kane (and later, Kane and Michael White)[44] offered three potential explanations for the relatively low number of officers who were involuntarily terminated as a result of abuse of authority allegations: (1) historically, the actual incidence of excessive force incidents has been lower in the New York Police Department than other large police departments across the United States (as measured by rates per 1,000 officers employed for use of deadly force incidents and rates per 1,000 officers employed for civil rights complaints filed with the US Department of Justice); (2) it is often very difficult to prove allegations of excessive force by police officers; and (3) there seems to be a high degree of tolerance among fellow officers for police who use excessive force against citizens. Onlookers sometimes assume that police officers are acting within the law during violent street encounters. Sworn law enforcement officers assigned to patrol duties have very little direct supervision during their shifts.

Problems and Solutions

Each of the methodologies used to study police misconduct has limitations. Government data collection efforts to learn about the incidence and prevalence of police violence have been lacking. The work of independent commissions and human rights organizations have yielded large amounts of information about police violence, and more generally police corruption, but only about specific high-profile incidents or dealing with only one or a few large police departments. Investigative journalism similarly has shed light on previously hidden problems of police misconduct, corruption, crime, and violence, but it too typically deals with specific high-profile incidents or problems within single law enforcement agencies or jurisdictions. Observational field research of policing is limited to one agency at a time and may not be generalizable to policing in other places at other times. It is possible that police officers act differently in encounters with citizens when officers are aware of the presence of researchers, resulting in fewer observed use of force incidents.[45] There is often a social desirability effect in survey research, and that is true in surveys of police officers and police departments. Edward Maguire and Craig Uchida found that police administrators completing surveys on community policing were less than truthful, exaggerating when answering questions on US Department of Justice surveys.[46] In another study of community policing, error with data sets "doomed" researchers' ability to make any meaningful findings because survey responses from local law enforcement agencies "represent more about the image they wish to portray to the external world than about their agencies' actual activities."[47] Janet Fishman doubted the value of surveying police officers about corrupt practices within law enforcement agencies because she assumed they would maintain a code of silence and not answer truthfully.[48]

I have been studying police crime—that is, crime committed by nonfederal sworn law enforcement officers—since the early 2000s using news articles as the primary data source. My methodology utilizes the Google Alerts email update service and the Google News search engine. In 2005 I set up forty-eight automated Google Alerts search terms that persistently crawl the Google News search engine and deliver daily real-time search results. The Google News search engine algorithm offers some advantages over other aggregated news database services and draws content from more than fifty thousand news sources.[49] It allows for access to a larger number of police misconduct cases than is available through other research methods.[50]

As with all social science research, there are some strengths and limitations to my data collection methods. First, my police crime data are limited to cases that involve an official arrest based on probable cause for one or more crimes committed by individual sworn law enforcement officers. My data set of police crime does not contain any cases of alleged criminal behavior of police who were not arrested. Second, the amount of information on each case in my data is limited by the content analyzed and the quality of information available to my research group for each case. The amount of information available on each case varies, and sometimes there are missing data on variables of interest. Third, I do not purport to include in my data set every single instance of a nonfederal sworn law enforcement officer who was arrested across the United States during the study years. My data collection methods have, however, consistently found approximately eleven hundred cases each year, for more than a decade, in which officers across the country were arrested for committing a crime. Finally, the primary data sources for cases in my database are media reports. News articles are the result of a filtering process that includes an exercise of discretion by media sources themselves in terms of both the types of news covered and the nature of the content devoted to particular news events.[51] Even so, Justin Ready, Michael White, and Christopher Fisher found that media coverage of police misconduct news is consistent with official police records of the events.[52] Other research suggests that police departments are not effective in controlling news media accounts of police misconduct.[53]

CRIMINOLOGICAL THEORY AND POLICE VIOLENCE

Police violence has become an area of concern for many people in the past several years, especially in the context of police shootings across the United States. And yet, police violence is understudied as a criminological phenomenon. This book presents the phenomenon of police violence through a social-ecological approach drawing on relevant criminological literature that largely studies the behavioral and social consequences of interactions between human beings (here, police officers) and their environment. The social ecology of crime investigates the relationship between social control and crime in communities. It draws on both individual-and community-centered theories and research.[54] A social-ecological approach is especially appropriate because a core principle of social ecology is interdisciplinary study of a phenomenon (here, police violence) and framing the discussion as an effort to understand people's relationships with their surroundings in terms of place, space, and time. As Daniel Stokols noted, social ecology embraces the integration of "academic and nonacademic perspectives to more effectively analyze and manage complex societal problems."[55] Douglas Smith conceptualized police behavior as social ecology when he noted that the police patrol both people and places.[56] His research found that discretionary police behavior was influenced both by characteristics of individual encounters with citizens and by characteristics of neighborhoods and may be impacted by interaction with the structure and policies of specific law enforcement agencies. Building on Smith's conceptualization of police behavior as social ecology, David Klinger recognized that it was necessary to further define the ecological communities of policing.[57]

Policing in the United States is decentralized, with more than eighteen thousand state and local law enforcement agencies (e.g., primary state police agencies, county sheriff's offices, county police departments, municipal police departments, etc.) in fifty states and the District of Columbia, each agency having its own jurisdictional boundaries.[58] These jurisdictional boundaries that define the geographic areas of policing also define the ecological communities of policing. Further delineation is defined through geographic patrol areas (sometimes referred to as beats, districts, or precincts) within the jurisdictional boundaries of a law enforcement agency. As John Liederbach and others have noted, all policing is local.[59] Robert Kane first applied the social-ecological criminological framework to police misconduct in his research on career-ending misconduct of New York City police officers, finding that some police officers exploit people they encounter through "conflict or an opportunity structure created in the places" they patrol within communities.[60]

The purpose of criminological theory is to gain an understanding of crime and criminal justice through social science. Criminological theories are useful in informing public policy and practice about human behavior and society. A theory can be evaluated on the criteria of clarity and consistency, scope and parsimony, testability, practical usefulness, and empirical validity.[61] Some criminological theories focus on making and enforcing criminal law by studying the operation of criminal law in the criminal justice system and are concerned with how and why certain behavior and people are defined and dealt with in terms of their criminality. Other criminological theories address criminal (or delinquent) behavior and focus on why legal and social norms are violated in terms of why some individuals are more likely than others to commit delinquent or criminal acts and why there is variation in group rates of crime. Some criminological theories are social structural (or macro) theories that focus on differences in group rates of crime, while others are micro theories that address individual differences and social processes.

Very little is known about police crime and police violence. Criminologists have been slow to apply most criminological theories to police behavior, largely due to a lack of available official data and the methodological difficulties that researchers encounter when working with law enforcement agencies. Criminological theories are often attempts to explain deviance rather than crime, and there are not necessarily clear distinctions between criminological and noncriminological theories. This is especially true in the study of police violence. It is for the reader of this book to determine to what extent criminological theory is a valid lens with which to examine the phenomenon of police violence.

The remaining chapters of this book each address specific areas of criminological theory. Chapters 2 through 7 are each organized to provide an overview of the relevant group of theories, as well as an overview of unit theories within the group. The relevant research on police violence is applied to the unit theories in each chapter, and implications for criminal justice policy and practice that arise from the theories are discussed.

CRITICAL THINKING QUESTIONS

1. Why is police violence understudied as a criminological phenomenon?
2. What are the methodological limitations of using media reports (such as newspaper articles) to study the phenomenon of police violence?
3. What are the methodological advantages of using media reports to study police violence?
4. Why have efforts by the federal government to collect data on the incidence and prevalence of police violence been unsuccessful?

TWO

Deterrence, Rational Choice, Victimization, and Lifestyle Theories

Deterrence and rational choice theories of criminology emerged in the early 1500s at a time when the prevailing European views were that crimes were sins against God. Persons prosecuted by the state were punished for their crime and their sin. Sixteenth-century philosophers started to adopt naturalistic views of human behavior. Thomas Hobbes argued that people are rational beings who will pursue their own interests and that a social contract was necessary to provide a safe and orderly society in exchange for giving up certain individual freedoms.[1]

The deterrence doctrine of classical criminology later evolved from the writings of Cesare Beccaria (in Italy) and Jeremy Bentham (in England).[2] Both Beccaria and Bentham sought to provide a utilitarian rationale for reforming the legal system and argued that individuals possess free will and can choose behaviors that avoid pain and maximize pleasure. They viewed crime as the result of a person making a rational decision to commit the act because he or she decides that the benefits (pleasure) outweigh the costs (pain). As such, the central premise of classical criminological thought is that "actions are taken and decisions are made by persons in the rational exercise of free will."[3]

The deterrence doctrine is based on Beccaria's argument that to deter crime, punishment should be swift, certain, and proportional in severity to the seriousness of the crime for which an individual is convicted. Beccaria posited that the primary purpose of criminal law is to deter individuals from committing crimes, and that can only happen if the legislature has defined crimes and punishments. Punishment must fit the crime for which an individual is convicted: punishments that are too severe are unjust, and punishments that are insufficient and not severe enough will not deter crime. In the philosophical context of crime and the operations of the criminal justice system, punishment is "the pain or deprivation inflicted on an offender" upon conviction for his or her offense.[4] This chapter explores contemporary criminological theories and legal concepts based on these classical conceptualizations of deterrence and rational choice that impact on police violence and other police behaviors, including routine activities, opportunity, and victimization lifestyle theories.

DECIDING TO OFFEND

Substantive criminal law recognizes numerous theories and purposes of punishment, one of which is deterrence. The deterrent effect of a particular crime is the total number of crimes it prevents.[5] Criminal law distinguishes between general deterrence and specific deterrence.[6] General deterrence punishes an offender to deter others from committing crimes in the future as a form of crime prevention. Specific deterrence punishes an individual specifically to deter him or her from reoffending; it is sometimes also referred to as direct or simple deterrence.

Classical criminology had a lasting impact on the development of the criminal justice system in the United States. The idea that criminal behavior is free will was challenged by the fields of biology, psychology, and sociology in the twentieth century with claims that outside influences and forces exert strong pressures on choices to offend.[7] Deterrence theories of criminological offending and crime prevention reemerged—with US criminologists and criminal justice policymakers alike—starting in the late 1960s and continuing for several decades thereafter, largely as a result of failed criminal justice policies that many viewed as favoring rehabilitation programs.[8] Joan Petersilia has argued, however, that crime prevention policies based on notions of rehabilitation were never "really" embraced, and to a large extent criminologists and policymakers still do not know what will "work" to reduce reoffending and recidivism in the United States.[9] Nevertheless, deterrence theories based on the premise that criminals are rational actors have driven criminal justice policymaking for much of the past five decades.

Modern Deterrence Theories

Scholarly research interest in the deterrence doctrine and the effect of the criminal sanction was rekindled in the late 1960s and early 1970s. Herbert

Packer proposed broadening the scope of general deterrence hypotheses to include the effects of all components of the criminal justice system, including punishment, in considering the totality of behavioral motivations.[10] He recognized that deterrence was more than a philosophical theory, because criminals know that "punishment is an unpleasantness that is best avoided."[11] But Packer also recognized that there were limitations of the criminal sanction, especially for individuals living on the fringes of society and experiencing weak social influences, because "deterrence does not threaten those whose lot in life is already miserable beyond the point of hope."[12]

Early research on deterrence studied capital punishment and conducted secondary analyses, comparing data from states with and without capital punishment for homicide offenses. These studies found that states with the death penalty typically did not have lower homicide rates than states without capital punishment.[13] Jack Gibbs and Charles Tittle both looked at official government crime and sentencing data to examine the certainty and severity aspects of deterrence, both finding some empirical support for deterrence theory.[14] These studies did not, however, examine any measures of punishment celerity (swiftness). Gibbs later argued that deterrence-theory research should expand beyond the core elements of certainty, celerity, and severity to include measures of individual perceptions and other properties of punishment.[15]

Mark Stafford and Mark Warr offered a reconceptualization of the deterrence doctrine, arguing that both specific and general deterrence can actually operate on the same person.[16] They posited that general deterrence is the result of a person's vicarious experiences and that specific deterrence is the result of a person's own experiences with the criminal justice system. The main premise of Stafford and Warr's reconceptualization is that people are likely to have a mixture of both "indirect experience" (the general deterrence component) and "direct experience" (the specific deterrence component) with both punishment and punishment avoidance.[17] Criminological theory-testing research suggests that the Stafford and Warr reconceptualization may be helpful in the further development of deterrence theory.[18]

Other research assesses the deterrent effect of police. These studies can be divided into two distinct areas: research focused on "the deterrent effect of the aggregate police presence measured" and research focused on "the crime prevention effectiveness of different strategies for deploying police."[19] Both areas of research assessing the deterrent effect of police fall within the realm of general deterrence. Aggregate studies of police presence have consistently demonstrated that assigning more police officers to patrol/street duties has a deterrent effect on major crimes, both in jurisdictions where more officers were hired and also in jurisdictions where existing police personnel were reassigned to uniformed patrol duties.[20] These findings are consistent with historical events worldwide over the past century where police have gone on strike, creating situations in which no police officers were working citywide and everyone knew it. Police labor strikes in Boston in 1919, Montreal in 1969, and Helsinki in 1973 all had the same result: "all Hell breaks loose," with sudden surges in the number of robberies, burglaries, assaults, and various property crimes.[21]

Additional studies have focused on deterrence based on police activities that averted crimes from being committed, some of which are consistent with the broken windows theory of policing. James Wilson and George Kelling's broken windows theory argues that intensive police efforts to reduce and mitigate neighborhood blight, disorder, and disrepair can reverse the breakdown of social controls that is often accompanied by rampant minor crime in a community.[22] Others have argued that broken windows theory is too simplistic, treating only the symptoms of poverty rather than the causes.[23] Wilson and Kelling's idea for broken windows policing came from an experiment by Philip Zimbardo more than a decade earlier. In 1968 Zimbardo arranged to have two Oldsmobile sedans parked on public streets, one in the Bronx of New York City and the other in suburban Palo Alto, California.[24] The license plates were removed from each car, and each was left unattended with the hood up, exposing the engine compartment. Within minutes the automobile parked in the Bronx was vandalized repeatedly, first by a family (man, woman, and their young boy) who removed the car's battery and radiator. A day later, the car had been completed stripped of all usable parts while researchers observed from a safe nearby location. Soon other vandals started to randomly destroy what remained of the car by smashing the windows and ripping up the upholstered seats. Most of the vandalism occurred in daylight hours. Meanwhile, the automobile parked on a street in Palo Alto was untouched for more than a week, so Zimbardo started to smash the car with a sledgehammer. Within a few hours, people passing by had joined in and the automobile was completely destroyed and flipped upside down. All the people observed vandalizing both vehicles were "clean cut, well-dressed, middle-class" white people.[25] Zimbardo concluded that the people engaging in the vandalism were encouraged by a sense of community, which occurred immediately in the blight-ridden neighborhood where the first car was located, but only occurred in the middle-class suburban Palo Alto neighborhood after the car was eventually vandalized by Zimbardo himself.

Anthony Braga and his colleagues' systematic reviews and meta-analyses have found that a variety of policing strategies based on deterrence are largely effective crime prevention strategies. Problem-solving policing interventions designed as strategies to change social and physical disorder conditions at particular places had strong effect sizes, but aggressive order maintenance strategies targeting disorderly behaviors of individuals were found to be less effective at reducing crime.[26] Braga and his colleagues also analyzed the existing studies on hot spots policing and found "small but noteworthy crime reductions," with diffusion of crime control benefits into the areas immediately surrounding the targeted hot spot locations.[27] Hot spots policing targets interventions at the very few specific geographic places that generate the majority of calls to the police.[28] It is an ecological approach consistent with routine activity theory, discussed in more detail below. Research has also found that police hot spot patrol strategies are effective in reducing repeat victimization and calls for service at small geographic locales.[29] Other effective deterrence strategies include patrols that target repeat offenders[30] or focus on specific types of criminal offenses.[31]

Police do not need the research of criminologists to know that these deterrence strategies work. When I worked at the Arlington County Police Department in Virginia from 1982 to 1986, officers routinely positioned unstaffed marked police vehicles at strategic locations during robbery season, the period between Thanksgiving Day and New Year's Day. There were always extra police cruisers not being used by the patrol units, and during robbery season several times each day a supervisor would determine where to park the marked cars in ways that made it appear to a casual observer that there must be a police officer nearby. For example, police cruisers would be left for five or six hours—with the parking lights on—parked on the sidewalk directly outside the escalators leading down to a subway station. Other police cruisers would be parked in front of convenience stores, doughnut shops, or banks. A team of police officers was assigned each day to move the cars from one location to the next one on the supervisor's list. A few years ago I was staying at the Crystal Gateway Marriott hotel in Arlington while working on a consulting project for the National Institute of Justice at the US Department of Justice. On my first night at the hotel I noticed an Arlington County Police cruiser parked just outside the doors of the main hotel lobby. I looked around to see if an officer was in the lobby as I headed to the elevator.

The next evening I again noticed a cruiser parked in the hotel driveway and assumed an officer was nearby. Not until later did it dawn on me that the cruiser was assigned as a take-home vehicle to an officer who lived outside the county, and the officer parked the cruiser in a high-visibility location whenever he or she was not working. More than thirty years later, the Arlington County Police Department was still adhering to the same deterrence strategy of making it look like there is a police presence even when no officer is anywhere nearby.

Rational Choice Theory

Ronald Clarke and Derek Cornish offered a criminological theory called rational choice perspective that focuses on the self-interests and sequencing of offender decision-making processes.[32] The rational choice perspective is squarely within the classical deterrence doctrine developed by Becarria hundreds of years ago that posits crime as the result of a person making a rational decision to act because he or she decides that the benefits outweigh the costs. Clarke and Cornish developed the rational choice perspective in the 1980s as a research and policymaking framework where criminal behavior is seen as the outcome of an offender's rational choices and decisions. It borrows heavily from scholarly research on human rationality in the academic fields of sociology of deviance, criminology, economics, and cognitive psychology.

The rational choice perspective assumes that offenders make decisions that are "purposive" and that crimes are deliberate acts "committed with the intention of benefiting the offender."[33] In committing a crime, offenders are confronted with risks and uncertainty, so they do not always succeed in making the best decisions. Their rationality is "bounded" by imperfect and hasty decision-making, poor planning, limited information about costs and benefits, inadequate resources, and failure to consider the full consequences.[34] Decision-making by offenders varies considerably depending on the motives for and methods of committing specific crimes. Some criminals are "generalists" who commit a wide range of street crimes with varying methods and motives.[35] Other offenders are "specialists" who commit violent crimes such as robberies or rapes, while others might limit their criminal offending to residential burglaries.[36] The decision-making processes of offenders vary considerably depending on the type of crime.

Another proposition of the rational choice perspective is that offender "involvement decisions" about becoming involved in a specific type of crime are very different from offender "event decisions" relating to the commission of a specific criminal incident.[37] There are three stages of involvement: initiation, habituation, and desistance. Initiation is the involvement decision to begin committing crime; habituation is the involvement decision to keep committing crimes; and desistance occurs when an offender decides to no longer commit crimes. Clarke and Cornish specified that, in research studies, each stage of involvement must be modeled separately with different sets of variables for each of the three stages of involvement that separately consider background factors, current lifestyle circumstances and routines, and situational variables that take into account an offender's motives, needs, and opportunities.

Clarke and Cornish developed their rational choice perspective as a criminological theory to provide a theoretical foundation to situational crime prevention.[38] Situational crime prevention "focuses on the settings in which crimes occur, rather than on those committing criminal acts."[39] There are several theoretical assumptions of situational crime prevention: crime is the result of an interaction between an offender's situation and disposition; offenders choose to engage in crime; opportunity causes crime; and crime can be stimulated by situational factors. Numerous criminologists, nevertheless, have been critical or dismissive of the Clarke and Cornish rational choice perspective. Some of the hostility seems to be directed at the notion that rational choice is economic theory. Then there is the problem for criminologists raised by Raymond Paternoster in 1987 when he suggested that maybe human beings are not rational creatures.[40] Indeed, Daniel Kahneman, an economist, found that cognitive errors in human intuition and reasoning can result in flawed decision-making that would impact on mapping bounded rationality.[41] Future research on the criminological rational choice perspective, according to Clarke, should focus less on the "rationality" component and more on the "bounded" component by incorporating advancements in the fields of behavioral economics, neuroscience, and psychology into developing a fuller criminological decision-making theory that can be applied to situational crime prevention.[42]

Routine Activity Theory

Lawrence Cohen and Marcus Felson developed a theory that was unique in that it broadened the focus from the criminality of the offender to include opportunity and other aspects of the crime. Their routine activity theory posits that "structural changes in routine activity patterns can influence crime rates by affecting the convergence in time and space of the three minimal elements of direct-contact predatory violations: (1) motivated offenders, (2) suitable targets, and (3) the absence of capable guardians against a violation."[43] Felson later expanded the applicability of routine activity theory to include situational crime prevention well beyond violent predatory crimes. A wide range of criminal offenses are now amenable to routine activity analysis, such as telecommunications crimes (including electronic terrorism, money laundering, and electronic fraud), drug crimes, auto theft, burglary, and many other nonviolent crimes.[44] Clarke and Felson have argued that the assumptions of routine activity theory are consistent with the rational choice perspective.[45] A motivated offender makes a calculated decision to proceed with the commission of a crime only after also making a determination that there is a good target and an absent guardian. In that situation, an offender's focus is on the immediate rewards and punishments but "not the eventual punishment of a slow criminal justice system."[46]

Crime Places

Felson and Cohen theoretically placed their routine activity theory within the framework of Amos Hawley's human ecological theory of community structure by "treating criminal acts as routine activities which feed upon other routine activities."[47] Hawley defined human ecology in terms of interwoven sustenance activities and relationships among people within the physical environment of community structure over both space (spatial aspects) and time (temporal aspects).[48] The application of Hawley's theory of human ecology to Cohen and Felson's routine activity theory of crime differs from other criminologists' work in the area of human ecology (such as Clifford Shaw and Henry McKay's social disorganization theory that included spatial analyses)[49] by also considering the interdependence of temporal aspects in criminal offending and crime rates.[50] Robert Sampson, however, has been critical of applying Hawley's view of human ecology to the study of criminal offending and crime rates in a neighborhood context, because Hawley's theoretical conceptualization focuses on the interdependence of physical environment and sustenance mechanisms but "neglects cultural symbols, change, and social mechanisms of reproduction" within the structure of communities.[51]

A growing body of criminological research focuses on specific places where crime occurs and is concentrated. In 1989 Lawrence Sherman and his colleagues applied routine activity theory to police calls-for-service records and spatial data of street addresses/intersections in their seminal research of geographic "hot spots" that produce the most reported predatory crimes.[52] In the three decades since publication of their study of predatory crimes in Minneapolis, there has been growing interest in research focused on the relationship between opportunity and physical space utilizing microgeographic units of analysis to explore why crime occurs at specific places. David Weisburd argued, however, that the "emergence of a large and sound body of empirical evidence about crime places contrasts with the fact that this body of knowledge has been largely overlooked by criminologists."[53]

Content analysis studies of the articles published in two leading crime policy journals provide some context for Weisburd's contention. John Eck and Emily Eck found that only 8 percent of the articles published during the years 2001–10 in both *Criminology and Public Policy* and *Criminal Justice Policy Review* examined crime opportunity policies and that "no articles [in *Criminal Justice Policy Review*] described policies toward crime places."[54] But that is simply not true. I served as managing editor of *Criminal Justice Policy Review* from 2005 to 2009, and during that time the journal published numerous policy articles addressing crime places and blocking opportunities to offend. Among them were seven articles on the geographic aspects of sex offender residency restrictions that were published in a 2009 special issue.[55] Jennifer Huck, Jason Spraitz, and I analyzed all the content published in *Criminal Justice Policy Review* from 1986 to 2008 and found that crime prevention was the primary research topic in 5.1 percent of the articles published (and secondary research topic in 2.4% of the articles).[56] We also found that the number of crime prevention articles published in the journal increased over time under four of the five journal editors at *Criminal Justice Policy Review* during the twenty-three-year study period. The trend of more research articles focused on crime places and crime prevention is consistent with a larger pattern that Huck, Spraitz, and I observed in our study of *Criminal Justice Policy Review* articles: the academic discipline of criminology has been in transition for much of the three decades since the mid-1980s.

Policing in the United States is decentralized, with more than eighteen thousand state and local law enforcement agencies across the country. David Klinger argued that there is an ecological context to police patrol work whereby police behaviors are derived geographically in local work groups within each police department.[57] While Klinger's negotiated order perspective was conceptualized as an ecological theory of police response to neighborhood violence, Robert Kane applied the theory to the social ecology of police misconduct in his study of variations of social conditions in New York City police precincts and divisions from 1975 to 1996.

Each police precinct in New York City is a geographic patrol area of approximately 3.5 square miles with an average of ninety-four thousand residents, and police divisions consist of three to five geographically contiguous precincts.[58] Kane was the first criminologist to apply both spatial aspects of community structure and temporal aspects of time (over years) in a social ecological framework to the study of police misconduct. He acknowledged that one limitation of reliance on administratively defined units of spatial analysis as proximate indicators of neighborhoods "is that the spatial zones created by cities may have little meaning to local residents, rendering ecological inferences questionable."[59] Kane posited that the "natural area" within which police misconduct occurs is different than the "natural area" of neighborhood where crime and delinquency occurs, because the daily routines of on-duty police officers are defined by duty assignments.[60] Police officers are generally assigned by a supervisor to patrol an area beat within a precinct (although terminology and the number/levels of structure vary with the size of the local law enforcement agency and its area of primary geographic jurisdiction). Kane's research of police misconduct is limited to policing within New York City. The New York Police Department is like no other local law enforcement agency, however, because it employs approximately forty thousand sworn officers. My own research also uses an ecological approach to study police crime at more than thirty-four hundred state and local law enforcement agencies where officers have been arrested during the years 2005–14, treating counties and independent cities conceptually as if they were neighborhoods in order to generate state-level geographic heat maps to determine hot spots of police crime across the United States.[61]

DETERRENCE OF POLICE VIOLENCE THROUGH FORMAL AND INFORMAL GUARDIANSHIP

Routine activity theory is simple and intuitive. It posits that crime results from the convergence of a motivated offender, suitable target, and absence of a capable guardian. Cohen and Felson defined a capable guardian as any person or thing that discourages crime from taking place.[62] Anyone can fill the role of a capable guardian when that person's simple presence alone prevents crime from happening at specific places and times, and his or her absence makes the occurrence of crime more likely.[63] While we often think of guardians in the formal context as police officers and security guards, informal guardians are individuals such as passersby and neighborhood residents who are able to discourage the commission of crime simply by being there, often at times and places where a formal guardian such as a police officer is absent.[64] According to Felson, routine activity theory includes a guardianship component of informal social control consistent with Travis Hirschi's social control theory.[65] The presence of formal and informal guardians is especially important in deterring acts of police violence. A variety of internal and external controls are also closely related to the concept of guardianship through routine activities and serve as situational crime prevention designed to deter police misconduct. Internal controls take place within each law enforcement agency to deal with its own personnel, including its sworn officers, whereas external controls often include aspects of citizen oversight outside of law enforcement agencies.

Early Intervention Systems

Herman Goldstein recognized the phenomenon of the "problem officer" in the 1970s as individual police officers who "are well known to their supervisors, to the top administrators, to their peers, and to the residents of the areas in which they work . . . but [about which] little has been done to alter their conduct."[66] Studies have shown that in some large police departments a very small number of officers are chronic offenders who account for a disproportionately high number of excessive force complaints by citizens and are rarely disciplined.[67] My own research found that 674 sworn officers at state and local law enforcement agencies across the United States were arrested more than once (and/or had two or more criminal cases because they had more than one victim) during the years 2005–11.[68] I also found that almost 10 percent of the officers arrested during those seven years—and who were then criminally convicted and/or lost their job after being arrested—were once again or still working as a police officer in 2016.[69]

The US Commission on Civil Rights recommended in 1981 that police departments develop systems to assist in early identification of violence-prone sworn officers.[70] Early intervention systems (sometimes referred to as early warning systems) are computerized risk management monitoring applications that provide data on officer performance and, more specifically, identify problem officers and officers considered to be at risk of engaging in acts of police misconduct. Law enforcement agencies using these information management systems also typically provide interventions designed to correct problematic behaviors, as well as follow-up processes that continually track officers who have been flagged for review by supervisors.[71] Items tracked or flagged by personnel early intervention systems typically include data on officer training, numbers of arrests made, citizen complaints, misconduct allegations, use of force reports, sick leave usage, workplace injury reports, officer-involved traffic accidents, disciplinary actions taken against officers, being named as a party-defendant in a civil action (lawsuit), and records of officers being arrested.

The US Department of Justice considers early intervention systems an effective management strategy to promote police accountability[72] and has required the use of such systems for all police departments who have entered into court-ordered consent decrees to resolve pattern-and-practice lawsuits initiated by the Department of Justice. Written policies on the use of personnel early intervention systems are required for police departments seeking voluntary accreditation through the Commission on Accreditation for Law Enforcement Agencies.[73] There are more than eighteen thousand state and local law enforcement agencies in the United States, and most of them are fairly small agencies that employ fewer than thirty-five sworn employees.[74] Presumably, many small local law enforcement agencies do not make use of formal early intervention systems, and there are indications that many police departments simply ignore the flags generated by the systems that identify violence-prone problem officers. Research has not demonstrated the validity of early intervention systems. It is not known if early intervention has any deterrent effect in reducing police violence and other forms of police misconduct.[75]

Fleet Management Systems and GPS

Police departments have long used technological devices that record the operation of an officer's police cruiser. When I was a police officer with the Dover Police Department in New Hampshire in the 1980s, each police vehicle was equipped with an analog tachograph machine installed in the trunk. Earlier academic research found that tachograph machines were effective in reducing police vehicle traffic accidents "through mechanically aided supervision."[76] The tachograph recorded twenty-four hours of data onto a round wax-coated paper disc (resembling a 45-rpm phonograph record) that was replaced daily by police supervisors. The collected paper discs were reviewed for irregularities and, presumably, saved in boxes somewhere. Data recorded on each disc included things such as date and time for vehicle speed, activation of emergency lights, activation of headlights, application of brakes, and whether any of the vehicle doors were open. Officers hated the machines and universally referred to them as "trunk sergeants." Fleet management systems utilized now by law enforcement agencies include digital tachographs and global positioning system (GPS) vehicle tracking devices that transmit real-time data for integration with computer-aided dispatch (CAD) systems and allow for server- or cloud-based archiving of all data collected from the operation of police cruisers.

These tracking devices that monitor and record the movement and activities of law enforcement agency patrol vehicles have proven to be instrumental forensic evidence in numerous cases of alleged police violence. The GPS location data have been critical in corroborating victim allegations, especially in cases where an accused officer denied being present where a victim claimed an act of police violence occurred. In one such incident in 2014, a fifty-six-year-old police officer in Pickens, South Carolina, was accused of sexually assaulting a woman outside a laundromat while the officer was on duty. Although the officer denied he had been at the laundromat while on patrol that day, investigators with the South Carolina State Law Enforcement Division were able to determine that the officer's patrol cruiser was located outside the laundromat for one hour and twenty-two minutes on the day the woman claimed to have been assaulted.[77] The officer's DNA was found on the woman's breast. The officer was fired and charged with first degree assault and battery, as well as official misconduct.

Fleet management systems that utilize GPS technology to record the location of police cruisers presumably serve as a deterrent for sworn officers who might be tempted to engage in various forms of police misconduct, but there is an absence of research in this area. Nevertheless, the systems have also been beneficial in uncovering alleged nonviolent crimes by police officers, including criminal cases in which an officer falsified time records, stole money from drivers during traffic stops, stole building supplies from construction sites, or was charged with arson for burning multiple vacant or abandoned houses.[78]

The GPS tracking device installed in the police cruiser assigned to Oklahoma City police officer Daniel Holtzclaw was instrumental in corroborating the allegations of several of his victims. Archived location data placed Holtzclaw at the exact places and times where victims alleged they had been sexually assaulted or raped by a uniformed police officer who was driving a marked police cruiser.[79] Investigators also determined that on one occasion Holtzclaw deactivated his cruiser's GPS by manually turning off the in-car fleet management computer system at some point prior to a 2:00 a.m. traffic stop where he was alleged to have forced the female driver to perform oral sex on him.[80] A detective testified at Holtzclaw's criminal trial that she initially had been unable to rule out that Holtzclaw was *not* at the location of the alleged sexual assault because records indicated that his GPS was turned off. She was able to determine, however, that the GPS tracking devices were operational in the cruisers of every other police officer working in the district that night and that none of the other cruisers were in the vicinity of the place and time where the victim said the traffic stop and assault occurred. A police captain with the Oklahoma City Police Department also testified at Holtzclaw's trial that it was against departmental policy for officers to operate their patrol vehicles without activating the fleet management computer GPS.[81] Holtzclaw was convicted of multiple crimes relating to acts of police sexual violence and received a 263 year prison sentence.

Video Recordings of Police Behaviors and Interactions with the Public

The President's Task Force on 21st Century Policing promoted the increased use of police body-worn cameras (bodycams) to strengthen police accountability and improve transparency of law enforcement agencies.[82] Transparency is important because theoretically it can improve trust in the police and perceptions of procedural justice. It is not clear, however, that police bodycams ultimately strengthen accountability or improve transparency.[83] Research studies on the efficacy of police bodycams have given mixed results. Some studies have found that the cameras have no meaningful impact on changing police behaviors and reducing use of force incidents and citizen complaints, while other studies have found the opposite.[84] Other research has found that police behaviors change immediately following implementation of wearing bodycams but that over time any deterrent effects weaken as the cameras become normalized in daily police routines.[85] Bodycam recordings do not seem to sway juries in criminal trials of police officers charged with violence-related crimes. Numerous officers, for example, charged with murder or manslaughter resulting from on-duty police shootings have been acquitted at trials that included video evidence of the incidents.[86] Many law enforcement agencies, especially small police departments, have delayed or decided against issuing bodycams because of the high costs associated with electronically storing video files on computer servers.[87] Some jurisdictions have also found that there are unexpected personnel costs for prosecutor's offices in responding to court discovery requests and preparing video files for court proceedings and trials.[88]

Perhaps the most significant development regarding informal guardianship of police officers as protection against acts of police violence has been the proliferation of smartphones with built-in video recorders. The Pew Research Center reported that 77 percent of Americans owned a smartphone in January 2018, up from just 35 percent seven years earlier.[89] Smartphone ownership is nearly ubiquitous among young adults aged eighteen to twenty-nine, and there have been sharp increases in smartphone ownership among adults aged fifty and older and, more generally, among low-income adults.[90] Smartphone ownership across race and ethnicities is strikingly similar: Pew Research Center surveys conducted in January 2018 found that 77 percent of white adults, 75 percent of black adults, and 77 percent of Hispanic adults own smartphones.[91]

Countless acts of police violence have been captured by smartphones, providing alternative narratives for incidents in which eyewitness accounts considered reliable by law enforcement would not otherwise be available. Some of these cases have garnered immediate national media attention solely as a result of the smartphone recordings. The smartphone recordings in some cases of police violence have shown that officers gave false narratives in their verbal statements and written reports to investigators. North Charleston, South Carolina, police officer Michael Slager, for example, claimed that he shot and killed Walter Scott in April 2015 when Scott wrestled the officer's Taser away from him and was trying to use the stun gun as a weapon against the officer. A bystander's smartphone video, however, showed that Scott—a fifty-year-old Black male—was unarmed and running away from the officer when Slager fatally shot him in the back. Slager was charged with murder, but his trial in state court ended in a hung jury and mistrial. He was later sentenced to twenty years in federal prison after pleading guilty to criminal deprivation of rights under the color of law. Slager would never have been charged with any crime for killing Scott without the bystander smartphone recording that provided an alternate narrative to the officer's false account of the shooting incident. Emerging technologies such as smartphone video recorders and police body-worn cameras will continue to develop as forms of internal and external controls used by law enforcement agencies to deter and uncover acts of police violence and other forms of police misconduct.

The Civil Rights Act of 1871 was enacted to provide federal civil remedies to former slaves whose constitutional rights were violated by local officials conspiring with the Ku Klux Klan. It was later codified at 42 U.S.C. § 1983 and is commonly referred to as Section 1983. The statute, which sat dormant for much of the ensuing century, provides redress for persons whose federally protected rights are violated by a state actor under the color of law. In 1961 the US Supreme Court held that individual police officers can be sued in federal court under Section 1983 for violating a plaintiff's constitutional rights.[92] Municipal liability under Section 1983 attaches when a court finds that a local government official (a) acted under the color of law (b) pursuant to some custom, policy, or law of the government entity (c) so as to deprive a plaintiff of some right, privilege, or immunity granted by the US Constitution or a federal law.[93] Prior to 1978 there was no municipal liability under Section 1983. The statute is now the cornerstone of federal civil rights litigation against police officers, their employing law enforcement agencies, and municipalities.[94]

Section 1983 litigation has greatly increased since 1978, in part because municipal liability provides greater likelihood of plaintiffs being able to obtain settlements and collect monetary judgments from local government entities and their insurance carriers. The threat of Section 1983, however, does not serve as a deterrent for individual police officers who use excessive force or engage in other forms of police violence. It is difficult to recover money damages from an individual police officer because, as a practical matter, most police officers are judgment proof or have limited financial assets. In any event, there is very little chance in most litigation pursuant to Section 1983 that an individual police officer named as a party-defendant would be personally liable for money damages. Police officers sued for money damages under Section 1983 may invoke an affirmative defense of qualified immunity, asking the court to dismiss the claims against them individually.[95] The legal rationale for this qualified immunity is based on the public policy consideration that such protections are appropriate for government officials who are required to exercise discretion, so long as they are acting in good faith, in conducting their official duties. Causes of action against a police officer in Section 1983 litigation arising out of excessive force allegations also require a threshold judicial determination (distinct from the question of qualified immunity) as to whether the facts alleged in the civil complaint show that the defendant police officer's conduct violated a plaintiff's constitutional rights.[96] Courts analyze a plaintiff's claims of police excessive force in the factual contexts of investigatory stops and arrests under an objective reasonableness standard pursuant to the Fourth Amendment.[97] The objective reasonableness standard frames a court's analysis of the facts on what *a reasonable police officer* on the scene would have perceived (without the benefit of hindsight) in terms of any imminent threat and the amount of force necessary given the circumstances of the particular case.

VICTIMIZATION, LIFESTYLE, AND OPPORTUNITIES

Criminological theories attempt to explain "differential involvement" in criminal offending and uneven distribution of crime across time and place, and victimology theories attempt to explain "differential risks" and skewed distributions of victimization across time and place.[98] The routine activity theory in criminology is closely linked to the lifestyle theory in victimology. Both theories treat the creation of an opportunity for criminal victimization as the convergence in time and place of a motivated offender, suitable target (i.e., the victim), and absence of capable guardianship. In this context, Michael Hindelang, Michael Gottfredson, and James Garofalo coined the term *routine activities* in 1978 and Lawrence Cohen and Marcus Felson subsequently adopted it.[99] The theories differ in how each views behaviors that create risk for victimization. Routine activity theory "*describes* the victimization event" (e.g., victimization occurs through the convergence of three elements—motivated offender, suitable target to victimize, and absence of capable guardianship—and victimization is avoided and does not occur in the absence of any one of the three elements), whereas lifestyle theory conceptualizes victimization as "risk in *probabilistic* terms" (e.g., the odds of a person being victimized increase with certain behaviors).[100] Both theories posit that crime occurs through the opportunities found in the lifestyles and routine activities of both offenders and victims.

The Lifestyle Model of Criminal Victimization

Hindelang, Gottfredson, and Garofalo offered a preliminary theoretical model of victimization applicable to the common law personal crimes of rape, robbery, assault, and larceny (the offenses are listed in descending order of crime seriousness).[101] In its original form, the theory was grounded in victim survey data from several major US cities in the 1970s. The premise of the theory is that personal victimization depends on the "routine daily activities, both vocational activities (work, school, housekeeping, etc.) and leisure activities," that are inherent to the concept of lifestyle.[102] The theory posits that lifestyle determines the likelihood of personal victimization through exposure to various events and associations. Victimization through the commission of crimes against persons is most likely to occur in high-risk places at high-risk times. Some people are at higher risk of being victimized than others, because individual lifestyle patterns "influence (a) the amount of exposure to places and times with varying risks of victimization, and (b) the prevalence of associations with others who are more or less likely to commit crimes."[103] It stands to reason that someone withdrawing cash from an ATM on a darkened street corner at midnight stands a greater chance of being targeted and is at higher personal risk for victimization in a robbery than someone who withdraws cash from the same ATM during daylight hours when the streets are crowded. Risky behavioral routines increase the likelihood of victimization in crimes against persons such as rapes, robberies, assaults, and larcenies.

Linking Rational Choice, Routine Activity, and Lifestyle

Ezzat Fattah argued that treating crime and victimization as two separate phenomena ignores that both perspectives "are simply two sides of the same coin" that should be linked theoretically to produce less fragmented research and scholarship.[104] Felson and others have continued to revise routine activity theory over the past three decades.[105] Hindelang, Gottfredson, and Garofalo's lifestyle theory was never revised (perhaps the consequence of Hindelang's death in 1982 at age thirty-six from a brain tumor). There is a body of research testing what has become a "conjoined lifestyle/routine activity theory" that, unfortunately, largely disregards the theoretical differences in how "risk" should be conceptualized in each of the two theories.[106] The result is that many of these studies ignore the probabilistic risk of victimization and, instead, view victimization solely in terms of the victimization event.

Targets and Opportunities for Police Violence Victimization

The context of police encounters with the public can predict increased opportunities for officers to engage in various forms of police violence. For example, an individual who is perceived by an officer as acting like an asshole during a street encounter is more likely to be arrested than if the officer thinks he or she is cooperative and nonargumentative.[107]

Other examples from my own police crime research also demonstrate the contexts and associations found in various opportunities to offend, routine activities, and victim lifestyle. The odds of an officer being arrested for a violence-related crime increase if the alleged act of police violence was detected by the filing of a citizen complaint.[108] The crimes for which school resource officers are arrested are more likely to be sex-related offenses than the crimes of arrested officers who are not assigned to work in schools.[109] Female officers are more likely to be arrested for profit-motivated offenses than violence-related ones.[110] Off-duty police officers who drive drunk are more likely to get arrested if (a) their drunk driving incident results in a traffic accident with injuries or (b) they flee from the scene of a hit-and-run that resulted from the officer's drunk driving.[111] The greatest predictors of an officer being convicted of a crime involving an act of police sexual violence are cases where an officer was terminated after being arrested for forcibly fondling a child victim.[112] In cases of officer-involved domestic violence, the odds of conviction increase if the arrested officer used a personally owned gun during the incident.[113]

The routine activity events and lifestyles of some individuals increase their opportunities and risk of being victimized through acts of police violence. The age of a victim predicts the type of crime for which an officer is arrested. The greatest predictors of an officer being arrested for a sex-related crime are cases where the victim is nineteen or younger, female, and either unrelated to the arrested officer or related but not the child of the officer.[114] On rare occasions police officers have been arrested for crimes involving the criminal misuse of conductive energy devices, such as a Taser. Victims in stun gun cases were typically persons who were no threat to the officer, including teenagers and homeless individuals.[115] Relationship of the victim to the arrested officer is the second greatest predictor of whether an arrested officer is convicted (the greatest predictor of conviction is the seriousness of the offense for which an officer is arrested). Officers stand the greatest chance of being convicted of a crime if the victim is a child or adult who is unrelated to the arrested officer (either nonstranger acquaintance or stranger).[116] When reading this chapter's policy box, "Easy Targets: Driving While Female," consider how the routine activities of offenders are linked to the lifestyles and routine activities of victims.

Traffic stops provide ample opportunity for police officers to victimize female motorists. Samuel Walker and Dawn Irlbeck refer to this situation as "driving while female."[a] Some of the "driving while female" traffic stops are initiated by an officer who spots an attractive girl or woman driving a car and wants to find out who she is and perhaps ask for her phone number. Other times the incidents result in an officer sexually harassing the female driver, and in rare instances the traffic stop leads to a violent rape of the female driver by the officer. Often the police officer conducting the "driving while female" traffic stop does not notify his dispatcher of the stop, as part of an effort to be able to deny the encounter if the female driver later files a complaint. Most of the "driving while female" encounters, however, are situations where victims are often reluctant to file a complaint, in large part because they do not think they will be believed or taken seriously.

During the years 2005–13 there were 211 arrest cases involving 142 individual police officers, each of whom was arrested for criminal offenses arising out of "driving while female" traffic stops. The arrested officers were employed by 123 state and local law enforcement agencies located in 105 counties and independent cities across the United States. The most serious offenses charged against the arrested police officer in these "driving while female" cases include forcible fondling (19.4%), forcible rape (17.1%), forcible sodomy (8.1%), simple assault (5.7%), intimidation and harassment (5.7%), criminal deprivation of civil rights (5.7%), bribery (5.2%), kidnapping and abduction (3.8%), official misconduct (3.8%), extortion or blackmail (2.8%), and aggravated assault (2.8%), among others.

Some of the cases in which sworn officers have been arrested for on-duty sex crimes occurring during traffic stops were taken seriously by investigators only when they were able to corroborate a victim's story by examining archived GPS data from an agency's fleet management system. In one such case, a sheriff's deputy in Tulare County, California, was charged with eighteen criminal offenses stemming from allegations by five women that he had demanded sexual favors during traffic stops in rural areas of the county. The deputy was sentenced to five years in prison after pleading no contest to two felony counts of oral copulation under the color of law and two counts of misdemeanor sexual battery. County detectives filed

a. Walker and Irlbeck, *Driving While Female.*

the criminal charges after confirming the location of the deputy's patrol car in each incident by using data from the cruiser's GPS tracking system.[b]

My research suggests that the crimes committed by officers in "driving while female" traffic stop scenarios are not isolated incidents but rather are crimes committed by serial sexual predators who happen to be employed as police officers. Often there is a pattern: once a female driver is believed by investigators and criminal charges are filed against a police officer, and the incident is reported in the news media, there are almost always more victims who come forward to report that they, too, were sexually assaulted by that on-duty officer. Most on-duty police officers who prey on vulnerable girls and women are never disciplined by their employing law enforcement agency and are rarely arrested.

b. Rose, "Ex-deputy William Nulick to Stand Trial for Sexual Assault."

CRITICAL THINKING QUESTIONS

1. How is deterrence theory helpful in understanding police violence?

2. What strategies using routine activities theory can be developed to reduce victimization caused by acts of police sexual violence?

3. Does the Exclusionary Rule promote or discourage police misconduct?

4. Using the interactive heat maps on the Henry A. Wallace Police Crime Database website,[117] where are the hot spots of police violence across the United States?

THREE

Individual-Level Theories

Since the late 1990s, there has been considerable interest within criminology in biological and biosocial research on the role of human genetics, neurological functioning, and hormones in relation to crime and delinquency. None of that research, however, has been specifically applied to the study of police behaviors and acts of police violence. This chapter focuses on individual-level theories that have been applied to the study of police misconduct and, more specifically, police violence. Much of the research involving individual-level theories takes place through the application of psychological theories to policing. Also discussed in this chapter are theories derived from the unique occupational aspects of policing.

PSYCHOLOGICAL ASPECTS OF POLICE MISCONDUCT

Richard Lundman observed in 1980 that the recruitment standards, selection criteria, and hiring processes of state and local law enforcement agencies had long produced a "remarkably homogenous" group of mostly high-school-educated white males from blue-collar backgrounds to work as police officers.[1] The police personality, however, is developed over time through exposure to formal police academy training and socialization to the police subculture. The psychological aspects and personality traits commonly found among individual police officers seem to be the product of exposure to the shared experiences of (a) quasi-military-style police academy training and (b) the realities of police work over time. Research has highlighted psychological factors in explaining use of excessive force and police violence.

Police departments have long used psychological instruments as a preemployment screening device to help identify and screen out job applicants who would not be suitable police officers. In 1916 the San Jose Police Department in California retained a psychology professor to conduct standardized testing of all individuals applying for police officer positions.[2] Both Wilmington, Delaware, and Toledo, Ohio, started using psychological and psychiatric preemployment screening of police applicants in 1938, and numerous other municipal police departments across the United States did so as well over the next three decades.[3] In 1967 the President's Commission on Law Enforcement and Administration of Justice recommended that local law enforcement agencies improve their preemployment screening.[4] Six years later another federal commission recommended that "police practitioners and behavioral scientists conduct research to develop job-related mental ability and aptitude tests, and personality inventories for the identification of qualified police applicants."[5]

The Minnesota Multiphasic Personality Inventory (MMPI) was published in 1940 and is one of several psychological instruments used extensively by state and local law enforcement agencies as part of their preemployment psychological screening of applicants for sworn officer positions.[6] I remember taking the MMPI prior to being hired as a police officer in 1986. The MMPI-2, a revised validated instrument consisting of 567 true/false items, was published in 1990.[7]

A large body of research examines the utility of the MMPI in the context of police personnel, such as studies that assess the validity of various MMPI scales and others that explore the predictive validity of the instruments regarding aspects of future job performance, police integrity, and problem behaviors. One group of researchers in 1988 derived an aggressiveness index from several MMPI scales and found that high index scores were associated with officers' self-reported physical aggressiveness toward others.[8] In another study, the same researchers examined personnel files of sworn officers employed by six local law enforcement agencies and created samples of fifty-three problem officers and fifty-three matched pairs of nonproblem officers. The problem officers had each experienced involuntary employment terminations, resignations in lieu of involuntary termination, or disciplinary suspensions for multiple days without pay. All the officers in both samples were previously administered the MMPI through preemployment psychological screening. When compared with the sample of nonproblem officers, the sample of problem officers was different in a number of statistically significant ways on several MMPI scales that have been associated in other policing studies with inappropriate aggression and poor performance evaluations by supervisors.[9] Curt Bartol developed an immaturity index from several MMPI scales and found high index scores to be strong predictors of involuntary termination in a longitudinal study of six hundred police officers in Vermont over a thirteen-year period (1975–88).[10] Bartol's study is unique because it examines preemployment psychological assessments and predictors of police misconduct in the context of sworn officers who work in small towns and rural communities.

More recent studies have examined the predictive validity of newer MMPI-2 instruments and scales to assess outcomes related to police integrity and problem officers. Some of these studies have found that certain MMPI-2 scales are not useful predictors of future police misconduct.[11] Recent research provides support for using the predictive validity of the MMPI-2-Restructured Form (MMPI-2-RF) to predict police officer problem behaviors.[12] This line of research might be limited by the possibility that samples are devoid of those job applicants who were washed out during preemployment screening and not hired as police officers. Some of the studies confound whether the purpose of preemployment psychological screening is to (a) identify candidates with preexisting psychological disorders that would somehow disqualify them from being employed as an officer or (b) identify candidates whose psychological profiles might be predictors of future problem behavior if they were to be employed as an officer. The MMPI was designed to assess various psychological disorders in a clinical setting. It was "not designed to evaluate job performance in so-called normal populations" of police officers.[13] There are newer instruments designed specifically for use in psychological preemployment screening, and presumably those will become more prevalent in the years ahead.

Changes to federal laws in the early 1990s have impacted on both the manner of preemployment psychological screening procedures and use of certain data and statistical operations to analyze test score results. The Americans with Disabilities Act of 1990 prohibits employers (including state and local governmental entities) from using preemployment tests or selection criteria in the hiring process that screen out or tend to screen out individuals with disabilities (including mental impairments), unless the test or other selection criteria as used by the employer is proven to be necessary for the job.[14] Similarly, the Civil Rights Act of 1991 prohibits the use of different cut-off scores or norms on the basis of a job applicant's race, color, religion, sex, or national origin in the analysis and interpretation of preemployment psychological screening tests.[15] Most state and local law enforcement agencies utilize extensive preemployment screening of job applicants for sworn officer positions. The process typically includes a background investigation (including a criminal history and credit check), standardized written tests, interviews with the applicant, medical examination by a physician (including a cardiovascular workup and testing for illicit drug use), physical fitness tests, polygraph exam, and psychological assessments. The effect of the federal prohibitions against certain discriminatory practices in preemployment testing and screening is that psychological instruments (such as the MMPI-2) are now administered to a perspective police officer only *after* a conditional offer of employment has been made by a hiring law enforcement agency.[16] Presumably a conditional offer of employment is contingent upon successful completion of psychological screening.

Many states mandate preemployment screening prior to hiring candidates for sworn positions in state and local law enforcement agencies. It is also a required standard for state and local law enforcement agencies that voluntarily elect to seek accreditation by the Commission on Accreditation for Law Enforcement Agencies.[17] One study of 355 police departments across the country found that more than 90 percent of those agencies use the MMPI-2 for preemployment screening.[18] Many small municipal police departments, however, do not use psychological screening as part of the hiring process for new officers. The Carroll Police Department in Iowa started using psychological assessments and polygraph examinations in preemployment screening only after a local newspaper reported on the misconduct of a problem officer who was hired after being fired by another local police department.[19]

In other police departments—even large ones employing hundreds of sworn officers—flags raised by clinical psychologists who conduct the preemployment screening are not always disqualifying. The Tacoma Police Department in Washington State ignored the recommendations of two clinical psychologists to *not* hire David Brame as a police officer in 1981. The first psychologist wrote in his report that he did "not recommend the candidate for employment" and a second psychologist indicated in a separate report that Brame was "a marginal police officer applicant and the prognosis for his developing into an above average officer is judged poor at this time."[20] Brame was hired and eventually became was the police chief in Tacoma. The records of

Brame's preemployment psychological screening were found in his personnel file by investigators after he killed his estranged wife and himself in 2003. More recently, prosecutors in Hennepin County, Minnesota, admitted irregularities in the 2015 preemployment psychological screening for Officer Mohamed Noor of the Minneapolis Police Department. Less than three years after he was hired, Noor was charged with third-degree murder and second-degree manslaughter for the July 2017 on-duty shooting death of Justine Ruszczyk Damond. Noor's preemployment MMPI-2-RF test results indicated "a level of disaffiliativeness that may be incompatible with public safety requirements for good interpersonal functioning," leading two psychiatrists to express concern after Noor "showed an inability to handle the stress of police work as well as a general unwillingness to be around people."[21]

When reading the policy box for this chapter, "Schenectady Police Officer Arrested Nine Times in Three Years," consider the potential psychological issues that are raised or inferred in the facts of the nine arrest incidents and how they might impact on policies within the officer's employing police department.

Rotten Apples in Policing

William Shakespeare wrote more than four hundred years ago in *The Taming of the Shrew* that "there's small choice in rotten apples," and Benjamin Franklin wrote in his *Poor Richard's Almanac* for 1736 that "the rotten apple spoils his companion."[22] Building on this metaphor, the rotten apple theory of police corruption posits that most acts of police corruption are committed by relatively few individual sworn officers within a police organization. Rotten apple theory sits in contrast to rotten barrel theory. Petter Gottschalk presents the metaphorical differences in the context of white-collar crime: occupational crime by individuals is associated with rotten apples (i.e., bad actor individuals) and corporate crime is associated with systems failure.[23] Rotten apple theory is an individual-level theoretical perspective within criminology that attempts to explain crime by individuals, whereas rotten barrel theory is an organizational crime theoretical perspective that attempts to explain crime by business enterprises. Applied to police misconduct, the rotten apple theory asserts that (a) individual police officers engage in acts of police misconduct without the knowledge or support of their fellow officers and supervisors; and (b) once the bad actor (i.e., the metaphoric rotten apple) is removed, "the problem is fixed—the rest of the apples and the barrel are fine."[24]

SCHENECTADY POLICE OFFICER ARRESTED NINE TIMES IN THREE YEARS

John Lewis was found dead at the age of forty-four in his home on February 20, 2014. His life had been unraveling for many years. Lewis was a police officer with the Schenectady Police Department in New York State for sixteen years until he was fired for the second time in April 2010. The first time Lewis was fired was in 1998 after he was accused of using a racial slur, but an arbitrator ordered the city to rehire him. Lewis was arrested in April 2008 following allegations that he shoved his wife during an argument, and he was suspended from his job for thirty days. He was acquitted at a bench trial but not before he was arrested in June 2008 for violating an order of protection that had been issued after the first arrest.[a] Lewis was also arrested in November 2008 after he allegedly threatened to kill his ex-wife, and he was again suspended for thirty days from his job as a Schenectady police officer.[b] He was also arrested for drunk driving in December 2008 and was again suspended from his job for thirty days.[c]

Lewis was also arrested twice in 2009. In January he was arrested for criminal mischief after his mother called 9-1-1 to report that he was "destroying the house" and fighting with his brother, an Albany police officer.[d] Lewis was also charged with computer tampering and eavesdropping felonies in December 2009 after he was accused of hacking into his ex-wife's email account. Also in December, Lewis was stabbed in his chest by a girlfriend during an argument with her in Massachusetts. While most of the criminal cases from the prior year were still pending, Lewis was arrested in January 2010 for driving while intoxicated and leaving the scene of a traffic accident in a hospital parking lot.[e] Around that time, contempt charges for violating the protection order the prior June were dropped by prosecutors. Lewis was acquitted in February 2010 for the first drunk driving arrest.[f] While incarcerated following the January arrest, Lewis was

a. Lamendola, "City Police Officer Innocent of Harassment in Domestic Dispute."
b. Cook, "Schenectady Police Officer Arrested for Third Time."
c. Goot, "Schenectady Police Officer Charged with DWI."
d. Web staff, "Schenectady Police Officer Charged with Criminal Mischief."
e. Crowe, "Suspended Schenectady Police Officer Charged with DWI."
f. Simons, "Schenectady Police Officer John Lewis Acquitted on Three Counts."

arrested in March 2010 for misdemeanor reckless endangerment of property after he broke a window in his jail cell block.[g]

On April 12, 2010, Lewis was terminated from his position as a police officer with the Schenectady Police Department. The firing "followed a lengthy disciplinary review hearing and report issued by an independent hearing officer."[h] Lewis was indicted in federal court the following month for violating the Lautenberg Amendment to the federal Gun Control Act, because he allegedly had possessed a handgun in November 2008 while under a domestic violence order of protection. He later pleaded guilty and was sentenced to sixteen months in federal prison, with credit for time served in the county jail.

g. Carleo-Evangelist, "Suspended Schenectady Police Officer Charged with Breaking Window in Jail Cell."
h. Schenectady Mayor's Office, "Stratton Fires Police Officer John Lewis."

Robert Kane and Michael White noted the appeal of rotten apple theory to many police chiefs across the country: police departments can maintain that the problem of police misconduct is "solved, and the organization is spared any real scrutiny for the problem" when an individual problem officer's employment is terminated.[25] In its report on police corruption in the New York Police Department during the late 1960s and early 1970s, the Knapp Commission wrote that the rotten apple theory explanation of police misconduct was the result of "stubbornness, hostility, and pride" that had served as "a basic obstacle to meaningful reform" in the city's police department.[26] The Knapp Commission found that corruption was widespread within the New York Police Department but that drastic changes were not possible because no one within the agency's command structure acknowledged the extent of the problem. Whitman Knapp, the federal judge who chaired the commission bearing his name, was quoted in the *New York Times* as saying, "We've finally blown the old rotten apple theory once and for all, and got even the highest police officials to admit to themselves and publicly that the police body has cancer. Now that the patient has admitted it, we can operate."[27]

Lawrence Sherman hypothesized in his sociological theory of police corruption that *all* police departments have at least a small amount of corruption resulting from a few bad apples (i.e., corrupt individual officers) and a few "rotten pockets" (i.e., small groups of corrupt officers) within the agency.[28] Others have suggested that bad apples in policing are the product of low hiring standards and that the problem can be resolved by law enforcement agencies adhering to high standards for the recruitment, selection, and hiring of new police officers.[29] While it is true that preemployment screening is an important aspect of police integrity, research has not resolved the chicken-or-egg question of whether propensities to engage in police violence or other forms of police misconduct preexist an individual officer's initial date of hire. A more plausible theoretical explanation is that most police officers start their careers as law-abiding individuals.

Authoritarian Personality

Numerous policing scholars have cited to Theodor Adorno, Else Frenkel-Brunswik, Daniel Levinson, and R. Nevitt Sanford's authoritarian personality research as an explanation of police misconduct.[30] But Adorno and his colleagues' study had nothing to do with police misconduct; they were working in the 1940s to develop a set of personality trait criteria to identify fascist individuals.[31] Their study—a book titled *The Authoritarian Personality*—grew out of a 1944 conference of the American Jewish Committee on religious and racial prejudice. The personality trait variables on Adorno and his colleagues' fascist scale (which they labeled the F Scale) are conventionalism, authoritarian aggression, anti-intraception, superstition and stereotypy, power and toughness, destructiveness and cynicism, projectivity, and exaggerated sexual concerns.[32] They defined conventionalism as "rigid adherence to conventional, middle-class values" and authoritarian aggression as the "tendency to be on the lookout for, and to condemn, reject, and punish people who violate conventional norms."[33] Arthur Niederhoffer noted that the F Scale variables are personality traits that manifest in the occupational role of police officers, which he called the "authoritarian police personality."[34] Several research studies have examined the relationship of authoritarian police personality traits to police misconduct.[35] None of those studies, however, utilized the F Scale developed by Adorno and his colleagues and applied to policing by Niederhoffer. Seven decades after the development of the fascist scale, the authoritarian personality research of Adorno and his colleagues is viewed as deeply flawed for its methodological assumptions and biases about types of dangerous individuals.[36]

Adorno and his colleagues defined cynicism as a generalized destructive hostility and "vilification of the human."[37] Niederhoffer applied this element of the F Scale to four stages of cynicism across the course of a police officer's career. According to Niederhoffer, the first stage is pseudo-cynicism, which recruits experience while attending the police academy. At this preliminary stage, the cynicism "barely conceals the idealism and commitment beneath the surface."[38] This pseudo-cynicism is replaced at some point during the first five years of an officer's career with a second stage, which Niederhoffer called romantic cynicism. The officers most vulnerable to the disillusionment of police work during this period of romantic cynicism are the very same young officers who were the most idealistic when they started their careers a few years earlier. Niederhoffer theorized that a third stage of cynicism, aggressive cynicism, occurs around the ten-year mark of an officer's policing career. The manner in which aggressive cynicism is manifested depends on the concurrence of an individual officer's cynicism and the subculture of cynicism already existing within an officer's employing law enforcement agency. The blatantly aggressive third stage of cynicism is overtaken in the last few years of a police officer's career with a fourth and final stage of resigned cynicism. Niederhoffer suggested that at this point in an officer's career he or she "comes to terms with the flaws of the system."[39]

My research on police officers arrested during the years 2005–7 found that 17.4 percent of the cases involved an officer with eighteen or more years of service at time of arrest.[40] Late-stage police crime is a problem not previously identified by criminologists. It seems at odds with Niederhoffer's view of resigned cynicism as an officer approaches his or her retirement. Perhaps not all police officers experience high levels of cynicism. Other research has found that police officers with high levels of cynicism are more tolerant of police misconduct than other officers. One study found that newly hired police officers with high levels of job satisfaction were less likely to adhere to a police code of silence, while more cynical rookie officers expressing a "fatalistic view of police efficacy were more likely to adhere to the code of silence."[41] Another study found that cynicism was a significant predictor of officers exhibiting problem police behaviors such as being the subject of formal citizen complaints, complaints by other officers, or internal affairs investigations or being involved in multiple use of force incidents.[42] Similarly, Beth Sanders found that police officers exhibiting high levels of cynicism in psychological testing were more likely than other officers to receive poor performance ratings in annual reviews by their supervisors and police chiefs.[43]

Aggression and Policing

Thomas Bernard's angry aggression theory posits that individuals who are chronically in a state of psychological arousal tend to interpret events as threatening more than other individuals do.[44] Bernard offered the theory as an explanation of a subculture of angry aggression among "truly disadvantaged" socially isolated individuals in inner-city neighborhoods who respond violently to seemingly trivial conflicts and insults.[45] He argued that angry aggression is an additive effect of the urban community, low social position, and discriminatory social factors leading to a "feedback loop" generating an aggressive environment that "increases the likelihood of aggression through vicarious and instrumental learning and through reasonable expectations of dangerousness."[46] It occurs in places where chronically aroused individuals are always in a socially isolated environment that is dangerous because everyone tends to see threats everywhere and they respond aggressively to the perceived threats. Over time the chronic physiological arousal becomes the basis for a subculture in which angry aggression is embedded in group values, norms, and worldviews.

Sean Griffin and Thomas Bernard applied angry aggression theory as an explanation of police violence.[47] While working, police officers are chronically aroused by many physiological stressors. They are socially isolated from the general public and are unable to remove the occupational sources of stress they experience as police officers. Angry aggression theory posits that police officers tend to see more threats and respond to them more aggressively than others do, and these perceptions and responses become embedded in the police subculture. Griffin and Bernard argued that police officers who do not have appropriate coping mechanisms might transfer and target their angry aggression to vulnerable individuals they come into contact with while working. The vulnerable individuals that police typically come into contact with during their work shifts are the people must likely to be victimized by acts of police violence. Many police officers do possess appropriate coping skills and exhibit high levels of self-control and would not be susceptible to manifestations of angry aggression. Individual-level differences among police officers are consistent with the expectations of angry aggression theory as applied to the phenomenon of police violence.

Police work is ugly. No one calls the police because they are having a good day. Police officers tend to encounter people who are having a really bad day. And if it was not a bad day already, certainly the day just got worse when the police showed up. Policing is an especially stressful occupation because the work often involves dangerous situations, repeated exposure to disturbing crime scenes, and stress-inducing bureaucratic rules.[48] Researchers have long recognized a link between the unique occupational stress experienced by police officers and a variety of negative outcomes, including poor health, chronic absenteeism, burnout, alcoholism, and officer attitudes regarding use of force.[49]

It has been said that police work involves many hours of sheer boredom punctuated by moments of sheer terror.[50] At times, the work is *very* boring. Scott Phillips argued that police work is often so boring that officers engage in discretionary nonwork activities during their shifts as a way to reduce stress and alleviate boredom.[51] Research on police workloads has consistently found that uniformed officers assigned to patrol duties in urban and suburban jurisdictions spend the bulk of their time on routine motorized patrol (i.e., just randomly driving around in a police cruiser), followed by tasks relating to administrative duties (e.g., shift preparation, attending roll call, and writing reports), driving to specific locations, waiting for other police officers, and handling personal tasks unrelated to their jobs as sworn law enforcement officers.[52] Officers assigned to community-oriented policing spend more time than beat officers on tasks related to problem-solving activities, gathering information, and meetings with nonpolice service providers, as well as on administrative duties and personal errands.[53] John Liederbach and James Frank found that police officers in small towns and rural communities also spend a large amount of time on routine patrol, driving to specific locations, and handling administrative and personal tasks, but they additionally devote a lot of time to things not typically dealt with by officers who work in urban and communities, including "situations involving utility problems, parade escorts, littering, performing house checks for citizens on vacation, transporting citizens who were not in custody, and animal-related problems (e.g., cows blocking traffic)."[54] Liederbach and Frank's research is consistent with Brian Payne, Bruce Berg, and Ivan Sun's observation that policing in small towns involves "dogs, drunks, disorder, and dysfunction."[55] Payne and his colleagues found that police officers who work in small towns fulfill overlapping roles of law enforcement: being a friend, being a social worker, providing animal control, and facilitating dispute resolution.

In some police departments in urban and suburban communities, patrol officers spend much of their time responding to and handling dispatched calls for service, and there is often little downtime between calls. When I was a dispatcher with the Arlington County Police Department in Virginia, patrol officers often worked their whole shift going from call to call, with very little uncommitted time to engage in discretionary activities, except on the weeknight midnight shift between 3:00 and 6:00 a.m. The uniformed officers in each district who were designated as crime scene agents (with specialized training and equipment to process accident and crime scenes) often spent most of their shifts responding to calls to back up the beat officers at a scene.

Arlington County is an urban area of twenty-six square miles with a population of 230,000 that swells to well over 500,000 during weekdays. It is directly across the Potomac River from downtown northwest areas of Washington, DC. The Arlington County Police Department employs more than three hundred sworn officers. It is very different from where I later worked as a police officer in Dover, New Hampshire, a small New England city of thirty thousand whose police department employs about forty-two sworn officers. In Dover, it was often very busy, but on a typical day each patrol officer handled fewer dispatched calls for service than when I worked in Arlington. Unlike Arlington, patrol officers in Dover handled many follow-up investigations; the detectives' caseloads were limited primarily to vice, drugs, and some juvenile work. Each day at the beginning of shift roll-call briefings, a supervisor would hand two or three case files to each patrol officer for follow-up investigations to be handled during the shift. The files (together with updated status reports) were turned in at the end of each shift. On most shifts, there was no downtime because all the time between dispatched calls was occupied by work on follow-up investigations. I liked the system in Dover because it provided young patrol officers with opportunities to gain experience as investigators (whereas in many police departments all criminal investigations are handled by detectives).

After I left the Dover Police Department—but before I moved back to the Washington, DC, area to attend law school—I spent a *long* winter working as a police officer in Barnstead, New Hampshire. They were shorthanded for the winter, and I did it to help out a friend who worked there. Barnstead is a rural community with a population of forty-five hundred and usually only one on-duty police officer working each shift. Calls for service to the Barnstead Police

Department were dispatched by the Belknap County Sheriff's Office, and often the only backup officers available when I worked in Barnstead were state troopers who were often fifteen or more miles away. On a typical night shift in Barnstead there were very few dispatched calls for service. I spent most of my working hours driving around mostly unpaved dirt roads, occasionally conducting traffic stops for speeding violations on Route 28 (a two-lane road that was the closest thing to a state highway in that area), and checking on unoccupied vacation homes and cabins that the police chief wanted checked several times each week. It was an incredibly boring place to work as a police officer.

Shift Work

Police officers often suffer negative consequences of shift work. Local law enforcement agencies typically have sworn officers on duty twenty-four hours a day, seven days a week. Federal law allows for police officers to work a maximum of 171 hours in a twenty-eight-day period without overtime compensation.[56] Police departments have great latitude in how they structure the scheduling of shift work within twenty-eight-day periods. Some agencies assign patrol officers to work permanent shifts, with the same days off each week. Other agencies assign officers to rotating shifts in which they work a combination of day, evening, and/or overnight shifts throughout the month, with different days off each week. Some agencies have two shifts of twelve hours each (a day shift and a night shift), whereas other agencies may have three shifts of eight hours each (days, evenings, and overnights) or may even utilize a combination of overlapping eight-hour, ten-hour, or twelve-hour shifts. Depending on how an agency structures duty assignments, officers may work with different colleagues regularly, or officers may always work with the same group of officers and supervisors. Shift work and overtime are reported as among the most difficult and stressful aspects of being a police officer.[57] Working atypical shifts puts police officers at risk for a variety of health problems, including sleep disorders, workplace injuries resulting from fatigue, metabolic syndrome, and other ailments resulting from chronic fatigue.[58]

Burnout

A large body of research addresses burnout in human services professions including mental health, public health nursing, and social work. Burnout in these helping professions occurs when an employee feels overwhelmed, overworked, lacking control, and chronically stressed from dealing with other people's problems. Burnout results from individual factors, client factors, and the organizational structure that affects how an employing organization functions.[59] Numerous studies have used a "measurement of experienced burnout" scale developed by Christina Maslach and Susan Jackson—the Maslach Burnout Inventory (MBI)—to assess various aspects of what the two researchers called "burnout syndrome" in human services professionals.[60] Burnout tends to vary by career stage. One study found that police officers exhibit the highest levels of burnout between sixteen and twenty-five years of service.[61] A study of police officers in Portugal found that burnout was a statistically significant predictor of self-reported verbal and physical aggression.[62] Other studies have found that police officers exhibiting suicidal ideation are more likely than other officers to self-report burnout and exhaustion,[63] as well as symptomology of post-traumatic stress disorder (PTSD).[64] An officer's inability to cope with the occupational stress and traumatic experiences is sometimes a precipitant to police suicidal ideation, suicidal behavior, and suicide.[65] Future research is needed to more thoroughly examine the relationship between various psychological aspects of policing, including burnout, and police violence.

CRITICAL THINKING QUESTIONS

1. Should preemployment screening of potential police officers include psychological testing? If so, what is the predictive validity in using the standardized psychological testing instruments (e.g., MMPI-2) to predict future problem behaviors such as propensities to engage in acts of police violence?

2. How does cynicism relate to police violence and other forms of police misconduct?

3. Is shift work in policing a factor that contributes to officers engaging in acts of police violence?

4. What role does stress have on officers engaging in acts of police violence?

FOUR

Social Structure Theories

This chapter explores a variety of social structure theories. These are macro-level criminological theoretical explanations that account for "variations in crime rates across communities by examining the variations in structural characteristics and conditions of each community."[1] According to Akers, social structure theories explain between-group variations and contend that people in certain groups, in certain locations, or encountering particular pressures created by the social structure will engage in more crime than other people in other groups and locations.[2] Social structure theories differ from social process theories discussed in chapter 5 that explain within-group variation. Both social structure theories and social process theories tend to consider interrelated aspects of processes and structural conditions that produce criminal behavior.

SOCIAL DISORGANIZATION

Émile Durkheim argued that increases in crime due to the breakdown of social controls were associated with rapid social change in society. This idea was at the core of research at the University of Chicago Sociology Department in the 1920s and 1930s as professors considered environmental factors associated with crime in neighborhoods. Their research focused on correlating neighborhood characteristics with neighborhood crime rates. One of the Chicago sociologists, Robert Park, conceptualized a parallel between the distribution of plant life in nature and human life in societies that he called the theory of human ecology. Using census tract data for Chicago, Park and his colleagues found a correlation between the percentage of residents who owned their own homes, land values, disease, and crime.[3]

Park and his colleagues Ernest Burgess and Roderick McKenzie mapped their data by neighborhood census tracts and conceptualized the city as a series of distinct concentric zones that radiated from the central city business district. The researchers found patterns where there were consistently fewer social problems, such as rampant disease and high crime rates, in the outer concentric zones farthest from the core zones. They identified five distinct concentric zones: zone 1 was the central business district of the city, zone 2 was an area of transition, zone 3 largely consisted of working-class homes, and zone 4 was the last zone within the city limits and home to middle-class families. Zone 5 was a suburban area outside the city limits. The most socially disorganized zone was zone 2, where new immigrants often lived in close proximity to where jobs were located at factories. As the relative economic positions of families improved, they often moved away from the city center into the zone where the working-class lived. As each wave moved to nicer and more expensive neighborhoods, they were replaced in the transition zone (zone 2) by new immigrants eager to find factory employment in Chicago's central business zone.

Clifford Shaw and Henry McKay, also sociologists at the University of Chicago, extended Park's theory of concentric zones to the study of juvenile delinquency in the 1930s and 1940s.[4] They found that many social problems, including delinquency, were closely related to a chronic state of social disorganization through continual processes of invasion, dominance, and succession in which the transition zone is invaded by successive waves of newly arrived immigrants. The families living in the socially disorganized inner concentric zones often did not participate in the social life of the neighborhood, and they failed to control their children while opportunities for delinquency flourished. The outer concentric zones were consistently characterized by lower rates of delinquency due to economic growth and stability, as well as cohesive family relationships and high levels of social organization.

Social Disorganization and Policing

Robert Kane argued that social disorganization theory provides context for the study of police misconduct.[5] He posited that residents of socially disorganized neighborhoods do not have effective social networks that could be used to organize against police misconduct and that these neighborhoods are often characterized by frequent police-citizen conflicts in police-citizen encounters and by lapses of police legitimacy.[6] Using the same longitudinal data set of career-ending misconduct in the New York Police Department as his study with James Fyfe, together with supplemental data from the US Census Bureau on the structural characteristics of census tracts, Kane found that increases in police misconduct within spatial police precincts were predicted by two indices of social ecology (structural disadvantage and population mobility) and percentage increases in Latino population. A major limitation of Kane's study, however, was absence of any organizational factors (such as officer-to-supervisor ratios) as control variables. Kane suggested that future research on the social ecology of police misconduct should test David Klinger's negotiated order perspective that posits police behavior is derived from local workgroup norms within a police department.[7] Kane also suggested that researchers should consider mechanisms of collective efficacy that may protect against police violence and other types of police misconduct.[8]

POLICE SUBCULTURE

It has long been recognized that the police operate in a social environment whereby systemic secrecy allows a subculture to thrive based on unwritten norms, in turn leading to permeation of police violence and police corruption. Writing for the Wickersham Commission in 1931, August Vollmer noted that "it is an unwritten law in police departments that police officers must never testify against their brother officers."[9] V. O. Key, also writing in the 1930s, noted that an informal rule of silence allows police misconduct to flourish in many police departments across the United States.[10] William Westley conducted extensive research of the police department in Gary, Indiana, in the 1950s and found that a code of secrecy served as a social bond between officers within the department but was also used as a shield against outsiders by officers who viewed the public as an enemy of the police.[11] Building on the concept of an informal social code within policing, Ellwyn Stoddard argued that a group deviation process of blue-coat crime prospers through the socialization of new police officers in which they are introduced into an unlawful informal code of secrecy that perpetuates illegal behaviors.[12] The socialization process occurs within the first weeks and months that a new police officer is on the street after he or she has completed police academy training. Stoddard noted that many police officers refer to these informal practices as "the code," which he defined as a functioning social system whose norms and practices are at variance with the law.[13] The existence of informal police codes of secrecy results in an us-versus-them social structure in policing wherein police officers tend to view everyone who is not also a police officer with extreme distrust, as if citizens were literally the enemy of law enforcement officers. It is this us-versus-them mentality that serves as the linchpin of the police subculture.

Much of the scholarship in the 1960s and 1970s on the police subculture comes from observational research studies, some of it by graduate students working on their doctoral dissertation projects. John Van Maanen's dissertation involved ethnographic fieldwork in 1970 where he assumed the role of a participant-observer. He attended a thirteen-week police academy and then rode with the new patrol officers and their field training officers for their first six months as rookie officers in a large police department of more than one thousand sworn officers. His work focused on locating individual action within the subculture of a patrol officer's structural surroundings in order to demonstrate the source and developmental nature of such action.[14]

Van Maanen was interested in studying the process of becoming a police officer. He identified four sequential stages in a paradigm of police socialization as each new recruit is initiated into the organizational setting of a municipal police department as a sworn law enforcement officer: choice (the preentry stage of police socialization), introduction (the admittance stage), encounter (the change stage), and metamorphosis (the continuance stage).[15] Van Maanen found that police officers "generally view themselves as performing society's dirty work" in jobs where they are outsiders who enter a "distinct subculture governed by norms and values designed to manage the strain created by an outsider role in the community."[16]

Van Maanen continued his fieldwork with the same police department for six weeks in 1973 and ten weeks in 1978. His status as a member of that agency's police subculture became evident when he later wrote that he had observed—and even taken part in—a variety of behaviors not typically seen by researchers, including helping other police recruits cheat on exams while at the police academy; carrying unauthorized equipment while on patrol, such as a backup gun, sap gloves, and a type of ammunition prohibited by departmental rules; observing veteran police officers stealing goods from a warehouse where an open door had been found after-hours; lying to police supervisors to cover for the bad acts of fellow officers; and drinking beer with officers while on duty working the midnight shift.[17]

The socialization process of new, typically young police officers involves distinct phases that inevitably lead to a changed occupational worldview over a period of several years early in an officer's law enforcement career. According to Van Maanen, the police recruit is drawn to work as a sworn law enforcement officer because he or she wants to work for an elite organization where the recruit can do meaningful work. Municipal police work is typically a deliberate career choice that attracts individuals with a strong sense of right and wrong. Over much of the twentieth century, the minimum educational requirements for entry-level police positions in many police organizations was a high-school diploma or equivalent. It is not uncommon, however, for newly hired police officers to have attended college or have prior military experience. Police academies are full-time training programs where newly hired officers are introduced to the formal structure of the police organization through coursework that lasts anywhere from two to six months, depending on state-specific training and certification requirements. The most crucial phase of socialization into the police subculture occurs after a recruit completes his or her police academy training and is assigned to shadow and work under the direct supervision and mentoring of a field training officer. It is not uncommon for a field training officer to introduce a rookie to "real" policing by suggesting that he or she forget everything that was learned in the academy. As Van Maanen noted, this is the encounter phase of socialization into the police subculture in which a new police officer learns "how to survive on the job . . . how to walk, how to stand, and how to speak and how to think and what to say and see."[18]

The process of socialization into the police subculture is completed with a metamorphosis where officers realize several years into their career that much police work is mundane and unsatisfying, where disenchantment with the social structure of policing is commonplace among veteran officers who now are resigned to just getting through the work day without making waves or getting hurt. Many sworn law enforcement officers wash out during their early years in police work when they become frustrated with the realities of the work. I have argued that there is another distinct phase in the police socialization paradigm: the exit strategy.[19] This occurs late in an officer's law enforcement career, often within three years of retirement eligibility. The exit strategy posits that long-term police officers are often unprepared to return to civilian life, which lacks the power that comes with carrying a gun and badge.

Policing scholars have struggled with the morality and legitimacy of police engaging in forms of street justice. Jerome Skolnick described as "justice without trial" the peacekeeping activities of police officers whose discretionary decisions in street encounters often provide resolution through a form of justice different from the structure of due process.[20] Gary Sykes offered a moral defense of street justice, arguing that it was situationally appropriate as a form of order-maintenance policing. Sykes argued that police officers engage in forms of street justice because it is "a community service demanded by citizens" and that the trade-off is that order-maintenance policing creates the potential for police abuses of their power.[21] In a direct rebuttal to Sykes, Carl Klockars defined street justice as police violence doled out in situations where an officer decides that someone needs a punishment more severe than would likely result through the formal processes of law and the criminal courts.[22] The police subculture provides context for street justice. More than one-third of police officers surveyed by Westley thought they would be justified in "roughing up a man" who was disrespectful to police.[23] Assholes are often subjected to street justice as a way of teaching a lesson. An asshole, according to Van Maanen, is a person who challenges a police officer's authority by being difficult, talking back, or simply refusing to accept an officer's view of a situation.[24] The more a police officer perceives that someone is acting like an asshole, the more likely that person is going to be arrested, and the more likely that person will become a victim of gratuitous acts of police violence.

One aspect of police work that provides unique opportunities for police violence is the use of conductive energy devices (CED), commonly referred to as stun guns. The most popular brand of CED used by law enforcement agencies across the United States is the Taser.[25] The Taser has been widely adopted because it offers a less lethal method for gaining control of individuals. These CEDs are shaped like a handgun and use nitrogen cartridges to fire two barbed projectiles into the target, delivering an electrical current that temporarily overrides a person's motor and sensory functions, thereby incapacitating the individual. It can incapacitate a person from up to thirty-five feet away and penetrate up to one inch of clothing when a CED is used in probe mode. Tasers can also be used in drive-stun mode at close range by pressing the barbs directly against a person's body. Although Tasers are categorized by law enforcement as less-than-lethal weapons, each year dozens of

CRIMINAL MISUSE OF CONDUCTIVE ENERGY DEVICES BY POLICE OFFICERS

Bradford W. Reyns, John Liederbach, and I conducted a mixed-methods content analysis of news articles reporting the arrests of twenty-four police officers for offenses involving the criminal misuse of Tasers.[a] The study found that none of the cases involved situational risk or danger to the officer. The criminal misuse of Tasers often involves criminal suspects who are already handcuffed, or even citizens who are clearly not criminals at all. Tasers were deployed against people the officers knew quite well, including spouses, other relatives, friends, and even other police officers. Tasers were deployed against girlfriends, cheating spouses, or troublesome citizens—persons who needed to be "taught a lesson"—rather than resistant criminal suspects. Sometimes the Taser served no purpose other than to provide some form of amusement to the officer or others. Some of the cases included foolish behavior by officers and a clear lack of judgment. One officer drive-stunned dozens of high-school students at a career fair. A group of officers casually deployed a Taser against a restaurant employee. Another officer foolishly stunned a fellow officer as they caroused after roll call. An officer stunned a Waffle House restaurant waiter with a Taser after the officer was repeatedly chided by two other officers at the table to "tase" him if he "picked a song they didn't like on the jukebox or when telling him not to mess up their order."[b]

Angry aggression theory may provide a basis for understanding some of these cases,[c] especially those in which the Taser was primarily used as a tool of torture.[d] In some cases, police used the Taser in conjunction with serious verbal threats or violent ultimatums to threaten or further traumatize the victim either prior to or during the attack.[e] Coercive force may hold seductive qualities[f] for police who confront individuals who fail to acknowledge an officer's authority or whom the officer perceives as assholes.[g] The Taser may provide rogue police

a. Stinson, Reyns, and Liederbach, "Police Crime and Less-than-Lethal Coercive Force."

b. Stinson, Reyns, and Liederbach, 13.

c. Bernard, "Angry Aggression among the Truly Disadvantaged."

d. Amnesty International, *"Less than Lethal"*?

e. On violent ultimatums, see Athens, "Violent Crime"; Goffman, *Interaction Ritual;* and Goffman, *Strategic Interaction.*

f. Crank, *Understanding Police Culture.*

g. Van Maanen, "The Asshole."

officers a less-than-lethal tool to deliver street justice.[h] Many police departments require officers to "take a shock" as part of their training before being certified to use the device. Dozens of training session videos can be found on YouTube. The videos invariably depict both trainers and trainees responding to stunning sessions with bouts of cheers, claps, jokes, and laughter. Most police officers never use their Taser as a toy or a tool of torture, but Taser training that includes jokes and laughter may promote the misuse of these weapons, especially among officers who experience psychological problems or trouble dealing with the occupational stressors associated with police work.

h. Skolnick, *Justice without Trial.*

people die after being subjected to an electrical shock from a police Taser.[26] Sometimes Tasers are misused by officers to violently inflict pain on someone who poses little or no threat to the police. When reading this chapter's policy box, "Criminal Misuse of Conductive Energy Devices by Police Officers," consider how the police subculture and social structure theories might explain the criminal misuse of Tasers by police officers and how law enforcement agencies could reduce misuse of CEDs by their officers.

In a highly personalized view of their occupational position of legal authority, police operate under a "moral mandate" that they are representatives of respectable society and what is "right," and this thinking justifies the use of street justice tactics in dealing with the "wrong and not-so-respectable" assholes.[27] Violent street justice tactics proliferate because police distinguish between legality and morality. This is often the case in instances of police brutality or illegal searches. Police officers do not recognize criminal procedure in the same moral class as substantive criminal law.[28] Substantive criminal law is *what* is applied to control the behavior of law breakers, whereas criminal procedure provides the process of *how* the legal authorities apply the law. Law enforcement officers have a general disdain for constitutional due process considerations and are adherents to what Herbert Packer referred to as a "crime control model" of the criminal justice system.[29] They focus on a suspect's factual guilt (and not legal guilt) and view the role of the police as quickly determining guilt or innocence so that courts can quickly process guilty defendants.

The ubiquity of video recordings of police-citizen encounters has provided the public with examples of street justice being delivered in numerous high-profile cases. The brutal beating of Rodney King by four Los Angeles police officers on March 3, 1991, provided the first peek into street justice for many Americans. King had led officers on a ten-minute high-speed freeway chase that ended with a traffic stop at 12:50 a.m. on a suburban street corner of Pacoima in the northeastern San Fernando Valley of Los Angeles. A nearby resident, George Holliday, heard the commotion and went outside with his newly acquired video camcorder to record the police activity. While the whole traffic stop encounter was not recorded, the video did show officers strike King with fifty-six baton blows and six kicks prior to handcuffing him and dragging him on his stomach across the street to await an ambulance for the now-injured man.[30] The next day Holliday called the Foothills Station of the Los Angeles Police Department to offer his videotape, but he was rebuffed. Holliday then offered the videotape to local television station KTLA for broadcast on the evening news, and soon CNN and other national media aired the video and reported on the incident.

Many were shocked by the raw display of police brutality. The video offered the public an image of policing very different than the professionalism seen on widely popular television shows of the era. As Jerome Skolnick and James Fyfe later noted, the video showed the police "teaching a lesson of retribution outside the bounds of the penal code."[31] Typically the police own the narratives in allegations of police violence because there are no credible witnesses who can rebut the factual averments in police reports and police testimony in criminal court proceedings. In recent years, however, alternative narratives provided by video recordings have contradicted the police version of events, as in the case of Walter Scott, who was shot in the back and killed in April 2015 by North Charleston, South Carolina, police officer Michael Slager. The proliferation of police encounters recorded on video—through security/surveillance cameras, citizen smartphone cameras, and police dash-cam and bodycam recorders—has resulted in increased public awareness of violent police street justice tactics.

STRAIN THEORIES

Like social disorganization theory, anomie and strain theories are largely grounded in Durkheim's view that the breakdown of social controls is associated with rapid social change in society, which leads to increases in crime and other social problems. Writing in the 1890s, Durkheim described anomie as a state of normlessness and disharmony in modern society caused by lack of moral guidance and social regulation, leading to deviant behaviors such as suicide.[32]

Anomie theories differ from social disorganization theory by positing that crime results from an individual's inability to achieve economic goals. Robert Merton applied Durkheim's ideas to the development of a strain theory of social structure and anomie that sought to explain deviance and criminal offending within the context of a contemporary American culture that emphasizes the goal of economic success.[33] Merton argued that many individuals, particularly in the lower class, are prevented from attaining the goal of economic success through legitimate socially approved means of educational and occupational achievement. The inability to achieve economic success creates frustration, or strain, that leads some (but not all) individuals in the lower class to reject legitimate means while still aspiring to achieve monetary success through illegitimate means by committing crimes.

Although popular with criminologists in the 1950s and 1960s, especially to explain delinquency and gang behaviors, Merton's strain theory was rejected by Ruth Kornhauser and other criminologists who argued the theory was logically inconsistent and lacked sufficient scope to explain criminal offending by anyone other than strained lower-class individuals.[34] Strain theory research later regained prominence in two divergent theoretical frameworks: Steven Messner and Richard Rosenfeld's institutional anomie theory of crime and "the American dream" and Robert Agnew's general strain theory.[35] Institutional anomie theory is not helpful to our discussion of police violence and social structure theories because it is a macro-level theory that does not apply to the behaviors of individual police officers.[36]

General Strain Theory

Agnew's general strain theory broadened the theoretical focus to encompass sources of strain or stress beyond the disjunctions between aspirations/expectations and actual achievements in traditional strain theories. According to Agnew, strain—conditions or events that are disliked by an individual—is often the result of negative relationships, such as when an individual does not like the way someone else is treating him or her. Agnew identified three major types of actual or anticipated strain: the inability to achieve positively valued goals (e.g., money, status, occupational goals), the loss of positively valued stimuli (e.g., the end of a romantic relationship), and the presentation of aversive or negatively valued stimuli (e.g., physical abuse).[37] Anticipated strains occur when an individual has an expectation of either current strains continuing or new strains developing in the future. There are also vicarious strains that occur when others around the individual, such as family members or friends, experience "real-life" strain.[38] Strain makes people feel bad, and some individuals with poor coping skills may engage in crime as a way of trying to alleviate their strain. According to Agnew's general strain theory, strains lead to negative emotions such as anger, fear, frustration, hopelessness, jealousy, malicious envy, or shame. Anger may be the most relevant negative emotion in explaining why strains increase the likelihood of violent crime. In the context of general strain theory, Agnew argued that anger "reduces the ability to engage in effective problem solving, reduces awareness of and concerns for the costs of crime, creates a desire for revenge, fosters the belief that crime is justified, and energizes the individual for action."[39] General strain theory posits that crime is most likely to occur when several strains cluster together in time and an individual is overwhelmed with negative emotions, and Agnew has suggested that research in this area is needed, with more attention paid to the interaction between and timing of various strains.

Strain in Policing

Law enforcement officers encounter numerous sources of strain. Often the strain experienced by police officers results from the inability to achieve desired goals. Police officers often feel that their salaries and benefits are low, especially compared to other occupations.[40] Research has shown that police officers' job satisfaction is positively associated with their perceptions of the importance of police work, autonomy to perform their job, and being recognized by their supervisors for doing a good job.[41] Hans Toch found that "slower-than-hoped-for advancement and less-than-anticipated recognition can become sources of frustration" for police officers.[42] My research found that policewomen are more likely than their male counterparts to be arrested for profit-motivated crimes.[43] It is possible that crime by policewomen may be motivated by financial insecurities related to the lack of promotional opportunities and their perceived lack of acceptance within the police subculture.

College-educated police officers often experience a gap between aspirations and expectations. Compared with police officers who did not earn a college degree, college-educated officers report lower levels of satisfaction and fulfillment, less tolerance of inequities, and higher levels of job frustration.[44] Arthur Niederhoffer described a process within the social structure of police organizations in which new police officers are committed to the ideals of police work when they graduate from the police academy, but exposure to the realities of police work quickly leads them to periods of decreased job satisfaction, frustration, disenfranchisement, and eventually, cynicism. According to Niederhoffer, cynicism can lead to anomie when a police officer has lost faith in humankind, has lost his or her professional integrity, and no longer has enthusiasm for policing. He described it as a "continuum stretching from commitment at one end to anomie at the other, with cynicism at the critical intervening stage."[45] Niederhoffer hypothesized that college-educated police officers will exhibit higher degrees of cynicism because the unfulfilled expectations of promotion within the police organization were greater than the promotion expectations of officers who never attended college. Assuming there is a correlation between high levels of police cynicism and police misconduct, Niederhoffer's hypothesis is not supported by research suggesting that college-educated officers are less likely to engage in police misconduct.[46]

Strain can also be experienced through the loss of something valued by an officer. Some officers become so disenchanted with police work that they experience psychological burnout.[47] Burnout occurs when job frustration, chronic stress, and cynicism lead to a state of emotional exhaustion and an inability to cope with the day-to-day demands of policing.[48] It happens when enthusiasm for policing is replaced by paralyzing feelings of stagnation and procrastination. Sometimes police officers experience strain that manifests in their personal lives through incidents of officer-involved domestic violence.[49] One research study suggested that there are higher rates of officer-involved domestic violence among police who suffer from post-traumatic stress syndrome.[50] Several researchers have suggested that officer-involved domestic violence is related to a work-family spillover effect from police officers' constant or repeated work exposure to violence.[51] Robyn Gershon surveyed Baltimore City police officers and found that on-the-job exposure to violence was one of the most significant stressors experienced by the officers.[52] Another study found statistically significant bivariate relationships between police stress and poor family functioning.[53] Toch's research found that older police officers were more stressed than younger officers and that stress levels increase as officers approach retirement.[54] There is something about the anticipated loss of the power and authority associated with having a police badge and gun that strains many police officers in the waning years of their careers as they near retirement. I found that 16.5 percent of the cases in years 2005–11 in which an officer was arrested for a violence-related crime involved an officer with fifteen or more years of service.[55] My earlier study of late-stage police crime found that 17.4 percent of the cases from years 2005–7 involved an officer who was arrested within three years of retirement eligibility (with eighteen or more years of service).[56]

Strain can also take the form of the introduction or presence of something an officer does not like. Police work is a constant stream of exposure to negative stimuli. Every call for service involves the potential for a violent encounter. Police officers often view the public as an enemy; everyone they encounter is a potential threat of some sort, ranging from threats or actual violence to citizens threatening or actually filing complaints against an officer. Some complaints involve allegations of police brutality or other officer misbehavior during an encounter with a citizen. But many complaints are made because of something an officer allegedly did *not* do that angered a citizen, such as a motorist perceiving an officer as rude when issuing a warning for speeding instead of an expensive traffic ticket. Even when a citizen complaint is unfounded, the process of being investigated by internal affairs can be very stressful for officers. Police officers also experience stress over a variety of threats to their physical health that are unique to their jobs. Law enforcement officers are often exposed to hazardous materials, including lead exposure from firearms and firing ranges, chemical exposure from clandestine methamphetamine labs, chemical exposure from fingerprint powders, blood-borne pathogens from needlesticks when dealing with illicit drug users, and even potential transmission of infectious diseases from exposure to dead bodies.[57]

Police officers are vulnerable to post-traumatic stress because they are often exposed to traumatic incidents. In 1974 Jeffrey Mitchell first recognized that public safety personnel—police officers, firefighters, emergency medical technicians, and paramedics—had difficulties coping in the aftermath of witnessing horrific incidents in their work. I remember hearing Mitchell speak at a conference many years ago where he told the story of his brother, a firefighter in New York City, responding to a call for a fire at an abandoned tenement house in the Bronx. As the fire truck pulled up to the curb in front of the burning building, he looked up and saw a mother leaning out a window several floors up holding a baby in her arms as the flames darted behind the woman. The firefighter motioned with his hands indicating that he wanted the woman to wait to be rescued. As he turned away from the burning building to reach for a ladder on the fire truck, he heard the baby hit the concrete on the sidewalk behind him. The woman had misunderstood his hand gestures, thinking that the firefighter was going to catch the baby if she dropped the baby to firefighter standing below. Around the same time as this incident, Mitchell was a psychology graduate student and working as a paramedic in Maryland. One day he responded to a traffic accident where a young woman was impaled by a metal pole. Unable to shake the gruesome image, he later shared the story with his brother, at which time his brother told him about the baby dying when it was dropped from the window.[58] Mitchell later developed the critical incident stress debriefing process that has been utilized by police and fire departments for over thirty years to help emergency services personnel cope with their stress following on-the-job exposure to traumatic incidents.[59]

Some strain is caused by the police organization. Police departments across the United States have long used quotas as a way of making sure that officers are on the job.[60] In some departments, officers are under constant pressure from supervisors to meet monthly quotas. Quotas can be formal or informal, and sometimes they are called something other than a quota, as if that somehow makes it better. When I worked at the Arlington County Police Department in Virginia in the 1980s, each employee's performance was periodically evaluated based on "key elements" of their job.[61] For patrol officers, key elements included the number of traffic tickets written and arrests made each month. The quotas for patrol officers assigned to the evening and midnight shifts included monthly expectations for the number of drunk driving arrests to be made. Officers developed their own strategies for making their monthly quotas, and some became obsessed with meeting their monthly key elements. Some officers were aggressive in making traffic stops during the first few days they worked each calendar month, and then they slacked off over the next several weeks, rarely making any proactive traffic stops. Other officers seemed to focus all their proactive traffic enforcement activities into the last few days of each month.

I recall several officers on the midnight shift parking their cruisers at Rosslyn Circle on the Virginia side of Key Bridge in Arlington on the last Friday and Saturday nights of each month, diligently watching cars come across the bridge from the area of Georgetown bars in Washington, DC. It was like shooting fish in a barrel; cars that drifted out of their traffic lane, driving too slow or too fast, or driving without their headlights were always pulled over once they crossed the state line at the high-water mark on the

Virginia side of the Potomac River. The drivers of the targeted cars were always drunk, and they were always arrested. Many years later, in 2012, someone leaked an internal Arlington County Police Department memorandum to a local television news reporter. The memorandum was titled "Proactivity Expectations 2012" and stated that officers who "consistently fail to attain these goals may be subject to corrective or disciplinary action."[62] Arlington County police chief Douglas Scott rescinded the memorandum soon after media reports made it public, falsely claiming that the department "does not support a quota system with regard to enforcement efforts."[63]

A state law in New York prohibits discriminatory personnel actions by law enforcement agencies against their police officers (e.g., reassignments, scheduling changes, adverse performance evaluations, constructive dismissals, denial of promotion, denial of overtime assignments) for failure to meet quotas for tickets or summonses issued, arrests made, or stop-and-frisks of individuals in street encounters.[64] Even so, quotas still exist within some New York police departments. New York City settled a whistleblower lawsuit brought by New York Police Department officer Craig Matthews for $280,000 after the he alleged an illegal quota system in the Forty-Second Precinct of the Bronx.[65] The settlement came months after a federal appellate court ruled that Matthews had a right to sue under the First Amendment.[66] Matthews claimed in his lawsuit that supervisors retaliated against him when he complained about the illegal quota system and that the retaliation had caused "extreme stress" manifesting in physical and mental health problems.[67]

Courts are a great source of strain for many police officers. Most arrests that patrol officers make are for misdemeanor offenses, and in most jurisdictions 90–98 percent of those cases never go to trial because they are resolved through dismissals or plea bargains. With the exception of cases where the defendant is charged with assault on a police officer or resisting arrest, police officers usually do not care about what happens to misdemeanor cases.[68] They view their job as completed in a misdemeanor case when they finish booking paperwork and submit arrest reports. The experience of many police officers with the criminal courts represents their own "frustration, triumph, and crucifixion" all at once.[69] Police officers often spend long hours in courthouses mostly waiting for cases to be called, sometimes spending entire days in court sandwiched between working night shifts with little time for sleep in their off hours. Officers get frustrated with the prosecutors' charging decisions about whether to move forward with a case and with having no meaningful input in prosecutors' plea bargain offers to defendants. Some police think that prosecutors are arrogant and often treat police officers like they are idiots.[70] In some jurisdictions there is tension between the police and prosecutors over who is responsible for follow-up investigations that are necessary to obtain indictments, often resulting in dismissal of cases or delays in court proceedings.[71] Other times officers feel mistreated by defense attorneys who relish in making an officer look like a fool while testifying in court. Police officers tend to feel that their veracity and discretionary arrest decisions are constantly being questioned by prosecuting attorneys, defense attorneys, and even judges.

As a result of these experiences, many officers lose faith in the criminal courts. Many sworn law enforcement officers also experience strain as a result of being sued in court. Most civil lawsuits against the police are filed in state courts as tort claims.[72] Approximately thirty thousand police misconduct lawsuits are filed each year in federal and state courts across the United States against individual police officers, their employing law enforcement agencies, and municipalities.[73] In my own research of 5,545 police officers who had each been arrested during the years 2005–11 for one or more crimes, I found that 29.3 percent of the officers who had been arrested for a violence-related crime had also been named at some point during their career as a civil party defendant in one or more federal civil rights actions pursuant to 42 U.S.C. § 1983.[74]

Strain Research and Police Misconduct

Several researchers have applied general strain theory to various forms of police violence, including some that conducted secondary analyses of the data set from Gershon's study of stress and domestic violence in families of Baltimore City police officers.[75] Chris Gibson, Marc Swatt, and Jason Jolicoeur found that general strain theory was useful in explaining officer-involved domestic violence perpetrated by male officers, but they cautioned that there were issues with using an existing data set to test criminological theory (in great part because of the potential that variance was caused by variables not included), potential problems with operationalization of strain theory, and concerns about the generalizability of the findings.[76]

Marc Swatt, Chris Gibson, and Nicole Piquero cited the same limitations in using the Gershon data set for secondary analysis. But they found support for general strain theory when they used the data set to examine the relationship between work-related strain and problematic consumption of alcoholic beverages by Baltimore City police officers.[77] Similarly, Don Kurtz, Egbert

Zavala, and Lisa Melander reanalyzed the Gershon data set and found that the odds of self-reported officer-on-officer violence among Baltimore City police officers increased by 133 percent for those who had experienced child abuse or maltreatment years earlier when they were growing up.[78] Robert Kane and Michael White noted that there are a number of limitations with the application of general strain theory to the study of police misconduct. Not everyone copes with strain in negative ways, and policing is unique in that sworn officers have the legal authority to use coercive force in the exercise of their official duties. The existence of the police subculture provides a structure for "unique strains to police officers not present to the general public," which may "mediate how officers cope with strain."[79]

BEHAVIOR OF LAW

Donald Black's behavior of law theory provides a sociological theoretical explanation for why police violence is rarely treated as deviant or criminal behavior. Although there are other definitions of law and social control, Black defined law as "governmental social control."[80] He conceptualized law as a quantitative variable that can be measured.[81] Black provided numerous examples of the quantification of law. For example, when someone calls the police, the theory posits that as an increase in law. An indictment on felony charges is more law than the issuance of a summons for a minor infraction. Pretrial detention is more law than when someone is released on bail to await trial. A conviction is more law than an acquittal. A presidential pardon is less law than parole revocation.

One of Black's early theoretical formulations involved the social context in which police officers make arrests of individuals during routine encounters while an officer is on patrol.[82] It evolved out of his ethnographic field observation dissertation research of police officers in Boston, Chicago, and Washington, DC, during the summer of 1966. Black made several generalizations about police behavior in routine patrol encounters where an arrest by the police was a possibility. Most of the observed arrests involved reactive policing and not proactive policing. They were largely arrests made as a result of a citizen complaint. Black referred to this process as mobilization, wherein citizen involvement mobilized the criminal law by calling the police. Many of the arrests reflected the desire of the citizen complainant, and rarely was someone arrested by the police when the complainant requested leniency.

Black noted that police officers often exercised their discretion, resulting in arrests being made less often than the law allows. There was a greater likelihood of an arrest being made if the incident involved serious felony crimes, and arrests were less likely when the alleged crime was a misdemeanor offense. There was also a greater likelihood of the police making an arrest in encounters where there was greater relational distance between the complainant and the suspect. As such, the police were most likely to make an arrest when the complainant and suspect were strangers to each other, less likely to make an arrest when the parties were friends or neighbors, and least likely to make an arrest when they were family members. Black also found that the probability that someone was going to be arrested by the police increased when a person was disrespectful of the police.

Black's theory posits that it is possible to formulate propositions to explain the quantity and style of law in which one or more aspects of social life—stratification, morphology, culture, organization, and social control—explain the behavior of law in all situations, places, times, and societies.[83] For example, one of the propositions relating to stratification of law is that law varies directly with rank. If we applied that proposition to develop a research hypothesis in a study of police violence involving excessive use of force, we could hypothesize that when all else is equal (i.e., controlling for age and years of service as a sworn law enforcement officer at time of the alleged incident) a patrol officer is more likely than a police chief to be arrested.[84]

CRITICAL THINKING QUESTIONS

1. How does Shaw and McKay's theory of social disorganization help to explain police violence?

2. Why are police subculture theories included in the group of social structure theories?

3. Does "street justice" justify police violence?

4. How might Agnew's general strain theory explain police misuse of conductive energy devices (e.g., Tasers) on individuals who pose no situational risk of violence against the police?

———————

Social Process Theories

Criminological social process theories attempt to explain within-group variation in terms of why some individuals engage in crime and yet others do not. This chapter explores a variety of social process theories applied to the phenomenon of police violence, including social learning theories, social control theories, self-control theories, noble cause corruption, and techniques of neutralization.

The police socialization process was discussed in the previous chapter on social structure theories, but it also fits well in this chapter because social structure theories and social process theories both consider interrelated aspects of processes and structural conditions that produce criminal or deviant behavior. Newly hired police officers are socialized into a police subculture whose code of secrecy serves as a social bond between fellow officers.[1] As officers gain experience and exposure to policing, they start to distrust anyone outside of law enforcement and soon develop an us-versus-them mentality that serves as the linchpin of the police subculture. Many officers become disenchanted with the mundane nature of most police work.[2] Policing, however, often involves violence that serves to break up the monotony. Police regularly encounter violent individuals, and sworn law enforcement officers are allowed to use coercive authority and that amount of force reasonably necessary to maintain order, defend themselves and others from threats of violence and other dangers, effectuate physical arrests, and execute search warrants.

Donald Black's behavior of law theory was also discussed in the prior chapter on social structure theories because that theory includes governmental social control and the unique structural nature of policing as a governmental organization. Behavior of law theory also fits well in the present chapter's group of social process theories that help explain the phenomenon of police violence, since Black's theory suggests that law (operationalized as a quantitative variable) varies with all other types and amounts of social control.[3] The distinction rests on whether law is being applied on a structural level between social groups or on an individual level within a social group.

SOCIAL LEARNING THEORIES

Edwin Sutherland's differential association theory of individual criminal behavior was presented in its final form in the 1947 edition of his criminology textbook. The theory consists of nine propositions that can be consolidated and summarized as follows:

- Criminal behavior is learned in interaction with other persons in a process of communication.
- When criminal behavior is learned, the learning includes (a) techniques of committing the crime, which are sometimes very complicated, sometimes very simple; and (b) the specific direction of motives, drives, rationalizations, and attitudes.
- A person becomes delinquent or criminal because of an excess of definitions favorable to violation of law over definitions unfavorable to violation of law.
- Differential associations may vary in frequency, duration, priority, and intensity.[4]

The gist of the theory is that criminal behavior is learned in a social process of symbolic interaction with other individuals. Sutherland's theory was written at a time when criminology was dominated by theories that primarily focused on biological and psychological abnormalities as the causes of criminal behavior. Sutherland's differential association theory shifted criminological research and development of theories to a view of crime as the result of environmental influences impacting on psychologically and biologically sound individuals. The legacy of his differential association theory within criminology is the proposition that criminal behavior is learned behavior.[5]

The eighth proposition of Sutherland's theory was that the process of learning criminal behavior through differential association "involves all of the mechanisms that are involved in any other learning."[6] Sutherland did not, however, identify or explain the mechanisms of learning. Building on

Sutherland's conceptualization of differential association, Robert Burgess and Ronald Akers specified the learning mechanisms in their differential association-reinforcement theory of criminal behavior.[7] They reformulated Sutherland's theory to specify that criminal behavior is learned through operant conditioning both in nonsocial situations that are reinforced and through social interaction that reinforces the behavior of other persons. Criminal behavior is the result of learning processes where such behaviors are reinforced more highly than noncriminal behavior. The amount and seriousness of criminal behavior, according to Burgess and Akers, is a function of frequency and intensity of its reinforcement.

Akers then developed his social learning theory of delinquent, criminal, and deviant behavior in general. Social learning theory retains the main principles of Sutherland's differential association theory and integrates it with Burgess and Akers's principles of differential reinforcement, together with additional principles of behavioral acquisition, continuation, and cessation processes.[8] Akers's social learning theory retains elements of symbolic interactionism found in Sutherland's theory of learning criminal behavior through processes of differential association. These are the major propositions of Akers's social learning theory:

- Criminal behavior is more likely to occur if a person believes that the behavior will be rewarded.
- A person who is rewarded for his or her criminal behavior is more likely to commit additional crimes.
- A person who is punished for his or her criminal behavior is less likely to commit additional crimes.
- A person is more likely to engage in criminal behavior if he or she sees other people committing crime.[9]

The main concepts of social learning theory are differential association, definitions, differential reinforcement, and imitation.[10] The theory posits that together these concepts determine whether someone is likely to engage in conforming or deviant behaviors. Akers and Christine Sellers explained that the differential association component of social learning theory includes dimensions that are behavioral-interactionist, as well as dimensions that are normative. The interactionist dimension consists of direct association and interaction with other individuals who engage in certain types of behaviors, as well as indirect association with reference groups that are more distant.

The normative dimension of differential association consists of the values and norms that a person is exposed to through the association. The definitions of social learning are meanings, rationalizations, and attitudes that a person attaches to specific behaviors. The third concept of Aker's social learning theory, differential reinforcement, "refers to the balance of anticipated or actual rewards and punishments that follow or are consequences of behavior."[11] Finally, Akers's social learning theory argues that criminal behavior is modeled after the behavior of others that is observed and imitated.

Differential Association and Police Behavior

Robert Kane and Michael White noted that "the primary differential association group is the peer group of fellow officers from whom an individual officer learns definitions" within the police subculture.[12] Police officers tend to view themselves and each other as morally superior to everyone else.[13] This leads to a solidarity among officers whereby definitions learned through the police subculture are much stronger than those learned from association with any individual or group outside of the law enforcement community. Police officers are often suspicious and distrustful of their own police supervisors and police administrators, as well as others who work in the criminal justice system outside of policing.[14] Even while not working, police officers tend to socialize only with other police officers. They become socially isolated.[15] They start to see the world through "cognitive lenses" that are distorted as a result of their unique social situation as police officers.[16] Many of the definitions favorable to police deviance are supported by the peer group "in the sense that they are not defined as deviant and actors who engage in them run little risk of exposure and sanction."[17] After all, law enforcement is exempt from law enforcement.[18]

Definitions of Social Learning in Policing

Limited research has found that officers' definitions of police violence are consistent with Akers's social learning theory. Allison Chappell and Alex Piquero surveyed a random sample of 499 Philadelphia police officers assigned to patrol duties and found that definitions about the use of excessive force in a binary logistic regression model were statistically significant predictors of citizen complaints.[19] To the extent that the Philadelphia officers surveyed did not consider using excessive force a serious problem, they were more likely to have a history of citizen complaints filed against them. But Kane and White argue that the "definitions" aspect of social learning theory "differs in the police subculture" and that "specific definitions of police deviance and misconduct need to be developed."[20]

Differential Reinforcement of Social Learning in Policing

The police subculture serves as a powerful reference group where corrupt behaviors are reinforced through powerful interactions with peers.[21] Police officers tend to engage in certain behaviors to maintain standing in the police subculture.[22] They do not want to call attention to things that will later cause problems for themselves or their peer officers. Sometimes police officers know that something violates departmental policy, but they continue to routinely engage in the behavior anyway. In the unique context of peer associations within the police subculture, it is often "difficult to separate whether peers are deviant or not."[23]

When I was a police officer in Dover, New Hampshire, I knew that departmental policy prohibited officers from accepting gratuities, including free or discounted restaurant meals. I also knew that uniformed police officers were charged only $2 for *any* meal at the local Burger King (more precisely, $1.92 plus 4% sales tax). Police officers frequented that particular Burger King in part because we would stop there to pick up "prisoner meals" for anyone held overnight in the cellblock at the police station. A prisoner meal consisted of a plain hamburger, small french fries, and a small Coke and was paid for with a city voucher. But it was the $2 meals for police officers— referred to by the Burger King staff as the "manager's special"—that appealed to me and my fellow police officers. We all knew there was little risk of getting in trouble for accepting the manager's special that was provided only to uniformed officers. As my field training officer explained to me, it actually seemed to be a bigger hassle to try *not* to get the discounted meals, because that would inevitably involve a discussion with the Burger King staff at the counter that could be overheard by other customers in line. It just seemed easier to pay the $2 and enjoy my double cheeseburger, extra-large fries, and extra-large Diet Coke several times a week. I certainly never thought that accepting the manager's special was deviant or unethical behavior. Other police officers with more seniority explained to me that the policy against accepting such favors was simply another sign of our overreaching police chief, Charles Reynolds, who was at that time also the president of the

International Association of Chiefs of Police. Lawrence Sherman, however, has argued that police accepting "perks" from a restaurant is the first step "on a career ladder" of morality leading up to accepting bribes and other more serious forms of corruption.[24]

Modeling Behaviors through Social Learning in Police Work

When applied to the deviant police subculture, Akers's social learning theory "would argue that as a new officer enters the peer group, he or she will be exposed to models of behavior that will influence his or her own attitudes and behaviors."[25] Sherman conceptualized police corruption as a form of social interaction using Erving Goffman's framework of contingencies, moral experiences, and stages to explain the process.[26] Goffman originally developed the framework in the 1950s to examine the moral behavior of mental patients as they negotiated periods of hospitalization at St. Elizabeth's Hospital in Washington, DC.[27] Corrupt behaviors are reinforced through the modeling of roles observed within the reference group within the subculture in a process of social learning. M. G. Aultman suggested that these processes are often at work within the police subculture, where a "police officer learns to behave corruptly because such behavior is effective in satisfying the requirements of major roles and because significant groups may control reinforcements."[28]

Social Learning Theory and Police Misconduct Research

Kane and White found that social learning theory was applicable to their study of career-ending misconduct by New York City police officers. Both black and Hispanic police officers were more likely than white officers to engage in misconduct, a finding the researchers have acknowledged as controversial.[29] Kane and White suggested that "it is possible that black and Hispanic officers came from backgrounds where deviant definitions were more accepted, and these definitions were translated into more tolerant views of police misconduct."[30] They also found that police officers in New York City were less likely to engage in police misconduct if their fathers had worked for the police department before them, speculating that maybe those second-generation officers were taught definitions favorable to ethical policing while growing up. The study also found that police officers with college degrees were less likely to experience career-ending police misconduct. Kane and White explained that it is possible that "being closely associated with peers in an educational environment causes individuals to learn definitions less favorable toward deviant behavior."[31]

There are limitations to the application of Akers's social learning theory to the study of police misconduct.[32] For example, social learning theory does not explain why some police officers engage in acts of police deviance, such as police violence through the repeated use of excessive force, and others do not engage in such deviant behavior. Similarly, social learning theory does not explain why some officers do not engage in acts of police deviance even when their peer officers do engage in deviant acts. While social learning theory might help explain certain types of deviant police behaviors, such as on-duty police violence, it really does not explain the full range of police criminality (unless we assume that the idea that police officers are exempt from law enforcement—and can do whatever they want in terms of committing crimes—is learned behavior from association with peers within the police subculture).

CONTROL THEORIES

Control theories have dominated much of the research in American criminology since at least the 1970s. This group of theories assume that crime is going to occur unless people conform to the social demands placed on them and then tries to explain why people conform. The main theoretical premise is that "when controls are present, crime does not occur," and "when controls are absent, crime is possible and often does occur."[33] Control theories are grounded in Émile Durkheim's nineteenth-century concepts of social integration and social regulation in the Industrial Revolution. Durkheim wrote that "when society is strongly integrated, it holds individuals under its control," and that individuals find their lives meaningful when "the bond that unites them with common cause attaches them to life and the lofty goal they envisage prevents their feeling personal troubles so deeply."[34] Akers and Sellers explained that the criminological notion of social control "includes both the socialization in which a person acquires self-control, and the control over the person's behavior through the external application of social sanctions, rewards for conformity, and punishments for deviance, with the understanding that the application of sanctions is a major process by which socialization occurs."[35]

Among the first criminologists to apply the social control conceptualization to the study of crime and delinquency in the mid-twentieth century were Albert Reiss, F. Ivan Nye, and Walter Reckless. Reiss attributed delinquency to the failure of personal and social controls.[36] He defined personal control as "the ability of the individual to refrain from meeting needs in ways which conflict with the norms and rules of the community."[37] Personal controls are internalized by the individual. Reiss defined social control as "the ability of social groups or institutions to make norms or rules effective."[38] Social controls are external and operate through the application of informal social sanctions or formal legal sanctions.[39] Nye identified three main forms of social control in family relationships that prevent delinquent behavior: direct control (consisting of the threat or application of punishment for misbehavior and rewards for compliant behavior), indirect control (where a youth refrains from delinquency to avoid parental disappointment), and internal control (where a youth is prevented from engaging in delinquency by his or her own consciousness or sense of guilt).[40] Reckless sought to explain conforming behavior in his containment theory of delinquency and crime.[41] He termed internal controls as "inner containment" (e.g., good self-concept, self-control, high tolerance for frustration) and external controls as "outer containment" (e.g., institutional reinforcement at school, social expectations, effective parental supervision).[42] Containment theory argued that youths are motivated to commit acts of delinquency by "pushes" (e.g., poverty and other social conditions) and "pulls" (e.g., illegitimate opportunities). Akers and Sellers explained that the basic proposition in Reckless's containment theory is that "pushes and pulls will produce delinquent behavior unless they are counteracted by inner and outer containment."[43]

Social Control Theory

In promulgating his 1969 theory on the causes of delinquency, Travis Hirschi argued that earlier control theories were largely tautological. Other criminologists often refer to Hirschi's social control theory as social bonding theory. The premise of Hirschi's theory is that "delinquent acts result when an individual's bond to society is weak or broken."[44] There are four elements of the bond: attachment, commitment, involvement, and belief. Strong bonds result in behavior that is controlled in the direction of conformity, and weak bonds result in behavior that is more likely to be delinquent. Attachment to others is the extent to which an individual has close affectional ties to other people, admires and identifies with them, and cares about the expectations of those other people.[45] Hirschi conceptualized the attachment of adolescent youth to others through their ties with parents, school, and peers. Commitment is an individual's investment of time and energy in things such as "getting an education, building up a business, [and] acquiring a reputation for virtue" that would be endangered by engaging in delinquent or criminal acts.[46] Involvement refers to "engrossment in conventional activities," as the theory assumes that "a person may be simply too busy doing conventional things to find time to engage in deviant behavior."[47] Hirschi's social bonding theory assumes the existence of common values within society, such as morals and laws that people believe should be followed. The theory sought to explain why individuals violate rules and norms in which they believe. Hirschi did not conceptualize belief in terms of religiosity in his original formulation of social control theory, although religious beliefs "are obviously representative of conventional values."[48]

Self-Control Theory

Michael Gottfredson and Hirschi promulgated a self-control theory of crime in 1990 that is distinct from Hirschi's earlier social bonding theory. It is a *different* theory, although numerous scholars criticized Hirschi for allegedly abandoning his earlier theory or somehow failing to explain the relationship between the two theories.[49] Hirschi responded to the criticisms by noting that reconciliation of separate theories is unnecessary because "consistency within a theory is crucial ... [but] consistency across theories is no virtue at all."[50] Gottfredson and Hirschi proffered their self-control theory as a general theory of crime that posits low self-control as the cause of delinquent and criminal behavior.[51] Individual differences in levels of self-control dictate the tendency to commit crimes, although a "lack of self-control does not require crime and can be counteracted by situational conditions" or other traits of an individual.[52] Individuals with low self-control are more likely to engage in delinquent or criminal behavior, and individuals with high self-control are less likely to engage in such deviant acts. Low self-control is primarily the result of incomplete or ineffective socialization through parental child-rearing processes that are "negative rather than positive" and occur "in the absence of nurturance, discipline, or training."[53] Gottfredson and Hirschi viewed self-control as a stable individual characteristic that should not change over time in adolescence and adulthood.

Hirschi offered a "slightly revised version" of the self-control theory in 2004.[54] It posits a new definition of self-control that includes social bonds by pronouncing that "social control and self-control are the same thing."[55] Hirschi came to define self-control as "the tendency to consider the full range of potential costs of a particular act."[56] The theoretical revision helps resolve past empirical tautology criticisms of Gottfredson and Hirschi's theory that argued that measures of self-control and criminality actually measured the same thing.[57] Hirschi argued that his revised self-control theory is consistent with the life-course perspective of Robert Sampson and John Laub's informal social control theory.[58] Hirschi recognized there are life events, turning points, transitions, and trajectories that serve as social bonds and may impact on an individual's future offending and desistance from offending.

Control theories have largely dominated criminology ever since Hirschi promulgated his social bonding theory in 1969.[59] Several recent studies have examined aspects of police behaviors and social control or self-control, although it is an underdeveloped area of criminological theory-testing research. The studies applying control theories to the study of police misconduct suggest that much can be learned that would guide the development of policies and practices to reduce police deviance. For example, one study found that higher social bonds were significantly related to lower intentions of police supervisors to engage in misconduct such as ticket-fixing and unauthorized use of law enforcement computer systems to run record checks.[60] The same study also found that age, sex, and education levels of police supervisors were significant predictors of police misconduct intentions.

Several studies have examined the relationship between self-control and police misconduct. First-line police supervisors from multiple law enforcement agencies were surveyed in a study that included separate regression models to test Gottfredson and Hirschi's self-control theory, as well as Hirschi's revised self-control theory. Measures of both theoretical formulations of self-control were found to be statistically related to both prior police misconduct and the likelihood of engaging in future police misconduct.[61] A multi-agency study of police recruits found that impulsivity was positively related to adherence to the police code of silence as manifested through an unwillingness to report misconduct of fellow officers.[62] A study of personnel records for 1,935 police officers in Philadelphia found that officers with lower self-control are significantly more likely to have been involved in a police shooting at some point during their law enforcement career.[63] Research has also shown that nonsupervisory patrol officers with low self-control are more likely to engage in police misconduct[64] and problematic alcohol consumption.[65] Kane and White suggested that self-control theory could be helpful in examining various aspects of police misconduct, such as whether police work results in officers' "self-control depletion" and whether indicators of low self-control can predict those officers who are at risk of engaging in career-ending misconduct.[66]

TECHNIQUES OF NEUTRALIZATION

Gresham Sykes and David Matza's theory of delinquency argued that juvenile offenders minimize and justify their deviant behavior through any of five behavioral techniques of neutralization: (1) denial of responsibility, (2) denial of injury, (3) denial of the victim, (4) condemnation of the condemners, and (5) appeal to higher loyalties.[67] Delinquency is the result of learning these techniques of neutralization that Sykes and Matza viewed as a crucial component of Edwin Sutherland's differential association process, wherein there are "definitions favorable to violation of law over definitions unfavorable to violation of law."[68] The idea for techniques of neutralization came from Sykes's experience in the military during World War II, where "neutralization had a military meaning of neutralizing the enemy to overcome their power by using defensive and offensive techniques," and Matza, who "interpreted neutralization from the point-of-view of the person or persons being neutralized."[69]

Over the subsequent decades, neutralization theory has been applied to many types of criminal offending outside the theoretical context of juvenile delinquency as originally conceptualized by Sykes and Matza. These include research topics as varied as elder abuse and neglect,[70] hate crimes against the Amish,[71] violent honor crimes by religious extremists in the United States,[72] Medicaid fraud by physicians,[73] white-collar crime by retail bankers,[74] and rationalizing continued horse betting while dealing with monetary losses from gambling.[75] Gerald Foster was the first scholar to apply Sykes and Matza's neutralization theory to police crime, in his study of the response of public officials in Denver in the aftermath of a 1961 scandal within the Denver Police Department. The scandal resulted in the dismissal and criminal prosecution of fifty-three police officers on charges of burglary, larceny, and related conspiracies. Foster found that three techniques of neutralization by police officers were "directly demonstrable": denial of injury ("the criminals in many cases viewed their acts as petty enough to be unnoticed and, if not, losses were covered by insurance anyway"), condemnation of condemners ("the brass had their forms of 'larceny,' why should we not have ours?"), and appeal to higher loyalties ("loyalties to the police solidarity group").[76]

Techniques of neutralization are justifications for deviance. In the context of police misconduct, and more specifically, police violence, techniques of neutralization help explain the rationalization of sworn law enforcement officers who engage in illegal behaviors that are not recognized as valid by the legal system or society at large. The police subculture provides the social process and conditions to neutralize the guilt associated with engaging in acts of police violence. Victor Kappeler, Richard Sluder, and Geoffrey Alpert conceptualized techniques of neutralizing police deviance as "they made me do it" (denial of responsibility), "no innocent got hurt" (denial of injury), "they deserved it" (denial of the victim), "they don't know anything" (condemning the condemners), and "protect your own" (appealing to higher loyalties).[77]

Denial of Responsibility

Blame is deflected through denial of responsibility as a technique of neutralization. Sykes and Matza explained that delinquent youth often view their own behavior as the result of forces outside of their own control, as if they were a "billiard ball" being helplessly propelled into new situations.[78] This technique of neutralization helps to understand the context of police violence within the police subculture, in which "defiant citizens" are viewed "as provocateurs in need of police control."[79] Further, "When police use violence or choose to use the force of law illegally against citizens, they are merely responding to the provocation of citizens—situations and events that they have little or no control over and for which they are not responsible regardless of their own contributions to the situation or their departure from social expectations."[80]

Abusive police officers often rationalize the illegal use of excessive force as the natural consequence of someone else's bad acts. I first witnessed this type of police behavior when I was a rookie police officer many years ago. One night on patrol I encountered several teenagers roughhousing on the lawn of a downtown funeral home. It was well after midnight, and the lawn was basking in the bright floodlights that illuminated the outside of the funeral home. I was soon joined by two other officers, including a police sergeant. While we were talking to the teenagers, I was startled when—without any apparent provocation at all—the police sergeant punched one of the boys in the face, knocking him to the ground. The sergeant then directed me to handcuff the teen and arrest him for assault. The sergeant later said he had no choice but to punch the boy in the face; he said he had been provoked when he noticed that the teenager's fist was clenched as he stood talking to us calmly with his hands at his sides. Of course, the teenager never clenched his fist and he posed no threat to the police officers there. But as the sergeant explained to me later that night, "The good guys always win."

Denial of Injury

Another technique of neutralization focuses on the harm or injury sustained by the victim in acts of police violence. Sykes and Matza theorized that with denial of injury neutralization "wrongfulness may turn on the question of whether or not anyone has been hurt by the deviance, and this is open to a variety of interpretations."[81] In the context of police violence and the police subculture, these are acts that police view as not really causing any great harm and should not be of any concern to the public. Kappeler, Sluder, and Alpert provided examples of police deviance that are "accompanied by a denial of injury: theft of evidence from suspects for personal gain; violation of the civil rights of citizens to make arrests or secure convictions; abuse of authority to establish or maintain a personal sense of order."[82] The denial of injury technique of neutralization is also commonly invoked by police officers accused of sexual misconduct by victims who allege rape by an on-duty officer. Some accused officers have claimed that sexual encounters were consensual, especially in jurisdictions where there is no specific criminal statute that prohibits sex between an on-duty officer and a person in police custody.[83]

In chapter 4, I discussed police violence involving the criminal misuse of conductive energy devices (e.g., Tasers) by sworn law enforcement officers. Most of the cases where police officers have been arrested for crimes involving use of a Taser consisted of little or no situational risk that would justify that use of force.[84] The cases typically involved victims who posed no threat to the officer, such as teenagers, homeless persons, individuals already handcuffed, or even other officers. The training that officers receive in the use of CEDs as tactical less lethal police weapons seems to reinforce the denial of injury technique of neutralization in instances where an officer later misuses a police-issued stun gun. Many police departments require officers to "take a shock" as part of the training before being issued and allowed to carry a CED, although some law enforcement agencies have stopped the requirement because of complaints regarding injuries to trainees.[85] Still, dozens of video clips of these sorts of training sessions can be viewed on popular video-sharing websites. The videos usually depict both trainers and trainees responding to stunning sessions with cheers, claps, jokes, and laughter. The trainer in one YouTube clip reassures the trainees, "See, that just shows you how safe this thing is."[86] The video clips may or may not be representative of most CED training programs, but they do call forth lessons from the legendary police gun battle known as "the Newhall Incident" that involved the tragic deaths of four California Highway Patrol officers in 1970.[87] Some of the officers killed in the firefight had spent shell casings in their pockets, indicating that they had inexplicably taken the time to collect and secure the casings as the gun battle raged. In fact, the officers had acted exactly how they had been trained on the police firing range, where they were expected and required to pick up their spent brass from their six-shot revolvers at the end of the day. The Newhall Incident showed that training—for better or worse—often dictates police actions.[88]

Some have argued that the part of the Newhall Incident involving the embattled officers collecting their spent brass is nothing more than urban legend.[89] Nevertheless, I do recall being told the story as a warning by a firearms instructor when I was a cadet at the New Hampshire Police Academy in 1986. The lessons learned from the Newhall Incident continue to have an impact on police policies and training decades later.[90] The content and tone of Taser training may promote inappropriate or even criminal behavior in some officers in much the same way that training contributed to the death of the four highway patrol officers in the Newhall Incident. Of course, the vast majority of officers go through Taser training and never misuse the weapon, but Taser training that includes jokes and laughter may promote misuse justified by the denial of injury technique of neutralization, especially among officers with psychological problems or who are particularly troubled by occupational stressors.

Denial of the Victim

Some acts of police violence target victims whom the police subculture sees as deserving of injury. This can happen when an officer decides that a potential target's social status neutralizes victimization in light of the circumstances. Sykes and Matza explained that with this technique of neutralization, offenders may rationalize their deviance as "not really an injury; rather, it is a form of rightful retaliation or punishment."[91] Members of vulnerable populations are at the greatest risk from police officers who abuse their authority through acts of police sexual misconduct. Officer Daniel Holtzclaw of the Oklahoma City Police Department, for example, targeted women whom he thought were especially vulnerable—such as poor women of color, some of whom allegedly were illicit drug users with criminal records—to sexually assault while he was on duty and in full police uniform. He wrongly assumed that his victims would not be believed if they filed a complaint. Holtzclaw was convicted of numerous crimes and sentenced to 263 years in prison.

Sex workers, including prostitutes and exotic dancers/strippers, are especially vulnerable as targets of police sexual misconduct. My research identified 105 cases where seventy-two police officers were arrested during the years 2005–13 for crimes involving a victim who was a sex worker. The arrested officers were employed by sixty-four state and local law enforcement agencies located in fifty-three counties and independent cities in twenty-six states and the District of Columbia. The victims were mostly female (97%) adults (93.2%) with ages ranging from fourteen to forty-seven. The arrested officers include a Melbourne, Florida, police officer who engaged in sex acts with prostitutes in his patrol car;[92] a police officer in Uplands Park, Missouri, who sexually assaulted and robbed four prostitutes;[93] a part-time Belgium, Illinois, police officer who sexually assaulted seven strippers (while he was on duty and in full police uniform) in repeated incidents over a three-year period in back rooms at a bar where the women worked;[94] and a Lowell, Massachusetts, police officer who admitted to having sex in his patrol car with prostitutes "about twenty times while on duty."[95]

Persons who identify as LGBTQ+ are also vulnerable to police misconduct where the victim is neutralized. Whereas Sykes and Matza explained that a delinquent youth might deny the victim by neutralizing "assaults on homosexuals or suspected homosexuals,"[96] my research on gender, sexuality, and policing for the Office of Community Oriented Policing Services at the US Department of Justice identified similar patterns of justifications for police violence against transgender women, sexual assault of transgender men by police officers, police violence against gay men, police harassment of gay men, police harassment of lesbians, prevalence of homophobia among police, as well as harassment, discrimination, and retaliation against LGBTQ+ police officers by other police officers within law enforcement agencies.[97]

A fourth technique of neutralization involves condemnation of the condemners and occurs when a deviant person "shifts the focus of attention from his own deviant acts to the motives and behaviors of those who disapprove of his violations."[98] Sykes and Matza described this technique of neutralization as a "jaundiced viewpoint" that "hardens into a bitter cynicism."[99] For the delinquent adolescent, that cynicism is typically directed against authority figures such as teachers or the police. For the corrupt police officer, that cynicism might be directed against anyone who disagrees with the police.

Kappeler, Sluder, and Alpert argued that when applied to police deviance, condemnation of the condemners as a neutralization technique manifests in three ways. First, "police condemn the edicts of the external and internal normative system when they conflict with police informal norms by imputing motive on those criminal justice personnel who attempt to curtail police autonomy and authority."[100] When reading this chapter's policy box, "Off-Duty Police Bizarre Gun Violence," consider how state and local law enforcement agencies might develop policies to reduce the incidence of police acts of "bizarre violence" involving firearms.

Kappeler, Sluder, and Alpert argued that police officers view certain aspects of the criminal justice system, such as the exclusionary rule and the practice of plea bargaining, as showing that others (including, perhaps, almost everyone outside of law enforcement) are "soft on crime" or use "loopholes" to undermine police authority.[101] Law enforcement officers generally adhere to a worldview consistent with Herbert Packer's crime control model of the criminal justice system. Packer developed two abstract models, the crime control model and the due process model, to help explain competing values in the criminal justice system.[102] Adherents of the crime control model are generally conservative and view the root causes of crime as a breakdown of individual responsibility. The focus of the criminal justice system, according to Packer's crime control model, should be to determine *factual* guilt, and the courts should operate efficiently almost like an assembly line in a factory. As such, courts should process guilty defendants quickly, with the understanding that police fact-finding investigations will have determined guilt or innocence through the discretionary power of arrest. The crime control model is not concerned with the rights of defendants, at least to the extent that adherents of the crime control model argue that technicalities often let crooks go free. The goal of sentencing, according to the crime control model,

Many police officers carry firearms while off duty. In some jurisdictions, off-duty officers are encouraged or required by their employing law enforcement agency to carry a gun while in public. Federal law allows off-duty state and local police officers to carry concealed firearms almost anywhere in the country.[a] James Fyfe once estimated that at any time there are probably more than 300,000 armed off-duty police officers across the country.[b] The rationale for off-duty officers carrying firearms includes the fact that police sometimes need to intervene in potentially violent encounters while off duty, that it serves as a deterrent for potential offenders, and that it is necessary for officer safety.[c] Police officers are sworn to uphold the law and have received specialized training in the proper use of firearms. Yet there are many instances each year where police officers are arrested for crimes stemming from acts of "bizarre violence" involving guns.[d] The following are some examples.

DeKalb County Police Department, Georgia. An off-duty detective, age forty-eight, pointed his handgun at the driver in the car in front of him at a McDonald's drive-through because the detective was upset that it was taking a while to get his lunch.[e]

Detroit Police Department. An off-duty twenty-five-year-old officer was arrested after he pulled a gun and pointed it at two men who intervened when they saw him arguing and trying to force a woman into his car outside a nightclub at 2:00 a.m.[f]

New York Police Department. An off-duty police lieutenant was arrested after he pressed his department-issued 9-millimeter handgun against his wife's head and threatened to kill her after becoming angry that she had not gotten him an ice-cream cake for his forty-seventh birthday party.[g]

Philadelphia Police Department. An off-duty twenty-eight-year-old police officer was charged with assault after he pulled his gun and threatened to kill the owners of a doughnut shop because they were

a. Law Enforcement Officers Safety Act (2004).
b. Fyfe, "Always Prepared."
c. Fyfe.
d. Fyfe, 77.
e. LaRenzie, "DeKalb Cop Arrested after Fight at Local McDonald's."
f. Siacon, "Police: Off-Duty Officer Arrested."
g. Samuels, Scalafani, and Moore, "Make a (Death) Wish!"

speaking to each other in Chinese and the officer thought they were talking about him.[h]

St. Louis County Police Department. An off-duty thirty-four-year-old officer attending a St. Patrick's Day parade with his family was arrested after he pulled a handgun and pointed it at a parking lot attendant who told him he could not park his car in the lot.[i]

Ware Shoals Police Department, South Carolina. While off duty at home, the police chief shot at his dog with a gun after the dog knocked over a small table in the living room. The chief, age forty-four, was arrested for discharging a weapon within city limits.[j]

h. Graham, "Two Philadelphia Police Charged with Crimes."
i. Merkel, "County Officer Charged with Pulling Gun."
j. Dominguez, "Ware Shoals Police Chief on Leave after Facing Gun Charge."

is that punishment will deter crime. The crime control model offers a law-and-order viewpoint based in substantive criminal law, and most police officers have great difficulty understanding the rationale of adherents of the due process model of the criminal justice system.

Procedural rights and determination of *legal* guilt are the benchmarks of Packer's due process model. The due process model is concerned with reliability and constitutional notions of procedural due process. A key value of the due process model is protecting the rights of citizens. Adherents of the due process model are considered to be politically liberal and think the root causes of crime are related to poverty and racial discrimination. They are suspicious of the police and argue that only formal fact-finding can protect the innocent from abusive police powers and overzealous prosecutors. Police officers often have distain for anyone who values the key elements of the due process model, because the police view procedural due process as a threat to their autonomy and authority.

The second way that deviant police invoke this technique of neutralization is through "condemnation of people who bring charges of deviance against the police."[103] Kappeler, Sluder, and Alpert explained that this is different from the denial of the victim technique of neutralization because the condemners are "hostile" to the police or are "money grubbing" persons who sue the police.[104] As previously mentioned, researchers estimate that at least thirty thousand police misconduct lawsuits are filed annually in state and federal courts across the United States against individual police officers, their employing local law enforcement agencies, and municipalities.[105] Many of these cases are filed as civil tort actions against police officers and local law enforcement agencies in state trial courts.[106] There is also considerable civil rights litigation arising out of police misconduct claims filed in federal courts alleging violations of 42 U.S.C. § 1983 (often referred to as Section 1983). Section 1983 provides civil remedies for persons aggrieved by a state actor who acts under the color of law to violate someone's federally protected rights. Some individual police officers are sued repeatedly for civil rights violations.[107] In my own research, I found that 29.3 percent of the police officers arrested during the years 2005–11 for a violence-related crime had also been sued in federal court pursuant to Section 1983 for violating someone's civil rights at some point during their law enforcement careers.[108] I also found that 21 percent of the arrested officers named as party defendants in a federal Section 1983 action were first sued in a state civil action that was later removed to federal trial court by defense counsel pursuant to 28 U.S.C. § 1441, because the plaintiff had asserted a federal question in their civil complaint. Some Section 1983 lawsuits are dismissed from court because they are frivolous.[109] Others are dismissed by a court on summary judgment or for failure to state a claim upon which relief can be granted. The majority of these lawsuits, however, are resolved through monetary settlements or judgments against the employing municipalities.

In the third form of this technique of neutralization, deviant police "condemn those persons who pass judgment on the police."[110] Sheriff Joe Arpaio of Maricopa County, Arizona, is an example of one sworn law enforcement officer who spent considerable energy and county resources condemning anyone who passed judgment on him or the actions of the sheriff's office. Arpaio's law enforcement career started in 1954 when he joined the Metropolitan Police Department in Washington, DC. He also briefly worked as a deputy sheriff in Clark County, Nevada, and in 1957 he joined the US Bureau of Narcotics, which later became the federal Drug Enforcement Administration. Arpaio retired from the DEA in 1982, settled in the Phoenix area where he and his wife opened a travel agency, and was elected sheriff of Maricopa County in 1992.[111]

For years Arpaio was criticized by many for his harsh treatment of inmates in Maricopa County jails. Arpaio built tent cities as jails to warehouse inmates in the desert heat, issued pink underwear to inmates either to shame them or deter them from stealing county-issued underwear, and often boasted about the cheap food that inmates were fed, costing the county just pennies per meal. He developed a reputation for being tough on illegal immigration and undocumented immigrants; he encouraged deputy sheriffs to target Latinos in traffic stops solely on suspicion they might be in the country illegally, and he and his deputies turned over detained undocumented individuals to federal immigration authorities. A federal judge issued an order in 2011 enjoining the Maricopa County Sheriff's Office and its officers from arresting any person unlawfully present in the United States unless the person was alleged to have committed some other state or federal crime. Arpaio ignored the court order and directed his deputies to continue enforcing federal immigration law. On July 31, 2017, Arpaio was convicted of misdemeanor criminal contempt for willful violation of the 2011 court order. The judge found that Arpaio had "announced to the world and to his subordinates that he was going to continue business as usual no matter who said otherwise."[112] Indeed, Arpaio publicly stated many times that his actions were legal and that his detractors and condemners were wrongfully passing judgment on him because he was tough on crime and on illegal immigration. President Trump pardoned Arpaio the following month, saying he was a "worthy candidate for a presidential pardon" because he was an "American Patriot" who "kept Arizona safe!"[113]

Appealing to Higher Loyalties

Sykes and Matza noted that the deviant individual "does not necessarily repudiate the imperatives of the dominant normative system, despite his failure to follow them."[114] Instead, deviant individuals resolves a dilemma— where they end up breaking the law or committing some deviant act—by rationalizing their appeal to a higher loyalty. This technique of neutralization is common in situations where police officers are "faced with the conflict of upholding the external norms of the larger society or violating the informal norms of their subculture."[115] Typical scenarios involve lying, falsification, and perjury—all of which are discussed in the pages that follow.

NOBLE CAUSE CORRUPTION

Crimes of police falsification are often motivated by officers' skewed perceptions of legitimate law enforcement ends.[116] Some police officers develop a profound utilitarian moral commitment to a crime control model of law enforcement that results in a willingness to do whatever it takes to get the desired result—typically an arrest and criminal conviction—through noble cause corruption.[117] Police officers who engage in noble cause corruption are concerned only with the "good end" and justify their illegal means in pursuit of larger law enforcement purposes and what they perceive as the greater social good in ridding the streets of a criminal.[118] Many consider policing a noble cause, and individuals who work in law enforcement often see their work not as just a job, but as a moral commitment. Noble cause corruption, however, involves a corruption of police power "that happens when police officers care too much about their work."[119]

Police Falsification

The practice of deception, including lying, is an integral part of policing.[120] Some forms of police deception are accepted and recognized by courts as legitimate law enforcement practices, such as use of trickery to elicit incriminating statements from suspects.[121] Thus, not all lies told by police officers are considered improper, and some lies are even encouraged as part of the secrecy found in police organizations and the police subculture as a feature of social control.[122] Thomas Barker and David Carter formulated a taxonomy of police lies, including accepted police lying, tolerated police lying, and deviant policing lying.[123] Accepted police lies are ones that are necessary for legitimate law enforcement purposes, such as a lie told by an officer preserve the integrity of an ongoing criminal investigation. Tolerated lies are those the police deem necessary to achieve legitimate law enforcement objectives, even though the police might privately question the appropriateness of the deception. Tolerated lies within policing are consistent with situational ethics, in which the act of lying is deemed morally right in the limited context of the situation at hand.[124] Deviant police lies, according to Barker and Carter, are those told by sworn officers that violate someone's due process rights pursuant to the Fourteenth Amendment.

Barker and Carter distinguish between deviant police lies told in support of perceived legitimate law enforcement goals and those told in support of illegitimate police goals. The police tend to focus on *factual* guilt, and sometimes there are weaknesses in a criminal case that are necessary to overcome to reach *legal* guilt and sustain a conviction. When that happens, an officer might "fluff up the evidence" and "supply the missing elements."[125] Officers might embellish the narrative in a police report or search warrant application, or they might even commit perjury by falsely testifying under oath in a court proceeding. Police lies in support of legitimate goals (such as obtaining an arrest warrant, search warrant, or conviction) are rationalized by officers as a technique of neutralization. Deviant police lies in support of illegitimate goals are lies told by the police "to effect an act of corruption or to protect the officer from organizational discipline or civil and/or criminal liability."[126]

The Mollen Commission found three primary areas of falsification among police officers: testimonial perjury involving lying under oath in a court proceeding, documentary perjury involving sworn or unsworn written false statements in an affidavit or criminal complaint, and falsification of police records such as false statements written in a police report.[127] Several New York City police officers told investigators with the Mollen Commission that police falsification was so common in cases involving narcotics or weapons that officers openly refer to the practice of police perjury as "testilying."[128] Perjury by police officers is so common among police departments throughout the United States that it is generally regarded as a cultural phenomenon.[129] According to Alan Dershowitz, the practice of testilying is "an open secret among prosecutors, defense attorneys, and judges" in courts throughout the country.[130] It is seemingly encouraged by prosecutors driven by a "win at all costs" mentality, where high conviction rates become the benchmark of measuring a successful prosecutor.[131] Police perjury is tolerated by prosecutors and judges who "subtly encourage" the widespread practice "because they think that most victims of police perjury are guilty of the crimes for which they stand charged."[132] Although I do not think he encouraged police perjury, Judge Robert Cullinane of the Dover District Court in New Hampshire told me in 1987 that he was always impressed with my testimony as a police officer in criminal trials he presided over, because there were numerous instances where he thought it would have been easier for me to lie on the witness stand. Underscoring the proliferation and passive tolerance of the problem, Dershowitz once joked that years from now people "will be 'shocked—shocked' at the pervasiveness of police perjury in the criminal justice system."[133]

Public awareness of police falsification practices has increased because of the existence of video recordings that contradict the police version of events in numerous high-profile fatal police shooting cases across the United States. In the past, police have owned the narratives in cases involving police shootings, largely because a dead person cannot talk and because there are often no eyewitnesses deemed credible by investigators and prosecutors. Video evidence increasingly provides an alternate narrative that can be inconsistent with the factual averments made by police officers in their statements, written reports, and sworn testimony. The ubiquity of video recording devices means that many police encounters with citizens are captured on video. Some of the video recording devices are deployed by law enforcement agencies, such as police dashcams mounted in police vehicles, police body-worn cameras, and security/surveillance cameras in public places. There is also widespread use of security/surveillance video cameras in commercial businesses and private residences that are always recording, as well as high-definition smartphone video cameras that are carried by virtually everyone and available to record police encounters at any moment. Even so, falsification practices are so engrained in the police subculture that the ubiquity of video cameras has not vanquished the lies, but just exposed more lies.[134]

Police falsification practices erode police legitimacy in communities across the country. It is difficult to assess the extent of the problem, but it seems to permeate many law enforcement agencies and is likely the most common form of noble cause corruption in policing. Most acts of police falsification that result in an arrest are never uncovered, because most criminal cases are resolved through guilty pleas without a trial where a police officer's testimony would be subject to cross-examination by a defense attorney.[135] In my study of sworn law enforcement officers arrested in years 2005–13 at agencies across the United States, I found that 6.3 percent ($n = 574$) of the arrest cases involved an officer who was charged with a falsification crime such as perjury or filing a false police report. Twenty-seven percent ($n = 155$) of the police falsification arrest cases also involved alleged acts of police violence.

CRITICAL THINKING QUESTIONS

1. What are some limitations of techniques of neutralization as a criminological theory to explain police violence?

2. How did Maricopa County, Arizona, sheriff Joe Arpaio use techniques of neutralization to justify his controversial actions?

3. Why are some lies told by police officers considered a valid form of social control and not deviant behavior?

4. Is low self-control a reliable measure of predicting future police misconduct?

SIX

Societal Conflict and
Legitimacy Theories

The theories presented in this chapter all involve some aspects of power, control, and social inequality. While it is impossible to remove race from most any criminal justice policy discussion, concerns of race and racial injustice are at the core of criminological thought and research related to police violence. Concern for racial disparities manifested in discretionary police behaviors—especially acts of police violence—were largely dormant in mainstream criminology and political discourse until the media aired a video recording of the 1991 beating of Rodney King by Los Angeles police officers.[1] The truth is that beatings "constitute an ancient and traditional part of police work" at local law enforcement agencies across the United States.[2] Much of the police brutality in the United States has long been directed at persons of color. As Jill Nelson noted, "The notion of the 'black male predator' is so historically rooted in the American consciousness that we have come to accept the brutalization and murder of citizens by the police as an acceptable method of law enforcement."[3] For good reason, many young black males are not willing to accept the legitimacy of the police in their own communities.

The first section of this chapter focuses on theories of societal conflict, including conflict theory, critical criminology, state crime, critical race theory, and institutional racism. The final section explores theories and concepts related to police legitimacy and restorative justice. It includes discussion of police militarization, procedural justice, and related topics such as the Ferguson effect, de-policing, and the Black Lives Matter movement. It is important to note that I have written this chapter from the perspective and place of privilege as a white male in my fifties. All of my life experiences and my professional work—as a police officer, attorney, professor, and criminologist—have been socially constructed in ways not experienced by people of color.

Inherent in the study of US police violence are concepts related to societal conflict, race, and the power that come with the legal authority possessed by sworn law enforcement officers in a decentralized policing system with more than eighteen thousand state and local law enforcement agencies. Some theories in this section are not traditional criminological theories that neatly present propositions to explain causes of criminal offending. Some may have limited scope, lack parsimony, and be difficult to empirically test in ways that scholars and students of criminology seek to evaluate theories. It is important, however, to acknowledge that police crime—and more specifically, police violence—is different than other types of crime and deviance studied by criminologists. Police officers are supposed to uphold and enforce the law, not break the law and commit crimes. Generally, law enforcement is exempt from law enforcement—meaning that police officers do not like arresting other officers, and rarely do. The theories in this section address the proverbial elephant in the room: police violence often involves elements of power, control, social inequality, race, and racism.

Conflict Theory

The mid-1960s to the mid-1970s was a period of unrest in American culture in which many people felt disenchanted with societal values. Conflict theories of criminology became popular during this time. These theories were in stark contrast to the sociology of law and social control that largely adhered to consensus theories, which explained societal norms as being achieved through the greatest normative consensus. Conflict theories posit the opposite: that conflict is natural to society and consensus is an aberration.[4]

Consensus is created through the use of power and control. Power is created by control of scarce societal resources, and conflict in society is caused by attempts to control these resources. Conflict theorists focus on lawmaking and law enforcement and are rarely concerned with the criminal offending of individuals. Formulation and application of the law enables those in power to maintain control over others in society who are less dominant and less powerful. Conflict theories argue that application of the law by dominant groups results in law enforcement that disproportionately criminalizes the behaviors of citizens in nondominant groups.[5]

George Vold was the first criminologist to propose conflict theory as an explanation of criminal offending when he suggested that "the whole process of law making, law breaking, and law enforcement becomes a direct reflection of deep-seated and fundamental conflicts between interest groups and their more general struggles for the control of the police power of the state."[6] According to Vold, the groups in control of police power can "dominate the policies that decide who is likely to be involved in violation of the law."[7] Vold's group conflict theory of crime posited that crime is minority group behavior in direct opposition to the rules of the dominant majority. The view of the minority group members is that the police represent the values and power of the dominant majority from which they are excluded. Vold argued that members of minority groups do not accept the definition of their own behaviors as criminal and that group conflicts and struggles for the control of power are always present in any society.

Critical Criminology

Building on Vold's conflict theory, Richard Quinney's early writings argued that crime is socially constructed as the product of legal definitions created through the exercise of political power.[8] He posited that crime is the product of reactions by legitimate authorities who use political power to impose criminal definitions on the types of behaviors they find objectionable. Those who are powerless are the ones whose behavior is most likely to be deemed objectionable and, thus, defined as criminal behavior. The social construction of crime takes hold through definitions spread by the media.

Critical criminology of the 1970s developed with a Marxist orientation. William Chambliss and Robert Seidman argued that law is a means of social control by the ruling class, who control resources. Control is exercised by creating laws that criminalize behaviors of the lower classes within society and by promulgating myths that the law serves the interests of everyone without regard for social class.[9] Quinney, similarly, espoused Marxist propositions to explain crime, arguing that the state is organized to serve the interests of the dominant capitalist ruling class; that criminal law is an instrument of the state and ruling class to maintain the existing social and economic order; that crime control is accomplished through a criminal justice system designed to establish domestic order in a way that preserves the interests of the elite ruling class; and that capitalism requires the subordinate classes to be oppressed by whatever means necessary, including through the use of power, coercion, and violence within the legal system.[10] Critical criminology has continued to evolve since the 1970s and now includes a wide range of criminological perspectives, including convict, critical race, cultural, feminist, Marxist, newsmaking, peacemaking, and radical criminology theories, as well as restorative justice, environmental justice, and state crime theories.

Newsmaking Criminology

Many Americans never have any direct contact with the police and the criminal justice system.[11] They mostly learn about crime, the police, and issues relating to the criminal justice system from the news media through newspaper articles and television news programs. Some research has found that media coverage of crime is often disproportionately represented when certain demographic and social characteristics of offenders and crime victims are present.[12] There is often a filtering process in reporting the news that includes the exercise of discretion by media organizations in terms of the types of news reported on and the nature of the content devoted to specific news reports.[13]

News coverage of police misconduct, however, is generally accurately reported by the media. Justin Ready, Michael White, and Christopher Fisher found that coverage of police misconduct incidents was consistent with official police agency records of the same events.[14] Research has also suggested that local law enforcement agencies are not very effective at controlling media reports of police misconduct.[15] My research relied exclusively on media reports to identify 6,724 arrest cases involving 5,545 nonfederal sworn law enforcement officers across the United States who were each arrested during the years 2005–11.[16] The arrested officers were employed by 2,529 state and local law enforcement agencies located in 1,205 counties and independent cities in all fifty states and the District of Columbia. Almost half (49.5%) of these arrest cases involved violence-related offenses. All of this research is within the theoretical framework of newsmaking criminology, which Gregg Barak defined as "the conscious efforts and activities of criminologists to interpret, influence or shape the representation of 'newsworthy' items about crime and justice."[17] Although a separate paradigm of newsmaking criminology focuses on criminologists' manipulation of public discourse by becoming part of the newsmaking process, the primary focus in studying police violence is within the paradigm concerned with empirical research that analyzes the content of media crime reports.

State Crime

Some crimes are committed by the government. While the criminological study of state crime has suffered from poor theoretical and methodological conceptualization, state crime is generally understood to include governmental crime, governmental lawlessness, official misconduct, and human rights violations.[18] Chambliss described state-organized crime as "acts defined by law as criminal and committed by state officials in the pursuit of their job as representatives of the state."[19] State crime differs from all other crime because of the exclusive legal authority of the government to use coercive power. David Friedrichs distinguished state crime from governmental crime by arguing that state crime consists of actions conducted by the state or on behalf of a state agency and that governmental crime more broadly includes all crimes committed in a governmental context.[20]

State crime is difficult to study because it often involves criminality that is hidden from the media and the public.[21] Jeffrey Ian Ross argued that the police are "principal state criminogenic actors" and that police departments are "state criminogenic organizations."[22] But not all crimes by the police are state crimes. Chambliss suggested that state crime does not include criminal offenses that only benefit individual officeholders, and he argued that acts of police violence are not state-organized crimes "unless such acts violate existing criminal law and are official policy."[23] Ken Menzies, however, posited that "state crimes may be committed for personal gain or on behalf of the employing organization."[24] Police officers are especially well situated to engage in such state crimes.[25] The us-versus-them mentality of the police subculture provides fertile ground for corrupt officers to engage in acts of state crime. My own research on police crime has shown that many police officers are arrested for crimes committed in their official capacity as sworn law enforcement officers and use the power of their legal authority to illegally violate the rights of citizen victims.[26] This underresearched area remains largely ignored by most criminologists because it is difficult to conceptualize and operationalize phenomena that are often hidden from public view. This is especially true when many assume that most acts of police crime and violence are perpetrated by just a few bad apples.

Critical Race Theory

The civil rights movement through the early twenty-first century has sought systemic progress and incremental change to the social order. Critical race theory developed starting in the 1970s with activists, lawyers, and legal scholars who were concerned that the forward progress of the 1960s civil rights era had largely stalled.[27] Derrick Bell went so far as to argue that advancements of civil rights in the United States were actually timed to benefit the economic conditions of elite white people. Focusing on the landmark 1954 Supreme Court decision in *Brown v. Education*, Bell suggested that substantive civil rights policymaking progress only occurs when there is convergence of racial interests.[28] He argued that at the time of *Brown* racial segregation was causing the United States to lose international prestige, and there was a sense that segregation was a barrier to continued industrialization of the South.

Critical race theory focuses on the study and transformation of power, race, and racism. Critical race theorists argue that the incremental progress through civil rights discourse is unable to truly transform relationships involving race, racism, and power. According to Richard Delgado and Jean Stefancic, there are several major tenets and propositions of critical race theory.[29] First, racism is experienced as a normal part of the everyday life of people of color in the United States. Racism is difficult to eradicate because most forms of it are ordinary and not acknowledged. Only the most blatant acts of racism are provided remedies in the law. Second, there is little incentive to address systemic racism because of the interest convergence and material determinism that benefits both white elites and the white working class. The social construction of race is also a theme of critical race theory. An aspect of this social construction is that genetic similarities of the races are ignored in favor of classifications and stereotypes based on skin color, facial features, and hair texture. Delgado and Stefancic noted that racial minority stereotypes change over time through societal circumstances and shared experiences. In the United States, Middle Eastern people who were once viewed as "exotic, fetishized figures wearing veils, wielding curved swords, and summoning genies from lamps" are now viewed by many Americans as "fanatical, religiously crazed terrorists bent on destroying America and killing innocent citizens."[30] Critical race theory also posits that persons of color are uniquely positioned to speak about race and racism because of their own life experiences, especially as to racism, racial oppression, racial disparities, and racial injustices in the criminal justice system. This often takes the form of legal storytelling through personal narratives told by scholars and activists alike.

Bennett Capers argued that critical race theory is an important element in criminal justice discourse and policymaking because "quite simply, race matters."[31] Race permeates all stages and processes of the criminal justice system, starting with police street encounters with citizens, interactions during police calls for service, and in the discretionary decision-making and powers of individual police officers. Elijah Anderson referred to a "code of the street," in which black people living in inner-city neighborhoods do not believe the police care about them and their communities, and "residents are aliened from the police and police authority."[32] There is a general sense among residents in these urban neighborhoods that it is best not to call 9-1-1 seeking police assistance, because the police often harass and arrest black residents they come into contact with on calls for service and in street encounters. The black people living by this code of the street are well aware that their experiences with the police are very different from the experiences of white people.

Racial profiling is a term that "embodies a widespread belief that minorities are disproportionately singled out by American police for scrutiny on a class basis—equating race or ethnicity with criminality—rather than on the basis of individual suspicion.[33] The term was first used in a 1990 article in the *New York Times* about an investigation to determine whether New Jersey state troopers were "using racial profiles when deciding which cars to stop" on the New Jersey Turnpike.[34] Critical race theory provides context to criticisms of criminological research on racial profiling by police officers. Karen Glover argued that mainstream criminology has largely embraced a "white logic orientation" in racial profiling research, because most criminological research studies of racial profiling have "avoided serious engagement of race and racism in large part because of the methodology and theoretical approaches that dominate the discipline, even when race itself is a fundamental component of the studies."[35] The essence of her argument is that much of the criminological research on racial profiling tends "to not address racial profiling as a manifestation of larger racial contexts that shape everyday life for communities of color."[36]

Institutional Racism

In the context of police violence, there are two forms of racism that permeate the criminal justice system. The first is individual racism. The second is institutional racism that is embedded in the police subculture and the practices of the criminal courts in many communities across the United States.[37]

A. Leon Higginbotham—whom I once heard speak of the racism he experienced as a newly appointed federal judge in 1964 when a Philadelphia police officer refused him access to the parking garage underneath the courthouse—argued that people of color have, historically and currently, been criminalized by virtue of skin color.[38] Shaun Gabbidon coined the term *blackaphobia* to describe fear of blacks as criminals[39] and separately argued that racial profiling practices are really "social subordination" efforts to keep the privileged feeling safe.[40]

The US Supreme Court has consistently deferred to the judgment and discretion of police officers in cases that involve police street encounters with people of color. The court has carved out an exception to the probable cause requirement of the Fourth Amendment through a series of cases since the 1960s that have allowed de facto routine police racial-profiling practices to continue to this day.[41] The seminal Supreme Court decision of *Terry v. Ohio* in 1968 laid the foundation for the continued proliferation of racially biased policing. In *Terry*, the court held that a police officer may temporarily detain a person and pat down outer garments in a stop-and-frisk street encounter if the officer has a reasonable suspicion that the person is about to engage in criminal activity.[42] The court's legal rationale was that an officer's safety and the governmental interests in detecting and preventing crime outweigh the brief intrusion a person experiences while detained by police during the investigatory stop. John Terry, a black man, was observed by a Cleveland, Ohio, police officer pacing back and forth on the sidewalk in front of a store. The officer thought that Terry and two other black men might be casing the store for a robbery. Terry and one of the other men on the sidewalk were arrested when police found that each of them were carrying concealed firearms. Some scholars have argued that there is a hidden racism inherent in *Terry v. Ohio* that is grounded in the prevailing view of the police subculture that black males are likely to be criminals. Adina Schwartz suggested more two decades ago, in the mid-1990s, that the "greater incidence of stops and frisks of blacks is attributable to racial animus and/or an unwarranted cognitive equation of being black with being dangerous."[43]

The hidden racism of Supreme Court jurisprudence involving cases of police-citizen encounters is also found in other cases, including *Whren v. United States*. In *Whren*, the court held that automobile stops by police are governed by the Fourth Amendment standard of reasonableness and that a police officer's underlying motivation is not relevant so long as the officer had probable cause to believe that a traffic violation had occurred.[44] Some states, however, have enacted legislation that criminalizes discriminatory police racial-profiling practices in street encounters, including motor vehicle investigatory stops.[45] State-level legislative efforts and opinions of lower trial and appellate courts have done little to change the police subculture of racially biased policing that is the norm at many of the more than eighteen thousand state and local law enforcement agencies throughout the United States. Blacks are almost three times more likely than whites to be pulled over by the police in a traffic stop.[46]

Research suggests that approximately 70 percent of all contacts that citizens have with the police are through police-initiated encounters.[47] Paul Butler argued that police *Terry* stops are "violent assertions of police dominance of the streets" that result in racial humiliation at the hands of the police.[48] Although available data are limited, research supports Butler's argument. Men of color—blacks and Latinos—are at higher risk than are white men for death by police-involved homicide.[49] The same study found that police officers were responsible for about 8 percent of all homicides in the United States between 2012 and 2016. Even so, the vast majority of fatal police shootings are found to be legally justified homicides and criminal charges are rarely brought against police shooters. See this chapter's policy box, "Does Race Play a Role in Fatal Police Shootings?" for a discussion of this issue.

Police Violence against Women of Color

Andrea Ritchie argued that women of color, especially black women, are especially vulnerable to victimization through police sexual violence, which is prevalent in many jurisdictions across the United States. It is normalized police behavior largely invisible to the general public.[50] Police sexual violence is a tool to enforce gender norms often perpetrated by police sexual predators against women of color—many of whom come into contact with the police only because they are already victims of other crimes—under the auspices of broken windows policing, the "war on drugs," stop-and-frisk practices, probation/parole enforcement, and the policing of prostitution.[51] Some predatory police officers seek out black women and other women of color as suitable targets to sexually assault as a calculated risk, based on the assumption that that such victims will either not file a complaint or will not be seen as credible complainants.

On-duty police officers across the United States shoot and kill people approximately one thousand times every year.[a] The best source of data on fatal police shootings is the open-source project of the *Washington Post*. The numbers of fatal police shootings have been remarkably similar each year since the *Post* started collecting data in 2015. The official statistics reported by the federal government on fatal police shootings each year are much lower.[b] Most fatal shootings by on-duty police officers are found to be legally justified. An officer is legally justified to use deadly force when he or she has a reasonable apprehension of an imminent threat of serious bodily injury or deadly force being used against the officer or a third person.[c]

Since 2005 (through late April 2019), only 101 police officers across the United States have been charged with murder or manslaughter resulting from an on-duty shooting. Of those 101 officers, to date only 35 have been convicted of a crime resulting from the shooting (16 by guilty plea, 19 by jury trial, and none by a bench trial). The victims were black in 22 of those 35 cases. In the cases where an officer was convicted of a crime, it was often for a lesser offense. Only 3 of the officers were convicted of intentional murder. The murder convictions of 4 other officers were overturned on appeal, but each was later convicted of federal crimes arising out of the same incident. As to the other officers, 10 were convicted of manslaughter, 4 of voluntary manslaughter, 5 of involuntary manslaughter, 2 of official misconduct, 2 of reckless homicide, 3 of negligent homicide, 5 of federal criminal deprivation of civil rights (including the 4 whose murder convictions were overturned), and 1 of reckless discharge of a firearm. The criminal cases for 43 of the officers ended in a nonconviction: 23 were acquitted at a jury trial, 9 were acquitted at a bench trial, 4 were dismissed by a judge, 6 were dismissed by a prosecutor, and in 1 instance no true bill was returned from a grand jury. The criminal cases for 23 of the officers were pending as of this writing.

It is difficult to draw statistically significant conclusions on the race and ethnicity of the officers charged in fatal police shootings and of

a. Sullivan et al., "Nationwide, Police Shot and Killed Nearly 1,000 People in 2017."

b. Zimring, *When Police Kill*.

c. Tennessee v. Garner, 471 U.S. 1 (1985); Graham v. Connor, 490 U.S. 386 (1989).

their victims. Most of the officers were white (84%) or black (14%). One of the arrested officers was Asian and another was Pacific Islander. Only 4 of the black officers were convicted (36%) (2 victims were black, and 2 were nonblack). Similarly, 31 of the nonblack officers were convicted (46%) (20 victims were black, and 11 were nonblack).

Relatively few of the victims were armed with a weapon when they were shot and killed by one of the 101 officers charged with murder or manslaughter. Only 32 (32%) of the criminal cases against an officer involved a victim who was actually armed with a dangerous weapon (e.g., gun, bat, scissors, screwdriver, automobile) when they were shot and killed by an officer. In the cases where an officer was convicted, just 10 (29%) involved a victim armed with a dangerous weapon.

LEGITIMACY AND RESTORATIVE JUSTICE

Whereas deterrence, incapacitation, and rehabilitation are utilitarian perspectives of punishment, restorative justice focuses on repairing the harm caused by crime through practices designed to reduce the likelihood of future harm. Restorative practices encourage criminal offenders to take responsibility for the harm caused by their actions, provide redress for their victims, and promote reintegration into the community for the purpose of restoring the pre-harm equilibrium of the offender, victim, and community.[52] Restorative justice practices are closely aligned with John Braithwaite's reintegrative shaming theory, which argued that reoffending can be reduced if shaming of an offender can result in genuine remorse and result in his or her successful reintegration into the community.[53]

Restorative justice differs from traditional criminal justice practices in several ways. Restorative justice views crime more comprehensively because it recognizes the harm caused to the offender, victim, and community rather than limiting the response of the criminal justice system to just the lawbreaker alone.[54] The success of restorative justice practices is measured in terms of how much harm has been repaired or prevented instead of how much punishment has been inflicted on an offender. Most importantly, restorative justice relies on community involvement and initiative in crime prevention and is not content solely with governmental responses within the formal structure of the criminal justice system. A few organizations across the United States have used mediation programs to resolve citizen complaints against police officers. Mediation programs are a form of restorative justice and could be used for informal dispute resolution to resolve complaints of police violence by providing a forum for citizen complainants and police officers to "discuss their interpretations of disputes."[55] Research has shown that citizens who complete a mediation process have greater trust in the police than do citizens whose complaints against the police went through traditional processes.[56]

Police Legitimacy

Legitimacy is defined by Tom Tyler as "the belief that legal authorities are entitled to be obeyed and that the individual ought to defer to their judgments."[57] Tyler argued that legitimacy is a belief, separate from an individual's self-interests, in accepting the judgments of the police and criminal courts. Individuals who believe in the legitimacy of the police and criminal courts are more likely to self-regulate their own behaviors to comply with the law and legal authority. Braithwaite argued that legitimacy of the criminal justice system can be improved if the system "becomes more effective at preventing crime and helping victims."[58] He suggested that police could be more effective if they solve fewer problems through formal case processing in the criminal justice system and focus, instead, on seeking community-based restitution and reconciliation between individual offenders and their victims.[59] Braithwaite reconciled restorative justice and police legitimacy by recognizing that democracy is strengthened through community policing when "it proceeds through a bottom-up rather than top-down implementation."[60] This can be done only when police officers become "more in and of the community than they are and less seen as standing above it."[61]

A major impediment to police legitimacy, however, is that police officers often arrest an offender simply because the police lack viable alternatives to arrest.[62] The hope of many policing scholars and other stakeholders of problem-solving policing has been that community policing initiatives would somehow ingratiate officers with the residents of the communities where officers work. That has not happened, especially in many urban neighborhoods where high percentages of the residents are people of color and ethnic minorities. Police legitimacy is lacking in those places, in large part because the police who *work* there do not also *live* there. The police are not *of the community* where they work each day, because their own communities are in the suburbs, small towns, and places that typically lack racial and ethnic diversity.[63] Not only do the police live in different places from where they work each day; they shop in different stores, they worship in different places, and their children attend different schools from the children whom the officers encounter on the job. No matter where they live, however, police officers tend to engage in social avoidance behaviors. In one study, John Violanti and his colleagues found that social avoidance was associated with poor health outcomes for police officers.[64] Changing the us-versus-them mentality of policing has the potential to improve police legitimacy and the health of officers working in communities where police currently lack legitimacy.

Procedural Justice

Robert Worden and Sarah McLean argued that the legitimacy of the police is important for three reasons: people who perceive the police as legitimate are (1) more likely to comply with police directions and requests during citizen-police encounters; (2) more likely to cooperate with police and other criminal justice officials; and (3) less likely to break the law and commit crimes.[65] The public confers legitimacy on the police only when the public believes that the police are acting in procedurally just ways.[66] People want the police to use fair procedures in carrying out their law enforcement duties. Procedural justice "refers to the idea of fairness in the processes that resolve disputes and allocate resources."[67] This concept is important because police legitimacy is established through informal judgments people make about procedural justice. Research has found that citizen perceptions of the police are often based more on the process (through notions of fairness and procedural justice) than on outcomes of citizen-police encounters.[68] One study, for example, found that citizens who received traffic tickets had more favorable views of the police after the traffic stop and were more willing to cooperate with police than before the traffic stop when they thought the officer had treated them fairly.[69] A meta-analysis of thirty police-led intervention research studies found that police use of procedurally just dialogue in encounters with citizens enhanced police legitimacy, reduced offending, and resulted in higher levels of citizen satisfaction and cooperation with the police.[70] Future research should address whether procedural justice can reduce the incidence and prevalence of police violence.

In 2015, the President's Task Force on 21st Century Policing identified "building trust and legitimacy" as the first of six "pillars" upon which the task force organized its recommendations "on how policing practices can promote effective crime prevention while building public trust."[71] The task force's first recommendation was that "law enforcement culture should embrace a guardian mindset to build public trust and legitimacy ... [and] police and sheriff's departments should adopt procedural justice as the guiding principle for internal and external policies and practices to guide their interactions with the citizens they serve."[72] Central to this recommendation was the argument that state and local law enforcement agencies must shed the warrior mentality instilled during recruit academy training of new sworn officers and engrained within the culture of most policing organizations throughout the United States. Newly hired recruits are required to successfully complete several months of academy training for certification as a sworn law enforcement officer. Many police academies are modeled after military basic training boot camps that were "designed to produce a warrior ready for battle and ready to follow orders and rules without question."[73]

That certainly was my experience. I spent three months at the New Hampshire Police Academy as a cadet in 1986. The academy staff seemed to delight in harassing and yelling at the cadets. The slightest infraction resulted in being ordered to do sets of twenty-five push-ups. The days were spent marching from place to place, even to get our meals at the dining hall on the adjacent community college campus. Once in the dining hall, we were required to square our meals, meaning that we had to move our arms at right angles every time we raised a fork to our mouths. Apparently nothing has changed since the mid-1980s, as the website for the New Hampshire Police Standards and Training Council explains that the sixteen-week residential police academy "is paramilitary in nature, and requires military discipline (marching, saluting, etc.)."[74] As Sue Rahr and Stephen Rice noted, however, a police academy modeled after military boot camps "has little to do with the daily reality of policing."[75] It is little wonder that police officers trained in such a hostile environment—where those in power (police academy staff) prey on the powerless (police cadets)—soon embrace the us-versus-them mentality of the police subculture.

The history of policing in the United States is often divided into distinct time periods distinguished by each era's primary policing strategies. The political era of policing, from the 1840s to the early 1900s, was characterized by politically corrupt influences caused by the close ties between municipal politics and policing.[76] Police officers in the political era were not trained in the law, and civil rights violations by the police—such as "third degree" tactics to beat or trick confessions out of suspects—became routine.[77] The reform era of policing (sometimes referred to as the professional era), from the 1920s to 1980, developed as an effort to remove local political corruption from municipal police departments. The early years of the reform era were characterized in the 1920s and 1930s by rapid industrialization, urbanization, and population growth through large-scale immigration. It was during this period when large police departments were organizationally restructured according to principles of military science and when police officers abandoned foot patrols in favor or patrolling in motor vehicles.[78] As early as the 1890s in some cities, call boxes were installed on street corners so that police officers could be dispatched without having to return to the police station for each assignment.[79] The Bayonne Police Department in New Jersey was the first municipal police agency to utilize a mobile two-way radio system, in 1933.[80] Eventually, call boxes were replaced with two-way radios in patrol cars that allowed for rapid deployment of officers. By the 1970s it was common for police officers to also carry two-way portable walkie-talkies that provided additional communications abilities—beyond the radios mounted in police cruisers—for when officers were away from their vehicles. In many ways, the technological advancements in two-way radio communications corresponded with the increasing militarization of state and local law enforcement agencies across the United States.

The military model of policing was especially attractive to police administrators starting in the 1950s during the reform era of policing. Rank structures within state and local law enforcement agencies aligned with paramilitary terminology, using titles such as sergeant, lieutenant, captain, and so on. This provided structure and internal discipline within the ranks and appealed to many police officers who had served in the military. Egon Bittner argued that the military model of policing made sense because both the military and the police are instruments of force whose personnel must maintain a high level of preparedness because opportunities for using force "are unpredictably distributed" throughout both types of organizations.[81] Others have suggested that the war on crime and the war on drugs have led to increasing militarization of police organizations.[82] Jerome Skolnick and James Fyfe argued that "the 'war model' of policing encourages police violence of the type that victimized Rodney King" because "when any soldier goes to war, they must have enemies" and "when cops go to war against crime, their enemies are found in inner cities and among our minority populations."[83]

The Aftermath of Ferguson

The August 2014 fatal shooting of Michael Brown—an eighteen-year-old black male pedestrian—by a Ferguson, Missouri, police officer was a tipping point that brought the issue of police violence against people of color to the forefront of public discourse throughout the United States. An investigation by the US Department of Justice in the aftermath of Brown's death found that Ferguson police officers routinely violated the Fourth Amendment rights of black citizens by stopping them without reasonable suspicion, using unreasonable force against them often, and arresting them without probable cause.[84] Brown's death was one of several police homicides of black males that fueled the Black Lives Matter movement. Others were twelve-year-old Tamir Rice, fatally shot by a Cleveland, Ohio, police officer in 2014; Walter Scott, fatally shot by a North Charleston, South Carolina, police officer in 2015; and Eric Garner, suffocated by New York Police Department officers on Staten Island in 2014. Black Lives Matter has successfully used social media platforms to call attention to police violence.[85] Some scholars and commentators have suggested there was a "Ferguson effect" that resulted in higher crime rates in cities across the country, but criminological research has found little empirical evidence to support the contention.[86] Others have suggested that de-policing has occurred in some cities, wherein police officers have become less likely to engage in proactive activities such as traffic stops in response to the negative public perception of policing.[87] There is no evidence to suggest, however, any reductions in the incidence and prevalence of police violence against people of color.

CRITICAL THINKING QUESTIONS

1. How does restorative justice promote police legitimacy?
2. Do acts of police violence constitute state crime?
3. Is newsmaking criminology an appropriate theoretical framework to study the phenomenon of police violence?
4. How might "blackaphobia" contribute to the incidence and prevalence of police violence?

SEVEN

Integrationist Perspectives

The criminological theories presented in this book have been largely stand-alone theories that each offer explanations of crime. Criminological theories are sometimes subjected to theory competition, in which two or more theories are compared in efforts to determine which offer the best explanations of criminal behavior. Some mainstream criminological theories seem inapplicable to the study of police behaviors and causation of police violence without borrowing propositions from other theoretical frameworks. Theoretical integration offers a way to construct and assess criminological theories by identifying components from two or more theories and merging them into a synthesized and integrated theory that provides a better explanation of crime than each stand-alone theory.[1] Criminological theory integration is especially useful for the development of theories that might help explain police violence and improve policing. This final chapter does not attempt to create an integrated theory of police crime or police violence but rather discusses integrationist research relevant to the study of police violence. It explores several integrationist theoretical perspectives, including Charles Tittle's control balance theory, developmental criminology, and life-course criminology theories. The chapter ends with a brief discussion of applying the life-course approach to the phenomenon of police violence, drawing on literature from policing scholars.

CONTROL BALANCE THEORY

Tittle's control balance theory is a general theory of deviance that integrates aspects of deterrence, rational choice, labeling, strain, social learning, social control, and routine activities theories. The central premise of Tittle's theory is that "the amount of control to which an individual is subject, relative to the amount of control he or she can exercise, determines the probability of deviance occurring as well as the type of deviance likely to occur."[2] Control balance is defined as the ratio of how much an individual is able to control. The denominator in the control ratio is the amount of control an individual is able to exercise, and the numerator is the amount of control to which an individual is subject. The theory predicts conformity when these two forces of control are balanced. The theory conceptualizes control balance as a continuum with control deficits on one end, control balance in the middle, and control surpluses at the other end. The probability of deviance occurring is higher when an individual's control ratio is imbalanced either negatively or positively on the continuum, and it is lower when an individual's control is balanced in the middle of the continuum. Control balance theory posits that some individuals who experience control deficits (i.e., persons situated on the left side of the control balance continuum) will be predisposed to engage in behavior in the nature of predatory, defiant, or submissive deviance, while some individuals who experience control surpluses (i.e., persons situated on the right side of the control balance continuum) will be predisposed to engage in behaviors that constitute exploitative, plundering, or decadent deviance.

Tittle argued that control balance is the unifying causal process of deviant behavior. An unbalanced control ratio, together with an individual's desire for autonomy and personal needs, predisposes an individual to engage in acts of deviant behavior. The theory views deviant behavior as a device that helps individuals escape control deficits and extend surpluses of control. Control balance is operationalized through four primary variables: predisposition (i.e., deviant motivation), provocation (i.e., negative and positive situational stimulation), opportunity (i.e., circumstances favorable to engaging in specific types of deviant behavior), and constraint (i.e., an individual's perceived or actual likelihood of being subject to restraining reactions of others). Control balance theory posits that a predisposed individual engages in deviant behavior to alter his or her control ratio, even if the deviance brings only temporary relief. Deviance occurs when a predisposed individual (1) perceives that engaging in a deviant act will alter his or her control balance, (2) is in a situation that provides an opportunity to commit the deviant act, and (3) anticipates that his or her chances of countercontrol are not high enough to overwhelm the rebalancing of control that will likely result from the deviant act.

Recognizing problems with the logical consistency, parsimony, testability, and empirical validity of his theory, Tittle later refined it. Specifically, Tittle acknowledged that the original formulation of control balance theory needed revisions "to address a logical flaw, mistaken characterization, and inconsistencies and conceptual ambiguity . . . and to accommodate empirical findings that challenge some of its premises."[3] Tittle's revised theory makes a distinction between an individual's level of self-control and the type of deviant behavior predicted. Individuals with low levels of self-control seek immediate gratification and often do not have the ability to consider the long-term consequences of their actions. The revised control balance theory posits that individuals with low self-control are more likely than others to engage in deviant behavior that requires personal contact, and that individuals with high self-control are more likely to commit impersonal acts of deviance because they have the ability to resist urges for instant gratification.

Control balance theory has been subjected to less empirical theory-testing research than other contemporary criminological theories, perhaps because it is "much more complicated than other extant general theories of crime."[4] Control balance theory has been somewhat useful, but with mixed results in relatively few studies, in explaining various types of deviant behavior such as student cheating,[5] physical violence,[6] family violence victimization,[7] corporate crime,[8] and sexual predation.[9] These studies use survey methodologies, often involving the use of vignettes where respondents answer questions after reading one or more short paragraphs that provide descriptions of hypothetical situations. The questions are often grouped in scales so that researchers can measure concepts such as self-control, control balance, and control ratios. Matthew Hickman and his colleagues found that control balance theory "may serve as a useful foil to study the deviant proclivities of police officers."[10] They surveyed a random sample of 499 Philadelphia police officers and found that patrol officers with control deficits were more likely than other patrol officers to report colleagues who engaged in the deviant behaviors portrayed in the survey vignettes.

DEVELOPMENTAL CRIMINOLOGY

Developmental theories in criminology posit that an individual's likelihood of engaging in delinquency or crime changes across time. Proponents of developmental theories argue that individuals experience good life events and bad life events that can affect an individual's propensity for criminal offending. Exactly what life events and related factors increase an individual's propensity for offending vary among developmental theorists.[11] Prior to the 1980s, most criminologists and criminological theories did not consider risk factors and life events relevant to causation of crime and delinquency.[12] The usefulness of developmental theories has caused some leading criminology theorists to rethink their own theories and explanations of criminal offending. As noted in an earlier chapter, Michael Gottfredson and Travis Hirschi argued that offenders have a stable propensity for offending that does not change over time.[13] Hirschi later recognized that some life events, transitions, turning points, and trajectories serve as social bonds and may impact on an individual's offending and desistence from offending.[14] There are three categories of developmental theories: theories of continuity, theories of continuity *or* change, and theories of continuity *and* change. An individual's developmental pattern over the life course can be stable and continuous (i.e., marked by continuity) or can follow pathways of behavior that lead in different directions (i.e., marked by change).[15] Each theory of developmental and life-course criminology differs on how it addresses the processes and factors related to continuity or discontinuity in patterns of criminal offending.

Life-Course Persistent Theory and Adolescent-Limited Theory

Terrie Moffitt offered a dual-taxonomy developmental theory to explain delinquency and criminal offending. Her two theories were based on concepts from developmental psychology and neuropsychology and were apparently developed in response to Gottfredson and Hirschi's assertion that self-control is the only enduring personal characteristic implicated in an offender's decision to engage in delinquent or criminal activity. While most criminologists refer to Moffitt's dual-taxonomy as one theory, she was clear in defining the theoretical framework as two distinct theories that focus on the distinction between temporary and persistent antisocial conduct to explain criminal behavior.[16] Moffitt argued that a large number of individuals engage in antisocial and delinquent behavior during adolescence, while a much smaller number of individuals continue to engage in antisocial and criminal behavior throughout adulthood. She termed the first group adolescent-limited offenders and the second group life-course persistent offenders. According to Moffitt, adolescent-limited offending is normative behavior unlikely to continue into adulthood and is influenced by peer associations, whereas life-course persistent offending is pathological behavior linked to neuropsychological deficits.

Adolescent-limited offenders largely restrict their offending to teenage episodes of antisocial behavior and acts of delinquency. Moffitt posited that there is a maturity gap created by a teenager's biological development and the expectation of modern society that he or she refrain from certain adult behaviors. Dissatisfaction with the gap between biological maturity and social maturity leads to delinquent behavior in which "every curfew broken, car stolen, joint smoked, and baby conceived is a statement of independence."[17] The maturity gap closes with young adulthood, and the availability of conventional roles proliferate and the consequences for criminal offending and other forms of antisocial behavior escalate. Adolescent-limited delinquents are "able to abandon antisocial behavior when prosocial styles are more rewarding."[18] Transition to adulthood is characterized by discontinuity that results in desistence from criminal offending and other forms of antisocial behavior for the adolescent-limited offender.

Moffitt argued that life-course persistent offenders exhibit continuity in stable antisocial behavior from early childhood to adulthood. Neuropsychological deficits are produced when a child's normal brain development is disrupted, often through exposure to environmental factors at different stages of child development. These childhood neuropsychological deficits (e.g., poor self-control, irritability, high activity levels, an inability to delay gratification, and low cognitive ability) are traits or individual differences directly linked to a lifetime of antisocial behavior for the life-course persistent offender. Moffitt argued that these neuropsychological deficits serve to ensnare individuals into a life of crime by the cumulative consequences of their antisocial behavior that "prune away the options for change" and produce stability in offending over time.[19]

Research undertaken later by Moffitt and her colleagues found that some constructs of personality traits differ in young adult individuals who engage in general crime versus those who engage in domestic violence and other forms of intimate partner abuse.[20] Analyses of personality inventories measured at age eighteen and again at age twenty-one found that individuals engaged in both general crime and partner abuse shared a strong propensity for a negative emotionality personality trait, but only those involved in general crime (not partner abuse) were associated with a constraint personality trait of low self-control. Moffitt and her colleagues also analyzed longitudinal data from the

Dunedin Multidisciplinary Health and Development Study in New Zealand and found that at all ages males exhibit more violence and physical aggression than females.[21] They also found that high rates of violent behaviors and serious crimes are concentrated among relatively few people in the population for both male and female offenders. The most active female offenders engage in delinquency and crime at a rate much lower than the most active male offenders, and rarely are females life-course persistent criminal offenders.

The Dunedin Study is unique in that it provides "one of the few contemporary data sets that allow for a detailed examination of sex differences in criminal activity over the life course."[22] It was a longitudinal cohort study of the health, development, and behavior of all live births delivered at Queen Mary Hospital in Dunedin (a city with a population of 120,000 on the South Island of New Zealand) from April 1972 to March 1973.[23] One thousand individuals in the birth cohort were followed from age three to age twenty-one, and subsequent secondary studies have tracked criminal convictions well into adulthood. In one secondary data analysis study, Alex Piquero, Robert Brame, and Moffitt used the Dunedin data set to replicate the findings of Raymond Paternoster, Brame, and David Farrington's study of adolescent and adult criminal offending among the 411 cohort members in the Cambridge Study in Delinquent Development of mostly boys who were born in 1953.[24] Piquero and his colleagues found that very few members of the Dunedin birth cohort have been convicted of any crimes, boys were more likely than girls to engage in crime (as measured by criminal convictions), and distributions of convictions across time in the life-course were "entirely attributed to adolescent offending tendencies."[25] Both Paternoster and colleagues' and Piquero and colleagues' secondary data analyses of adolescent and adult offending behaviors among members of birth cohort longitudinal studies are consistent with Moffitt's dual-taxonomy theoretical framework of adolescent-limited offenders versus life-course persistent offenders.

Age-Graded Life-Course Theory

Sheldon and Eleanor Glueck were criminologists at Harvard Law School who together conducted empirical research on delinquency and crime for more than forty years from the late 1920s through the early 1970s. The Gluecks generated large data sets in lengthy research projects and follow-up studies that were primarily interested in developing delinquency and crime control correctional treatment programs. Their research subjects included

510 young men previously incarcerated at the Massachusetts Reformatory for Men at Concord, 500 young women previously incarcerated at the Massachusetts Reformatory for Women in Framingham, 1,000 juveniles who had been processed in the Boston Juvenile Court, and 500 additional juvenile offenders from the Boston area who had been in various correctional schools.[26] The Gluecks followed each of the juveniles for up to five years following the initial studies, and they followed all but the 500 women for fifteen to eighteen years after the expiration of the individuals' court-imposed sentences. Much of the work from these studies was met with disdain by sociologists and theoretical criminologists. Albert Reiss, for example, was highly critical of the methodological criteria used by the Gluecks in their book *Unraveling Juvenile Delinquency* to generate matched pair samples (of delinquent youth and nondelinquent youth) and delinquency prediction tables.[27] Three important methodological features, however, typified the Gluecks' research projects: they emphasized longitudinal studies and follow-up prediction studies, they focused on the criminal careers of serious persistent offenders, and they triangulated their research data by collecting information from multiple sources to supplement available official records.[28]

The delinquent and nondelinquent boys in the Gluecks' *Unraveling Juvenile Delinquency* study were all born between 1924 and 1935. The sample of delinquents included 500 white boys ages ten to seventeen, each of whom were committed by the courts to one of two Massachusetts correctional schools. The 500 nondelinquent boys in the all-white control group were ten- to seventeen-year-old students from the Boston public schools. The samples consisted of pairs matched by age, ethnicity, intelligence, and neighborhood socioeconomic variables. All of the boys were from families that lived in neighborhoods characterized by high levels of poverty and social disorganization. Data were collected by the Gluecks from 1940 to 1965, and interviews were conducted around age fourteen, age twenty-five, and age thirty-two. Approximately 92 percent of the individuals in both samples were included for data collection at all three age periods.

Shortly after Eleanor Glueck's death in 1972, Sheldon Glueck deposited their professional files in the archives of the Harvard Law Library. More than a decade later, Robert Sampson and John Laub "stumbled across . . . the dusty cartons of data" from the Gluecks' *Unraveling Juvenile Delinquency* studies in the library's basement.[29] The data from the 500 delinquent individuals alone were neatly cataloged in more than fifty file boxes. Sampson and Laub embarked on what eventually became a multipart project that would last almost two decades. The first part involved reanalysis of the Gluecks' delinquency data using multivariate statistical methods. Laub and Sampson found that the most important predictors of serious and persistent delinquency were attachment to parents, supervision by mothers, and parenting discipline styles.[30] Next, they continued to reanalyze the Gluecks' data and developed a life-course theory of crime and delinquency. The life course consists of "pathways through the age differentiated life span," where age differentiation is "manifested in expectations and options that impinge on decision processes and the course of events that give shape to life stages, transitions, and turning points."[31] A large body of life-course research across numerous academic disciplines has resulted in four central concepts that underlie life-course theories: social pathways, trajectories, transitions, and turning points.[32] *Social pathways* are trajectories of family, residences, education, and work followed by individuals. *Trajectories* are the sequence of roles and experiences through long-term patterns of behavior often marked by a series of transitions. *Transitions* are personal and social changes that can provide impetus for an individual to make behavioral changes. *Turning points* are major life changes in direction that come about for an individual as a result of the intersection of trajectories and transitions.

There are several major tenets of Sampson and Laub's first formulation of their life-course theory of crime and delinquency.[33] Delinquency in childhood and adolescence is explained by structural context that is mediated by informal family and school social controls. There is, in turn, continuity in antisocial behavior that runs from childhood through adulthood in a variety of life domains. Changes in criminality over an individual's life span can be abrupt or incremental and are explained by informal social capital and informal social bonds to family and employment, without regard for prior criminal propensities. Sampson and Laub's conceptualization of social capital is an expansion of Hirschi's concept of social bonds. Social capital is the quality of an individual's interpersonal relationships that produces resources to draw upon. Social conformity often requires the availability of those resources. The crux of Sampson and Laub's theory is that "childhood pathways to crime and conformity over the life course are significantly influenced by adult social bonds."[34] Laub and Sampson disagreed with the proposition of Gottfredson and Hirschi that individual differences in antisocial behavior are stable across the life course. Instead, Laub and Sampson hypothesized that variation in adult criminal offending for many individuals cannot be predicted from childhood behavioral manifestations.[35]

Laub and Sampson modified their age-graded theory of informal social control in 2003 to better explain criminal behavior over the full life course.[36] Their theory now posits that trajectories of individual offending across the entire life span are shaped both directly and in interaction with social control, routine activities, and human agency.[37] Laub and Sampson located and interviewed fifty-two elderly men, each of whom were former delinquents from the Gluecks' studies many decades earlier. The research involved mixed methods and life-history narratives, with both quantitative and qualitative components. The men from the Gluecks' studies were heavily influenced by growing up during the Great Depression of the 1930s and World War II. The situational context of their childhoods and adolescence impacted on both their objective opportunities and subjective worldviews. Laub and Sampson also argued that the situational context of violent crime matters and that informal social controls may be contingent on situational and social context. Violent behavior may be normative in some specific situations and contexts. The use of life-history narratives proved useful in developing a better understanding of the processes of human agency in the adult lives of the former delinquents and the specific mechanisms that differentiated the life pathways of persistent offenders from those of men who desisted and thereafter led crime-free lives.

Laub and Sampson's life-course theory is most useful in explaining why some offenders desist from criminal offending over the life course and why some persist in criminal offending throughout their lives. The theory posits that some criminals decide to stop offending when there are strong institutional supports and informal social control providing appropriate "situational contexts and structural influences ... that help sustain desistance."[38] The desistance process often involves a "knifing off" from an offender's immediate social-ecological environment and the provision of new structural opportunities for a brighter future.[39] Laub and Sampson found that the elderly men from the Gluecks' studies who desisted from offending in adulthood had often made knifing-off life transitions through their reform school or military experiences. The desistance process also involved daily routines for the men that provided meaningful activities and structured role stability across various life domains, including work, marriage, and residency in a new or different neighborhood. The structure and stability were turning points that resulted in adulthood crime desistance through personal agency and disassociation from their former delinquent peer group.

The men who desisted from criminal offending in adulthood led orderly lives. Their lives were very different from those of the men who persisted with criminal offending. The persistent offenders led lives marked by frequent churning, chaos, and a chronic inability to form attachments to others and social institutions. Laub and Sampson argued that persistent offenders led lives conducive to crime largely because the routine activities are very different for individuals without structured daily activities, gainful employment, spouses, and children. Laub and Sampson found no evidence that life-course persistent offenders could be identified prospectively, as argued by Moffitt. Instead, Laub and Sampson concluded that there is something that sustains involvement in crime at each stage of the life course for individuals who persist in criminal offending throughout their lives. The Gluecks' men who were persistent offenders typically experienced long periods of incarceration, failure in schools and the military, and chronic instability in residency, employment, and marriages throughout adulthood.

Police Misconduct and Life-Course Criminology

Christopher Harris applied aspects of life-course theories to his longitudinal study of police misconduct at a large police department in the northeastern United States.[40] He stressed that application of the life-course paradigm to police misconduct does *not* mean that the underlying causes of criminal antisocial behaviors are the same underlying causes of police misconduct. Rather, his purpose was to explore whether patterns of police misconduct exist over time in the life course of officers' law enforcement careers. Using Moffitt's developmental terminology, Harris hypothesized that some officers may exhibit "adolescent-limited" misconduct during the first few years of their law enforcement careers, while other officers might engage in acts of "life-course persistent" police misconduct in a trajectory throughout their entire careers.[41] These alternate pathways of police misconduct, however, have not yet been explored by criminologists in terms of career transitions and turning points that would shed light on causes of desistance or persistence in police misconduct. Harris found that police misconduct peaks within the first five years of employment and then steadily declines as officers gain experience and progress through their careers. Harris's initial study did not address police misconduct committed near the end of officers' careers, although he speculated that some officers already eligible to receive their full retirement pension benefits might be more likely to engage in problem behaviors than officers not yet approaching retirement.

Harris argued more recently that criminologists studying police misconduct and problem officers should adopt concepts from the career criminal

Prior research has focused on the behaviors and negative attitudes of experienced police officers and the problems that some officers encounter near the end of their policing careers during the transition to retirement. David Rafky found that the relationship between cynicism and years of service was higher than expected for nonsupervisory patrol officers with sixteen to twenty years of service as a sworn law enforcement officer, and the cynicism levels were significantly higher among police supervisors with eleven to twenty years of service.[a] Robert Regoli and his colleagues found high levels of cynicism among police chiefs with sixteen or more years of service, during what they called the "demise" career stage.[b] Similarly, John Violanti described a preretirement crisis period of turmoil experienced by some longtime police officers who feel trapped in their jobs because of pension eligibility requirements requiring more years of service prior to retirement.[c]

My research study with John Liederbach and Tina Freiburger on late-stage police crime found that 17.4 percent of arrest cases in the years 2005–7 involved a nonfederal sworn law enforcement officer with eighteen or more years of service when arrested.[d] The late-stage officers (with eighteen or more years of service at time of arrest) were different than those arrested officers with fewer years of service in numerous bivariate associations. The late-stage officers were less likely to be female than were the arrested officers with seventeen or fewer years of service. In terms of rank, the late-stage officers were move likely to be administrators, line/field supervisors, or managers, and the arrested officers with fewer years of service were more likely to hold street-level positions (e.g., patrol officers or detectives) through the rank of sergeant. The less experienced officers were more likely to be arrested for a violence-related crime, whereas the arrested officers with eighteen or more years of service were more likely to be arrested for nonviolent crimes, such as embezzlement and stolen property offenses. The victims of the arrested officers with eighteen or more years of service were more likely to be a relative or intimate partner. Officers with seventeen or fewer years of service

a. Rafky, "Police Cynicism Reconsidered."
b. Regoli et al., "Career Stage and Cynicism among Police Chiefs," 597.
c. Violanti, *Police Retirement*.
d. Stinson, Liederbach, and Freiburger, "Exit Strategy."

when arrested were subjected to more severe adverse employment outcomes than late-stage police criminals. The late-stage officers were more likely to resign after being arrested than the less experienced officers and were also more likely to be demoted (although keeping their employment as a sworn officer). In contrast, the officers with seventeen or fewer years of service when arrested were more likely to be terminated from their employment. The outcome disparities, however, reverse in cases that resulted in a guilty plea or criminal trial. The conviction rate among the late-stage police officers was 89.1 percent, whereas the conviction rate for officers with seventeen or fewer years of service was 77.5 percent.

These findings are, in part, consistent with prior research suggesting an inverse relationship between years of service and police crime, with spikes in early years and a precipitous decline after about four or five years of service. My study with Liederbach and Freiburger is unique, however, in that we found a large number of police crimes committed by officers on the cusp of retirement from law enforcement.

paradigm of developmental criminology, especially by focusing on trajectories and turning points within officers' law enforcement careers over time.[42] Risk management systems such as the early warning systems utilized by many state and local law enforcement agencies provide rich data sources for studying police behaviors—including police violence—over time as life-course criminology. Consistent with my own findings regarding late-stage police crime (discussed in this chapter's policy box, "Late-Stage Police Crime and the Exit Strategy"), Harris found that a small number of police officers start to engage in problem behaviors as they near retirement at the end of their policing career.[43] While it seems odd that a police officer would suddenly engage in antisocial behaviors after decades of working as a sworn law enforcement officer, developmental life-course criminology offers a theoretical framework with which to further explore the phenomenon. Police officers at the end of their law enforcement career may not be prepared for the involuntary turning point of retirement—and concurrent loss of their legal authority, power, gun, and badge—that necessitates the transition to civilian life after many years as a sworn law enforcement officer. For some police officers, the return to civilian life may require a rebalancing of social-ecological factors in new pathways because their long-term trajectories are suddenly blocked or redirected into what they perceive as unwanted or unwelcome forays into different social-ecological dimensions or domains.

CRITICAL THINKING QUESTIONS

1. Should police departments exclude job applicants for sworn law enforcement officer positions if applicants self-report a positive history of adolescent-limited antisocial or delinquent behavior?

2. Is Tittle's control balance theory useful in explaining police violence?

3. The chapter 3 policy box summarizes the nine times that Officer John Lewis of the Schenectady Police Department was arrested for various crimes. Lewis was fired from the Schenectady Police Department in 2010 and arrested a few months later for allegedly "punching his wife in the face."[44] After Lewis's death at age forty-four in 2014, his attorney said "that bouts of depression, marital problems, and alcohol abuse were behind his legal problems."[45] How does age-graded life-course criminology help to explain these behaviors?

4. What are the strengths and limitations of using integrated criminological theories to understand and explain acts of police violence?

5. How might the social-ecological domains within which a police officer operates change over the life course of an officer's law enforcement career and into retirement?

NOTES

INTRODUCTION

1. Avila, Lynn, and Pearle, "Police Sergeant Had Secret Life as Serial Rapist."
2. Stinson et al., *Police Integrity Lost.*
3. Castaneda, "DUI Arrest Is Officer's 4th This Year."
4. P. Nelson, "Schenectady Cop Fired in 2010 Dies."
5. Perry, "Crooked Cop Helped Suspected Robbers."
6. Perry, "Cop Admits Promoting Prostitution, Misusing Database."
7. Meyer, "Former Police Officers Get Probation."
8. Associated Press, "Pittsburgh Detectives Charged in After-Concert Brawl."
9. Van Derbeken, "Ex-Fremont Cop Guilty of Post-concert Assault."
10. Kibler, "APD Officer Pleads Guilty to Role in Concert Incident."
11. The Pittsburgh Steelers won the game against the Cleveland Browns by a score of 41 to 9.
12. Miller, "State Trooper Accused of Drunken, Disorderly Conduct."
13. Ferrise, "Fired Trooper Gets His Job Back."
14. Gauntner, "Trooper Arrested in Austintown Pleads."
15. LaForgia, "Boynton Police Officer Allegedly Spouts Drunken Obscenities."
16. Scharr, "Marcus Hook Cop Allegedly Strikes Wrestling Coach."
17. Wootson, "Officer Charged with Assaulting Softball Coach."
18. McCarthy, "Ex-cop's 'Nightmarish Storyline.'"
19. Dollinger and Santora, "James Burke, Ex-Suffolk County Police Chief, Pleads Guilty."
20. Fyfe, "Always Prepared."
21. Stinson et al., *Police Integrity Lost.*
22. Samuels, Scalafani, and Moore, "Make a (Death) Wish!"
23. Donnelly, "Charges Dropped against Cop."
24. Stinson and Liederbach, "Fox in the Henhouse."
25. Lautenberg Amendment, Gun Ban for Individuals Convicted of a Misdemeanor Crime of Domestic Violence (1996).

26. United States v. Hayes, 555 U.S. 415 (2009).

27. Robinson, "The Brame Files."

28. Stinson et al., "Police Sexual Misconduct: A National Scale Study of Arrested Officers."

29. Silverstein, "Oklahoma City Police Ignored Early Sexual Assault Complaint."

30. Kelley, "Girls: Cop Molested Us."

31. Walker and Irlbeck, *Police Sexual Abuse of Teenage Girls.*

32. See Factual Basis, filed March 10, 2006, in *United States v. Frank James Goodwyn and O'Dell Draper III* (E.D. Tenn. Case No. 1:06-CR-00020-CLC-SKL).

33. Radnofsky et al., "Why Some Problem Cops Don't Lose Their Badges."

34. Guthrie, "Detroit Cop Charged with Felony Torture for Breakup Fracas."

35. Hunter, "Fallout Continues."

36. Schwartz and Urbonya, "Section 1983 Litigation."

37. Westley, *Violence and the Police.*

38. Dershowitz, "Controlling the Cops"; Goldstein, "'Testilying' by Police."

39. Reiss, *The Police and the Public.*

40. Garrity v. New Jersey, 385 U.S. 493 (1967).

41. Garrity v. New Jersey, 385 U.S. at 494.

42. Miranda v. Arizona, 384 U.S. 436 (1966).

43. Rabe-Hemp and Braithwaite, "An Exploration of Recidivism and the Officer Shuffle"; Radnofsky et al., "Why Some Problem Cops Don't Lose Their Badges."

44. Stinson, "The Henry A. Wallace Police Crime Database."

45. Kane and White, *Jammed Up.*

CHAPTER ONE. UNDERSTANDING POLICE VIOLENCE

1. Westley, *Violence and the Police.*

2. Sherman, "Causes of Police Behavior," 69.

3. Ross, *Making News of Police Violence.*

4. Reiss, *The Police and the Public.*

5. Cheh, "Are Lawsuits an Answer to Police Brutality?"; Klockars, "A Theory of Excessive Force and Its Control."

6. Skogan and Frydl, *Fairness and Effectiveness in Policing.*

7. Terrill, "Police Use of Force and Suspect Resistance."

8. Punch, "Police Corruption and Its Prevention."

9. Stinson, "Police Crime."

10. Sherman, "Causes of Police Behavior."

11. Blalock, *Conceptualization and Measurement in the Social Sciences*, 35. See also Blalock, "The Presidential Address."

12. Maguire and Uchida, "Measurement and Explanation in the Comparative Study of American Police Organizations," 4.

13. Blalock, *Social Statistics*.

14. Maguire and Uchida, "Measurement and Explanation in the Comparative Study of American Police Organizations."

15. See, for example, Anechiarico and Jacobs, *The Pursuit of Absolute Integrity*; Barak, "Media, Society, and Criminology"; Collins, *Shielded from Justice*; Kane, "Collect and Release Data on Coercive Police Actions"; Kutnjak Ivkovic, "To Serve and Collect"; and Sherman and Langworthy, "Measuring Homicide by Police Officers."

16. See Black, *The Manners and Customs of the Police*; Reiss, *The Police and the Public*.

17. See the Violent Crime Control and Law Enforcement Act of 1994.

18. Hickman and Poore, "National Data on Citizen Complaints About Police Use of Force."

19. Comey, "The True Heart of American Law Enforcement."

20. Elinson, "Federal Count in Deadly Police Shootings Is Slow to Get Going."

21. Kutnjak Ivkovic, *Fallen Blue Knights*.

22. Anechiarico and Jacobs, *The Pursuit of Absolute Integrity*.

23. Knapp Commission, *Commission to Investigate Allegations of Police Corruption*, 65–66.

24. Mollen Commission, *Commission to Investigate Allegations of Police Corruption and the Anti-corruption Procedures of the Police Department*, 17.

25. Mollen Commission, 45.

26. Mollen Commission, 48.

27. Mollen Commission, 48.

28. US Commission on Civil Rights, *Who Is Guarding the Guardians?*

29. Christopher Commission, *Report of the Independent Commission on the Los Angeles Police Department*.

30. Collins, *Shielded from Justice*.

31. T. Carlson, "DC Blues." See also Collins, *Shielded from Justice*, 382.

32. Burnham, *The Role of the Media in Controlling Corruption*.

33. See Scott, "Exclusive: New Data Show Police Rarely Arrested for Killings on the Job."

34. See Kindy and Kelly, "Thousands Dead, Few Prosecuted."

35. For this, the *Washington Post* was awarded the 2016 Pulitzer Prize in National Reporting.

36. Liederbach, "Controlling Suburban and Small-Town Hoods," 109.

37. Reiss, "Systematic Observation of Natural Social Phenomena."

38. Black, "The Social Organization of Arrest," 1089.

39. Reiss, *The Police and the Public*, 160.

40. Reiss, "Police Brutality—Answers to Key Questions."

41. Paoline and Terrill, "Police Education, Experience, and the Use of Force," 194.

42. Fyfe and Kane, *Bad Cops*.

43. Law Enforcement Officers Safety Act (2004).

44. Kane and White, *Jammed Up.*

45. Alpert and Dunham, *Understanding Police Use of Force.*

46. Maguire and Uchida, "Measurement and Explanation in the Comparative Study of American Police Organizations."

47. Maguire and Mastrofski, "Patterns of Community Policing in the United States," 27, 30.

48. Fishman, *Measuring Police Corruption.*

49. Bharat, "Google News Turns 10."

50. Payne, *White-Collar Crime.*

51. Carlson, "Order versus Access."

52. Ready, White, and Fisher, "Shock Value."

53. Chermak, McGarrell, and Gruenewald, "Media Coverage of Police Misconduct."

54. Reiss, "Why Are Communities Important in Understanding Crime?"

55. Stokols, *Social Ecology in the Digital Age,* 67.

56. D. A. Smith, "The Neighborhood Context of Police Behavior."

57. Klinger, "Negotiating Order in Patrol Work."

58. US Department of Justice, *Census of State and Local Enforcement Agencies (CSLLEA), 2008.*

59. Liederbach and Travis, "Wilson Redux"; Liederbach and Frank, "Policing the Big Beat"; Wilson, *Varieties of Police Behavior.*

60. Kane, "The Social Ecology of Police Misconduct," 891.

61. Akers and Sellers, *Criminological Theories.*

CHAPTER TWO. DETERRENCE, RATIONAL CHOICE, VICTIMIZATION, AND LIFESTYLE THEORIES

1. Hobbes, *The Elements of Law, Natural and Politic.*

2. Beccaria, *On Crimes and Punishments*; Bentham, *An Introduction to the Principles of Morals and Legislation.*

3. Akers and Sellers, *Criminological Theories,* 15.

4. Zimring and Hawkins, *Deterrence,* 33.

5. Zimring, *Perspectives on Deterrence.*

6. LaFave, *Criminal Law*; Lippman, *Contemporary Criminal Law.*

7. Kubrin, Stucky, and Krohn, *Researching Theories of Crime and Deviance.*

8. Clarke and Cornish, "Modeling Offenders' Decisions."

9. Petersilia, "Keynote Address," 13.

10. Packer, *The Limits of the Criminal Sanction.*

11. Packer, 149.

12. Packer, 45.

13. For example, Sellin, *The Death Penalty.*

14. Gibbs, "Crime, Punishment, and Deterrence"; Tittle, "Crime Rates and Legal Sanctions."

15. Gibbs, "Punishment and Deterrence."

16. Stafford and Warr, "A Reconceptualization of General and Specific Deterrence."

17. Stafford and Warr, 126.

18. Paternoster and Piquero, "Reconceptualizing Deterrence."

19. Apel and Nagin, "General Deterrence," 418.

20. Apel and Nagin.

21. Sherman, "The Police," 331.

22. Wilson and Kelling, "The Police and Neighborhood Safety."

23. Taylor, *Breaking Away from Broken Windows*.

24. Zimbardo, "Diary of a Vandalized Car."

25. Zimbardo.

26. Braga, Welsh, and Schnell, "Can Policing Disorder Reduce Crime?"

27. Braga, Papachristos, and Hureau, "The Effects of Hot Spots Policing on Crime," 633.

28. Sherman, Gartin, and Buerger, "Hot Spots of Predatory Crime."

29. Mastrofski, Weisburd, and Braga, "Rethinking Policing"; Skogan and Frydl, *Fairness and Effectiveness in Policing*.

30. Abrahamse et al., "An Experimental Evaluation of the Phoenix Repeat Offender Program"; Martin and Sherman, "Catching Career Criminals"; S. E. Martin, "Policing Career Criminals."

31. Sherman and Rogan, "Effects of Gun Seizures on Gun Violence."

32. Clarke and Cornish, "Modeling Offenders' Decisions."

33. Clarke and Cornish, "Rational Choice," 24.

34. Clarke and Cornish, 25.

35. Clarke and Cornish, 26.

36. Clarke and Cornish, 26.

37. Clarke and Cornish, 24.

38. Clarke, "Introduction to the Transaction Edition."

39. Clarke, "Situational Crime Prevention," 259.

40. Paternoster, "The Deterrent Effect of the Perceived Certainty and Severity of Punishment."

41. Kahneman, "A Perspective on Judgment and Choice"; Kahneman, "Maps of Bounded Rationality."

42. Clarke, "Introduction to the Transaction Edition."

43. Cohen and Felson, "Social Change and Crime Rate Trends," 589.

44. Felson, "The Routine Activity Approach."

45. Clarke and Felson, eds., *Routine Activity and Rational Choice*.

46. Felson, "The Routine Activity Approach," 43.

47. Felson and Cohen, "Human Ecology and Crime," 389.

48. Hawley, *Human Ecology*.

49. See Shaw and McKay, *Juvenile Delinquency and Urban Areas*.

50. Cohen and Felson, "Social Change and Crime Rate Trends."

51. Sampson, *Great American City*, 484n42.

52. Sherman, Gartin, and Buerger, "Hot Spots of Predatory Crime."

53. Weisburd, *Place Matters*, 3.

54. Eck and Eck, "Crime Place and Pollution," 282n2.

55. For example, Mulford, Wilson, and Moore Parmley, "Geographic Aspects of Sex Offender Residency Restrictions"; Zgoba, Levenson, and McKee, "Examining the Impact of Sex Offender Residence Restrictions"; Chajewski and Mercado, "An Evaluation of Sex Offender Residency Restriction Functioning"; Barnes et al., "Analyzing the Impact of a Statewide Residence Restriction Law"; Zandbergen and Hart, "Geocoding Accuracy Considerations in Determining Residency Restrictions."

56. Stinson, Huck, and Spraitz, "A Content Analysis of Criminal Justice Policy Review."

57. Klinger, "Negotiating Order in Patrol Work."

58. Kane, "The Social Ecology of Police Misconduct."

59. Kane, 889. See also Taylor, *Breaking Away from Broken Windows*.

60. Kane, "The Social Ecology of Police Misconduct," 889.

61. Stinson, "The Henry A. Wallace Police Crime Database."

62. Cohen and Felson, "Social Change and Crime Rate Trends."

63. Felson, "Those Who Discourage Crime."

64. Reynald, "Informal Guardians and Offender Decision Making."

65. Felson, "Those Who Discourage Crime." See also Hirschi, *Causes of Delinquency* (1969, 2002).

66. H. Goldstein, *Policing a Free Society*, 171.

67. For example, Christopher Commission, *Report of the Independent Commission on the Los Angeles Police Department*; US Commission on Civil Rights, *Who Is Guarding the Guardians?*

68. Stinson et al., *Police Integrity Lost*.

69. Radnofsky et al., "Why Some Problem Cops Don't Lose Their Badges."

70. US Commission on Civil Rights, *Who Is Guarding the Guardians?*

71. Alpert and Walker, "Police Accountability and Early Warning Systems."

72. US Department of Justice, *Principles for Promoting Police Integrity*.

73. Commission on Accreditation for Law Enforcement Agencies, "Standard 35.1.9."

74. US Department of Justice, *Census of State and Local Enforcement Agencies (CSLLEA), 2008*.

75. Walker, Alpert, and Kenney, *Early Warning Systems*.

76. Larson et al., "Reduction of Police Vehicle Accidents," 571.

77. Lee, "Woman Sues Pickens PD."

78. Burke, "BSO Sergeant Paid for Off-Duty Detail He Never Performed"; Kimball, "Oklahoma City Police Officer Accused of Falsifying Time Cards"; Gaspar, "Investigative Reports"; Faulk, "Former Birmingham Police Officer Denies Setting Fires."

79. Murphy, "Ex-Oklahoma City Police Officer Convicted of Rape."

80. Schwab, "Jurors View Video of Accused Former OKC Police Officer's Interrogation."

81. Schwab.

82. President's Task Force on 21st Century Policing, *Final Report of the President's Task Force.*

83. Alpert and McLean, "Where Is the Goal Line?"

84. Demir et al., "Body Worn Cameras, Procedural Justice, and Police Legitimacy."

85. Koslicki, Makin, and Willits, "When No One Is Watching."

86. Stinson, Wentzlof, and Swinehart, "On-Duty Police Shootings."

87. Kindy, "Some U.S. Police Departments Dump Body-Cameras."

88. Kindy.

89. Pew Research Center, "Demographics of Mobile Device Ownership."

90. A. Smith, "Record Shares of Americans Now Own Smartphones."

91. Pew Research Center, "Demographics of Mobile Device Ownership."

92. Monroe v. Pape, 365 U.S. 167 (1961).

93. Monell v. Department of Social Services, 436 U.S. 658 (1978).

94. Kappeler, *Critical Issues in Police Civil Liability.*

95. Harlow v. Fitzgerald, 457 U.S. 800 (1982).

96. Saucier v. Katz, 533 U.S. 194 (2001).

97. Graham v. Connor, 490 U.S. 386 (1989).

98. Fattah, "The Rational Choice/Opportunity Perspectives," 251.

99. Hindelang, Gottfredson, and Garofalo, *Victims of Personal Crime*; Cohen and Felson, "Social Change and Crime Rate Trends," See also Pratt and Turanovic, "Lifestyle and Routine Activity Theories Revisited," 2.

100. Pratt and Turanovic, 1.

101. Hindelang, Gottfredson, and Garofalo, *Victims of Personal Crime.*

102. Hindelang, Gottfredson, and Garofalo, 241.

103. Garofalo, "Reassessing the Lifestyle Model of Criminal Victimization," 26.

104. Fattah, "The Rational Choice/Opportunity Perspectives," 251.

105. See, for example, Felson and Eckert, *Crime and Everyday Life.*

106. Pratt and Turanovic, "Lifestyle and Routine Activity Theories Revisited," 12.

107. Van Maanen, "The Asshole."

108. Stinson et al., *Police Integrity Lost.*

109. Stinson and Watkins, "The Nature of Crime by School Resource Officers."

110. Stinson, Todak, and Dodge, "An Exploration of Crime by Policewomen."

111. Stinson et al., "Drink, Drive, Go to Jail?"

112. Stinson et al., *Police Integrity Lost.*

113. Stinson and Liederbach, "Fox in the Henhouse."

114. Stinson et al., *Police Integrity Lost.*

115. Stinson, Reyns, and Liederbach, "Police Crime and Less-than-Lethal Coercive Force."

116. Stinson et al., *Police Integrity Lost.*

117. Stinson, "The Henry A. Wallace Police Crime Database."

1. Lundman, *Police and Policing*, 77.

2. Terman et al., "A Trial of Mental and Pedagogical Tests."

3. Oglesby, "Use of Emotional Screening in the Selection of Police Applicants."

4. President's Commission on Law Enforcement and Administration of Justice, *The Challenge of Crime in a Free Society*.

5. National Advisory Commission on Criminal Justice Standards and Goals, *Task Force Report on Police*, 348.

6. See, for example, Lowmaster and Morey, "Predicting Law Enforcement Officer Job Performance"; Tarescavage, Corey, and Ben-Porath, "Minnesota Multiphasic Personality Inventory"; Weiss et al., "Impression Management in Police Officer Candidacy."

7. Drayton, "The Minnesota Multiphasic Personality Inventory-2."

8. Hargrave, Hiatt, and Gaffney, "F+4+9+Cn."

9. Hiatt and Hargrave, "MMPI Profiles of Problem Peace Officers."

10. Bartol, "Predictive Validation of the MMPI."

11. For example, Caillouet et al., "Predictive Validity of the MMPI-2 PSY-5 Scales"; Sellbom, Fischler, and Ben-Porath, "Identifying MMPI-2 Predictors of Police Officer Integrity and Misconduct."

12. Tarescavage, Corey, and Ben-Porath, "Minnesota Multiphasic Personality Inventory."

13. Arrigo and Claussen, "Police Corruption and Psychological Testing," 278.

14. 42 U.S.C. § 12112(b)(6) (1990).

15. 42 U.S.C. § 2000e-2(l) (1991).

16. Caillouet et al., "Predictive Validity of the MMPI-2 PSY-5 Scales."

17. Commission on Accreditation for Law Enforcement Agencies, "Standard 31.5.7."

18. Cochrane, Tett, and Vandecreek, "Psychological Testing and the Selection of Police Officers."

19. Strong, "Police Chief Was Slow to Address 'Problem Officer.'"

20. LaRosa, *Tacoma Confidential*, 310, 312.

21. Schladebeck, "Former Minneapolis Officer Charged with Fatally Shooting Australian Woman."

22. Shakespeare, *The Taming of the Shrew*, 39; Franklin, *The Papers of Benjamin Franklin*, 140.

23. Gottschalk, "White-Collar Crime and Police Crime."

24. Kane and White, *Jammed Up*, 124–25.

25. Kane and White, 125.

26. Knapp Commission, *Commission to Investigate Allegations of Police Corruption*, 6–7.

27. Davidson, "The Knapp Commission Didn't Know It Couldn't Be Done."

28. Sherman, *Police Corruption*, 7–8.

29. For example, Delattre, *Character and Cops.*

30. For example, Chappell and Piquero, "Applying Social Learning Theory to Police Misconduct"; Kane and White, "Bad Cops"; White and Kane, "Pathways to Career-Ending Police Misconduct."

31. Adorno et al., *The Authoritarian Personality.*

32. Adorno et al., 228.

33. Adorno et al., 228.

34. Niederhoffer, *Behind the Shield*, 109–60 (quotation on p. 109).

35. For example, Henkel and Sheehan, "Relation of Police Misconduct to Authoritarianism"; Laguna et al., "An Examination of Authoritarian Personality Traits among Police Officers."

36. J. L. Martin, "The Authoritarian Personality, 50 Years Later."

37. Adorno et al., *The Authoritarian Personality*, 228.

38. Niederhoffer, *Behind the Shield*, 104.

39. Niederhoffer, 104.

40. Stinson, Liederbach, and Freiburger, "Exit Strategy."

41. Donner, Maskaly, and Thompson, "Self-Control and the Police Code of Silence," 16.

42. Hickman, "On the Context of Police Cynicism."

43. Sanders, "Using Personality Traits to Predict Police Officer Performance."

44. Bernard, "Angry Aggression among the Truly Disadvantaged."

45. See W. J. Wilson, *The Truly Disadvantaged.*

46. Bernard, "Angry Aggression among the Truly Disadvantaged," 87.

47. Griffin and Bernard, "Angry Aggression among Police Officers."

48. Brandl and Stroshine, "Toward an Understanding of the Physical Hazards of Police Work."

49. For example, Corey and Borum, "Forensic Assessment for High-Risk Occupations"; Gershon et al., "Mental, Physical, and Behavioral Outcomes"; Goodman, "A Model for Police Officer Burnout"; Violanti, "Predictors of Police Suicide Ideation."

50. Paraphrasing an often used description of war, generally attributed to Anonymous British soldier, "The Baptism of Fire."

51. Phillips, "Police Discretion and Boredom."

52. Cordner, "Police Patrol Workload Studies"; Parks et al., "How Officers Spend Their Time"; Smith, Novak, and Frank, "Community Policing and the Work Routines."

53. Smith, Novak, and Frank, "Community Policing and the Work Routines."

54. Liederbach and Frank, "Policing Mayberry," 69.

55. Payne, Berg, and Sun, "Policing in Small Town America," 31.

56. 29 C.F.R. § 553.230 (2012).

57. Charles et al., "Shift Work and Sleep"; Vila, "Tired Cops"; Vila, Morrison, and Kenney, "Improving Shift Schedule."

58. Baughman et al., "Shift Work and Health Consequences in Policing"; Violanti et al., "Atypical Work Hours."

59. R. J. Burke, "Burnout in Police Work."

60. Maslach and Jackson, "The Measurement of Experienced Burnout," 99.

61. Cannizzo and Liu, "The Relationship Between Levels of Perceived Burnout and Career Stage."

62. Queiros, Kaiseler, and Da Silva, "Burnout as a Predictor of Aggressivity."

63. Burke and Mikkelsen, "Suicidal Ideation among Police Officers."

64. Violanti, "Predictors of Police Suicide Ideation."

65. Violanti, *Dying for the Job*; Violanti, *Police Suicide*.

CHAPTER FOUR. SOCIAL STRUCTURE THEORIES

1. Akers and Sellers, *Criminological Theories*, 160.

2. Akers, "Problems in the Sociology of Deviance."

3. Park, Burgess, and McKenzie, *The City*.

4. Shaw and McKay, *Juvenile Delinquency and Urban Areas*.

5. Kane, "The Social Ecology of Police Misconduct."

6. See, for example, Tyler and Wakslak, "Profiling and Police Legitimacy." This study conceptualized police legitimacy "as a measure of obligation to obey, confidence in the police and positive affect towards the police" (263).

7. See Klinger, "Negotiating Order in Patrol Work."

8. See Sampson, *Great American City*, on mechanisms of collective efficacy.

9. Wickersham Commission, *United States National Committee on Law Observance and Enforcement: Report on the Police*, 48.

10. Key, "Police Graft."

11. Westley, "Secrecy and the Police."

12. Stoddard, "The Informal Code of Police Deviancy."

13. Stoddard argued that this informal code of blue-coat crime included a variety of illegal and/or unethical practices, including mooching (police receiving free coffee, meals, etc., sometimes in consideration of possible future acts of favoritism), chiseling (police demanding free or discounted admission to entertainment), favoritism (extended by police through immunity to arrest or traffic tickets via courtesy window stickers given to citizens who donate to police fraternal organizations), prejudice (where persons in minority groups receive less than impartial treatment by the police), shopping (police picking up small items such as cigarettes or a candy bar at a store where the door has been left accidentally unlocked after business hours), extortion (police demanding purchase of tickets to police functions or the practice of settling traffic tickets informally through the payment of cash to the officer conducting a traffic stop), bribery (payment to avoid prosecution, where the value received by the officer is higher than in mooching and lies in the mutual understanding about services the officer will perform in return for the payment), shakedowns (police misappropriating the personal property of a citizen during a street encounter, traffic stop, or search), perjury (police lying to provide an alibi for a fellow officer apprehended while committing an act of blue-coat crime), and pre-

meditated theft. Stoddard did not consider acts of police violence in his theory of blue-coat crime.

14. Van Maanen, *Working the Street*.
15. Van Maanen, "Observations on the Making of Policemen."
16. Van Maanen, 408.
17. Van Maanen, *Tales of the Field*.
18. Van Maanen, "Observations on the Making of Policemen," 412.
19. Stinson, Liederbach, and Freiburger, "Exit Strategy."
20. Skolnick, *Justice without Trial*.
21. Sykes, "Street Justice: A Moral Defense," 507.
22. Klockars, "Street Justice: Some Micro-moral Reservations."
23. Westley, *Violence and the Police*, 121–22.
24. Van Maanen, "The Asshole."
25. *Taser* is an acronym for Thomas A. Swift Electric Rifle, a nod to a popular novel and adventure character from the early twentieth century.
26. White and Ready, "Examining Fatal and Nonfatal Incidents."
27. Van Maanen, "The Asshole," 227.
28. Skolnick, *Justice without Trial*.
29. Packer, *The Limits of the Criminal Sanction*.
30. Christopher Commission, *Report of the Independent Commission on the Los Angeles Police Department*.
31. Skolnick and Fyfe, *Above the Law*, 24.
32. Durkheim, *The Division of Labor in Society*.
33. Merton, "Social Structure and Anomie."
34. See, for example, Kornhauser, *Social Sources of Delinquency*.
35. Messner and Rosenfeld, *Crime and the American Dream*; Agnew, "Foundation for a General Strain Theory."
36. Kane and White, *Jammed Up*.
37. Agnew, "Foundation for a General Strain Theory," 47.
38. Agnew, "Experienced, Vicarious, and Anticipated Strain," 603.
39. Agnew, "General Strain Theory," 104.
40. Ross, *Policing Issues*.
41. Zhao, Thurman, and He, "Sources of Job Satisfaction among Police Officers."
42. Toch, *Stress in Policing*, 200.
43. Stinson, Todak, and Dodge, "An Exploration of Crime by Policewomen."
44. Kakar, "Self-Evaluations of Police Performance."
45. Niederhoffer, *Behind the Shield*, 103.
46. Cascio, "Formal Education and Police Officer Performance"; Fyfe and Kane, "Bad Cops"; Kappeler, Sapp, and Carter, "Police Officer Higher Education."
47. Martinussen, Richardsen, and Burke, "Job Demands, Job Resources, and Burnout among Police Officers."
48. Bishopp et al., "Negative Affective Responses to Stress among Urban Police Officers."
49. Stinson and Liederbach, "Fox in the Henhouse."

50. Mullins and McMains, "Impact of Traumatic Stress on Domestic Violence in Policing."

51. Johnson, Todd, and Subramanian, "Violence in Police Families"; Mullins and McMains, "Impact of Traumatic Stress on Domestic Violence in Policing."

52. Gershon, *Project Shields*.

53. Neidig, Russell, and Seng, "Interspousal Aggression in Law Enforcement Families."

54. Toch, *Stress in Policing*.

55. Stinson et al., *Police Integrity Lost*.

56. Stinson, Liederbach, and Freiburger, "Exit Strategy."

57. Violanti, "Police Work May Be Hazardous."

58. Groopman, "The Grief Industry."

59. Mitchell, "When Disaster Strikes."

60. Bittner, *The Functions of the Police*.

61. Martinez, "Officer Evaluations Are Based in Part on Their Ticket Totals."

62. Tepper, "Arlington County Police Denies Quota System, Rescinds Memo."

63. Tepper.

64. N.Y. Consolidated Laws, Labor § 215-a (2018).

65. Mathias, "NYC to Pay $280,000 over Cop."

66. Matthews v. City of New York, et al., 779 F.3d 167 (2nd. Cir. 2015).

67. Matthews v. City of New York, et al., Complaint, Docket no. 1:12-civ-1354 (S.D.N.Y. February 23, 2012).

68. Kohler-Hausmann, *Misdemeanorland*.

69. Westley, *Violence and the Police*, 76.

70. Van Cleve, *Crook County*.

71. Bach, *Ordinary Injustice*.

72. US Commission on Civil Rights, *Revisiting "Who Is Guarding the Guardians."*

73. Silver, *Police Civil Liability*.

74. Stinson and Brewer, "Federal Civil Rights Litigation."

75. See Gershon, *Police Stress and Domestic Violence in Police Families in Baltimore, Maryland, 1997–1999*.

76. Gibson, Swatt, and Jolicoeur, "Assessing the Generality of General Strain Theory."

77. Swatt, Gibson, and Piquero, "Exploring the Utility of General Strain Theory."

78. Kurtz, Zavala, and Melander, "The Influence of Early Strain on Later Strain, Stress Responses, and Aggression by Police Officers."

79. Kane and White, *Jammed Up*, 133–34.

80. Black, "The Boundaries of Legal Sociology," 1096.

81. Black, *The Behavior of Law*.

82. Black, "The Social Organization of Arrest."

83. Black, *The Behavior of Law*.

84. Stinson, "Police Crime."

1. Westley, *Violence and the Police.*
2. Van Maanen, "Observations on the Making of Policemen."
3. Black, *The Behavior of Law.*
4. Sutherland, *Principles of Criminology*, 6–7.
5. Vold, Bernard, and Snipes, *Theoretical Criminology.*
6. Sutherland, *Principles of Criminology*, 7.
7. Burgess and Akers, "A Differential Association-Reinforcement Theory of Criminal Behavior."
8. Akers and Sellers, *Criminological Theories.*
9. Kubrin, Stucky, and Krohn, *Researching Theories of Crime and Deviance.*
10. Akers and Sellers, *Criminological Theories.*
11. Akers and Sellers, 84.
12. Kane and White, *Jammed Up*, 138.
13. Crank, *Understanding Police Culture.*
14. Seltzer, Alonè, and Howard, "Police Satisfaction with Their Jobs"; Westley, *Violence and the Police.*
15. Skolnick and Fyfe, *Above the Law*; Skolnick, *Justice without Trial.*
16. Skolnick, *Justice without Trial*, 42.
17. Barker, "Peer Group Support for Police Occupational Deviance," 362.
18. Reiss, *The Police and the Public*; Stinson et al., "Drink, Drive, Go to Jail?"
19. Chappell and Piquero, "Applying Social Learning Theory to Police Misconduct."
20. Kane and White, *Jammed Up*, 139.
21. Aultman, "A Social Psychological Approach to the Study of Police Corruption."
22. Herbert, "Police Subculture Reconsidered."
23. Chappell and Piquero, "Applying Social Learning Theory to Police Misconduct," 95.
24. Sherman, *Police Corruption*, 20–21.
25. Chappell and Piquero, "Applying Social Learning Theory to Police Misconduct," 95.
26. Sherman, *Police Corruption.*
27. Goffman, "The Moral Career of the Mental Patient."
28. Aultman, "A Social Psychological Approach to the Study of Police Corruption," 330.
29. Kane and White, *Jammed Up.*
30. Kane and White, 142.
31. Kane and White, 142.
32. Kane and White.
33. Lilly, Cullen, and Ball, *Criminological Theory*, 80.
34. Durkheim, *Suicide*, 209–10.
35. Akers and Sellers, *Criminological Theories*, 114.

36. Reiss, "Delinquency as the Failure of Personal and Social Controls."

37. Reiss, 196.

38. Reiss, 196.

39. Akers and Sellers, *Criminological Theories*.

40. Nye, *Family Relationships and Delinquent Behavior*.

41. Reckless, "A New Theory of Delinquency and Crime."

42. Reckless, 44–45.

43. Akers and Sellers, *Criminological Theories*, 115.

44. Hirschi, *Causes of Delinquency* (1969), 16.

45. Akers and Sellers, *Criminological Theories*.

46. Hirschi, *Causes of Delinquency* (1969), 20.

47. Hirschi, 22.

48. Akers and Sellers, *Criminological Theories*, 121.

49. For example, Akers and Sellers, *Criminological Theories*.

50. Hirschi, *Causes of Delinquency* (2002), xiv.

51. Gottfredson and Hirschi, *A General Theory of Crime*.

52. Gottfredson and Hirschi, 89.

53. Gottfredson and Hirschi, 95.

54. Hirschi, "Self-Control and Crime," 548.

55. Hirschi, 543.

56. Hirschi, 543.

57. See, for example, Gibbs and Giever, "Self-Control and Its Manifestations."

58. Hirschi, "Self-Control and Crime." See also Sampson and Laub, *Crime in the Making*.

59. Vold, Bernard, and Snipes, *Theoretical Criminology*.

60. Donner, Maskaly, and Fridell, "Social Bonds and Police Misconduct."

61. Donner, Fridell, and Jennings, "The Relationship Between Self-Control and Police Misconduct."

62. Donner, Maskaly, and Thompson, "Self-Control and the Police Code of Silence."

63. Donner et al., "Quick on the Draw."

64. Donner and Jennings, "Low Self-Control and Police Deviance."

65. Zavala and Kurtz, "Using Gottfredson and Hirschi's General Theory of Crime."

66. Kane and White, *Jammed Up*, 149.

67. Sykes and Matza, "Techniques of Neutralization."

68. Sutherland, *Principles of Criminology*, 6.

69. Blomberg, "David Matza—Criminologist," 7–8.

70. Quinn and Tomita, *Elder Abuse and Neglect*.

71. Byers, Crider, and Biggers, "Bias Crimes Motivation."

72. Baak et al., "Honor Crimes in the United States."

73. Jesilow, Pontell, and Geis, *Prescription for Profit*.

74. Leasure, "Neutralizations in Retail Banking."

75. Rosecrance, "Adopting to Failure."

76. Foster, "Police Administration and the Control of Police Criminality," 459n6.

77. Kappeler, Sluder, and Alpert, *Forces of Deviance*, 113–14.

78. Sykes and Matza, "Techniques of Neutralization," 667.

79. Kappeler, Sluder, and Alpert, *Forces of Deviance*, 114.

80. Kappeler, Sluder, and Alpert, 114.

81. Sykes and Matza, "Techniques of Neutralization," 667.

82. Kappeler, Sluder, and Alpert, *Forces of Deviance*, 117.

83. See, for example, Durkin, "Councilman Pushing to Make It Explicitly Illegal."

84. Stinson, Reyns, and Liederbach, "Police Crime and Less-than-Lethal Coercive Force."

85. Amnesty International, *"Less than Lethal"?*

86. Joker3249, *Cop Gets TASER Ride.*

87. Ayoob, *The Ayoob Files*; Rayburn, "Shooting Outside of the Box."

88. Sharps, *Processing under Pressure.*

89. Schraer, "Setting the Record Straight on the Newhall Incident."

90. Phippen, "One Day in 1970 That Changed Policing"; Pool, "The Ambush Killings of 4 CHP Officers."

91. Sykes and Matza, "Techniques of Neutralization," 668.

92. *WESH.com*, "Cop Accused of Having Sex with Prostitute."

93. Gosling, "Former Uplands Park Officer Leon Pullen Sentenced."

94. Rhodes, "Perversion of Justice."

95. Redmond, "New Trial Date for Lowell Officer in Rape Case."

96. Sykes and Matza, "Techniques of Neutralization," 668.

97. Copple and Dunn, *Gender, Sexuality, and 21st Century Policing*; Stinson, *The Impact of Police Crime on LGBTQ+ People.*

98. Sykes and Matza, "Techniques of Neutralization," 668.

99. Sykes and Matza, 668.

100. Kappeler, Sluder, and Alpert, *Forces of Deviance*, 121.

101. Kappeler, Sluder, and Alpert, 121.

102. Packer, *The Limits of the Criminal Sanction.*

103. Kappeler, Sluder, and Alpert, *Forces of Deviance*, 121–22.

104. Kappeler, Sluder, and Alpert, 122.

105. Silver, *Police Civil Liability.*

106. US Commission on Civil Rights, *Revisiting "Who Is Guarding the Guardians."*

107. Puente, "Some Baltimore Police Officers Face Repeated Misconduct Lawsuits."

108. Stinson and Brewer, "Federal Civil Rights Litigation."

109. Fyfe, "Good Judgment."

110. Kappeler, Sluder, and Alpert, *Forces of Deviance*, 122.

111. Pearce, "Timeline: The Rise and Fall of Arizona Sheriff Joe Arpaio."

112. United States v. Arpaio, No. CR-16–01012–001_PHX-SRB, Findings of Fact and Conclusions of Law, July 31, 2017.

113. Hirschfeld Davis and Haberman, "Trump Pardons Joe Arpaio."

114. Sykes and Matza, "Techniques of Neutralization," 669.

115. Kappeler, Sluder, and Alpert, *Forces of Deviance*, 123.

116. Mollen Commission, *Commission to Investigate Allegations of Police Corruption and the Anti-corruption*.

117. Caldero and Crank, *Police Ethics*, 2nd ed.

118. Crank, Flaherty, and Giacomazzi, "The Noble Cause."

119. Crank and Caldero, *Police Ethics*, 3rd ed., 2.

120. Barker and Carter, "Police Lies and Perjury"; Panzarella and Funk, "Police Deception Tactics and Public Consent."

121. Vaughn, "Parameters of Trickery as an Acceptable Police Practice." See also, for example, Illinois v. Perkins, 496 U.S. 292 (1990).

122. Manning, "Lying, Secrecy and Social Control."

123. Barker and Carter, "Police Lies and Perjury."

124. Cf. Fletcher, "The New Look in Christian Ethics"; Fletcher, *Situation Ethics*.

125. Barker and Carter, "Police Lies and Perjury," 147.

126. Barker and Carter, 148.

127. Mollen Commission, *Commission to Investigate Allegations of Police Corruption and the Anti-corruption*.

128. Mollen Commission, 36.

129. Crank, *Understanding Police Culture*.

130. Dershowitz, *The Abuse Excuse*, 233.

131. Davis, *Arbitrary Justice*, 141.

132. Dershowitz, "Controlling the Cops."

133. Dershowitz.

134. Goldstein, "'Testilying' by Police."

135. Goldstein.

CHAPTER SIX. SOCIETAL CONFLICT AND LEGITIMACY THEORIES

1. Cannon, *Official Negligence*.

2. Hopkins, *Our Lawless Police*, 34.

3. Nelson, ed., *Police Brutality*, 13.

4. Williams and McShane, *Criminological Theory*.

5. Williams and McShane.

6. Vold, *Theoretical Criminology*, 208–9.

7. Vold, 209.

8. Quinney, *The Social Reality of Crime*.

9. Chambliss and Seidman, *Law, Order, and Power*.

10. Quinney, *Class, State, and Crime*.

11. Intravia, Wolff, and Piquero, "Investigating the Effects of Media Consumption."

12. Pollak and Kubrin, "Crime in the News."

13. Carlson, "Order versus Access."

14. Ready, White, and Fisher, "Shock Value."

15. Chermak, McGarrell, and Gruenewald, "Media Coverage of Police Misconduct."

16. Stinson et al., *Police Integrity Lost.*

17. Barak, "Doing Newsmaking Criminology," 191–92.

18. Ross, "Controlling State Crime."

19. Chambliss, "State-Organized Crime," 184.

20. Friedrichs, "State Crime or Governmental Crime."

21. Barak, "Crime, Criminology and Human Rights."

22. Ross, "Controlling State Crime," 15–16.

23. Chambliss, "State-Organized Crime," 184.

24. Menzies, "State Crime by the Police," 141.

25. Clinard and Quinney, "Crime by Government"; Menzies, "State Crime by the Police."

26. Stinson et al., "To Protect and Collect"; Stinson and Brewer, "Federal Civil Rights Litigation"; Stinson et al., "Police Sexual Misconduct: Arrested Officers and Their Victims"; Stinson et al., "A Study of Drug-Related Police Corruption Arrests"; Stinson and Watkins, "The Nature of Crime by School Resource Officers"; Stinson, Reyns, and Liederbach, "Police Crime and Less-than-Lethal Coercive Force."

27. Delgado and Stefancic, *Critical Race Theory.*

28. Brown v. Board of Education, 347 U.S. 483 (1954); Bell, "Brown v. Board of Education and the Interest-Convergence Dilemma."

29. Delgado and Stefancic, *Critical Race Theory.*

30. Delgado and Stefancic, 10.

31. Capers, "Critical Race Theory and Criminal Justice," 2.

32. Anderson, *Code of the Street*, 321.

33. Buerger and Farrell, "The Evidence of Racial Profiling," 272.

34. J. F. Sullivan, "New Jersey Police Are Accused of Minority Arrest Campaign." See also Hutchins, "Racial Profiling."

35. Glover, *Racial Profiling*, 39.

36. Glover, 47.

37. Jones, *Prejudice and Racism.*

38. Higginbotham, *Shades of Freedom.*

39. Gabbidon, "Blackaphobia," 232.

40. Gabbidon, "Racial Profiling by Store Clerks and Security Personnel in Retail Establishments," 348.

41. , "Racial Profiling"; Jones-Brown and Maule, "Racially Biased
p

, 392 U.S. 1 (1968).

Take Away Their Guns," 375.

d States, 517 U.S. 806 (1996).

rime of Official Deprivation of Civil Rights (2013).

46. Epp, Maynard-Moody, and Haider-Markel, *Pulled Over.*

47. Davis and Whyde, "Contacts between Police and the Public."

48. Butler, "Stop and Frisk and Torture-Lite," 57.

49. Edwards, Esposito, and Lee, "Risk of Police-Involved Death by Race/Ethnicity and Place."

50. Ritchie, *Invisible No More.*

51. Ritchie, 113.

52. Van Ness and Strong, *Restoring Justice.*

53. Braithwaite, *Crime, Shame and Reintegration.*

54. Van Ness and Strong, *Restoring Justice.*

55. Schaible et al., "Denver's Citizen/Police Complaint Mediation Program," 627.

56. Bartels and Silverman, "An Exploratory Study."

57. Tyler and Huo, *Trust in the Law*, xiv.

58. Braithwaite, "Building Legitimacy through Restorative Justice," 158.

59. Braithwaite, *Crime, Shame and Reintegration.*

60. Braithwaite, 183.

61. Braithwaite, 183.

62. Pepinsky, "Better Living through Police Discretion."

63. Allen and Parker, "Police Officers and Their Perceived Relationships with Urban Communities."

64. Violanti et al., "Social Avoidance in Policing."

65. Worden and McLean, *Mirage of Police Reform.*

66. President's Task Force on 21st Century Policing, *Final Report of the President's Task Force.*

67. Kunard and Moe, *Procedural Justice for Law Enforcement*, 3.

68. Sunshine and Tyler, "The Role of Procedural Justice and Legitimacy"; Tyler and Huo, *Trust in the Law.*

69. Tyler and Fagan, "Legitimacy and Cooperation."

70. Mazerolle et al., "Legitimacy in Policing."

71. President's Task Force on 21st Century Policing, *Final Report of the President's Task Force*, 1.

72. President's Task Force on 21st Century Policing, 11.

73. Rahr and Rice, *From Warriors to Guardians*, 4.

74. New Hampshire Police Standards and Training Council, "Full-Time Police Officer Academy."

75. Rahr and Rice, *From Warriors to Guardians*, 4.

76. Kelling and Moore, *The Evolving Strategy of Policing.*

77. Hopkins, *Our Lawless Police*, 191.

78. Oliver, *August Vollmer.*

79. Haller, "Historical Roots of Police Behavior."

80. Payton, *Patrol Procedure.*

81. Bittner, *The Functions of the Police*, 53.

82. For example, Balko, *Rise of the Warrior Cop*; Kappeler and Kraska, "Normalising Police Militarisation"; Kraska and Kappeler, "Militarizing American Police."

83. Skolnick and Fyfe, *Above the Law*, 116.

84. US Department of Justice, Civil Rights Division, *Investigation of the Ferguson Police Department*.

85. Jee-Lyn García and Sharif, "Black Lives Matter."

86. Pyrooz et al., "Was There a Ferguson Effect."

87. Nix, Wolfe, and Campbell, "Command-Level Police Officers' Perceptions"; Oliver, *Depolicing*; Shjarback et al., "De-policing and Crime in the Wake of Ferguson."

CHAPTER SEVEN. INTEGRATIONIST PERSPECTIVES

1. For example, Akers and Sellers, *Criminological Theories*; Lilly, Cullen, and Ball, *Criminological Theory*.

2. Tittle, *Control Balance*, 135.

3. Tittle, "Refining Control Balance Theory," 395.

4. Piquero and Piquero, "Control Balance and Exploitative Corporate Crime," 400.

5. Curry, "Integrating Motivating and Constraining Forces in Deviance Causation."

6. Baron and Forde, "Street Youth Crime"; Higgins, Lauterbach, and Tewksbury, "Control Balance Theory and Violence."

7. Delisi and Hochstetler, "An Exploratory Assessment of Tittle's Control Balance Theory."

8. Piquero and Piquero, "Control Balance and Exploitative Corporate Crime."

9. Piquero and Hickman, "An Empirical Test of Tittle's Control Balance Theory."

10. Hickman et al., "Applying Tittle's Control Balance Theory to Police Deviance," 513.

11. Williams and McShane, *Criminological Theory*.

12. Farrington, *Integrated Developmental and Life-Course Theories*.

13. Gottfredson and Hirschi, *A General Theory of Crime*.

14. Hirschi, "Self-Control and Crime."

15. Cullen and Agnew, *Criminological Theory Past to Present*.

16. Moffitt, "Adolescent-Limited and Life-Course Persistent Antisocial Behavior."

17. Caspi and Moffitt, "The Continuity of Maladaptive Behavior," 500.

18. Moffitt, "Adolescent-Limited and Life-Course Persistent Antisocial Behavior," 686.

19. Moffitt, 694.

20. Moffitt et al., "Partner Abuse and General Crime."

21. Moffitt et al., *Sex Differences in Antisocial Behaviour*.

22. Piquero, Brame, and Moffitt, "Extending the Study of Continuity and Change," 224.

23. Silva and Stanton, *From Child to Adult*.

24. Piquero, Brame, and Moffitt, "Extending the Study of Continuity and Change"; Paternoster, Brame, and Farrington, "On the Relationship between Adolescent and Adult Conviction Frequencies."

25. Piquero, Brame, and Moffitt, "Extending the Study of Continuity and Change," 238.

26. Glueck, *Lives of Labor, Lives of Love*.

27. Glueck and Glueck, *Unraveling Juvenile Delinquency*; Reiss, "Unraveling Juvenile Delinquency: II."

28. Sampson and Laub, *Crime in the Making*.

29. Sampson and Laub, 1.

30. Laub and Sampson, "Unraveling Families and Delinquency."

31. Elder, ed., *Life Course Dynamics*, 17.

32. Elder, Johnson, and Crosnoe, "The Emergence and Development of Life Course Theory."

33. Sampson and Laub, *Crime in the Making*.

34. Sampson and Laub, 243.

35. Laub and Sampson, "Turning Points in the Life Course."

36. Laub and Sampson, *Shared Beginnings, Divergent Lives*.

37. Laub, Sampson, and Sweeten, "Assessing Sampson and Laub's Life-Course Theory."

38. Laub and Sampson, *Shared Beginnings, Divergent Lives*, 145.

39. Laub and Sampson, 49, 145.

40. Harris, *Pathways of Police Misconduct*.

41. Harris, 21.

42. Harris, "Towards a Career View of Police Misconduct."

43. Harris, "Problem Behaviors in Later Portions."

44. White, "Former Schenectady Officer Charged Again."

45. Cook, "Former Schenectady Police Officer Found Dead."

BIBLIOGRAPHY

Abrahamse, Allan F., Patricia A. Ebener, Peter W. Greenwood, Nora Fitzgerald, and Thomas E. Kosin. "An Experimental Evaluation of the Phoenix Repeat Offender Program." *Justice Quarterly* 8, no. 2 (1991): 141–68. https://doi.org/10.1080/07418829100090971.

Adorno, Theodor W., Else Frenkel-Brunswik, Daniel J. Levinson, and R. Nevitt Sanford. *The Authoritarian Personality*. New York: Harper, 1950.

Agnew, Robert. "Experienced, Vicarious, and Anticipated Strain: An Exploratory Study on Physical Victimization and Delinquency." *Justice Quarterly* 19, no. 4 (2002): 603–32. https://doi.org/10.1080/07418820200095371.

———. "Foundation for a General Strain Theory of Crime and Delinquency." *Criminology* 30, no. 1 (1992): 47–88. https://doi.org/10.1111/j.1745-9125.1992.tb01093.x.

———. "General Strain Theory." In *Taking Stock: The Status of Criminological Theory*, edited by Francis T. Cullen, John Paul Wright, and Kristie R. Blevins, 101–23. Advances in Criminological Theory 15. New Brunswick, NJ: Transaction Publishers, 2008.

Akers, Ronald L. "Problems in the Sociology of Deviance: Social Definitions and Behavior." *Social Forces* 46, no. 4 (1968): 455–65. https://doi.org/10.1093/sf/46.4.455.

Akers, Ronald L., and Christine Sharon Sellers. *Criminological Theories: Introduction, Evaluation, and Application*. 6th ed. New York: Oxford University Press, 2013.

Allen, Terrence T., and M. Michaux Parker. "Police Officers and Their Perceived Relationships with Urban Communities: Does Living in the Community Influence Police Decisions?" *Social Development Issues* 35, no. 3 (2013): 82–95.

Alpert, Geoffrey P., and Roger G. Dunham, eds. *Understanding Police Use of Force: Officers, Suspects, and Reciprocity*. Cambridge Studies in Criminology. New York: Cambridge University Press, 2004.

Alpert, Geoffrey P., and Kyle McLean. "Where Is the Goal Line? A Critical Look at Police Body-Worn Camera Programs." *Criminology and Public Policy* 17, no. 3 (2018): 679–88. https://doi.org/10.1111/1745-9133.12374.

Alpert, Geoffrey P., and Samuel Walker. "Police Accountability and Early Warning Systems: Developing Policies and Programs." *Justice Research and Policy* 2, no. 2 (2000): 59–72. https://doi.org/10.3818/JRP.2.2.2000.59.

Amnesty International. *"Less than Lethal"? The Use of Stun Weapons in US Law Enforcement*. London: Amnesty International, 2008.

Anderson, Elijah. *Code of the Street: Decency, Violence, and the Moral Life of the Inner City*. New York: W. W. Norton, 2000.

Anechiarico, Frank, and James B. Jacobs. *The Pursuit of Absolute Integrity: How Corruption Control Makes Government Ineffective*. Chicago: University of Chicago Press, 1996.

Anonymous British soldier. "The Baptism of Fire." *New York Times Current History: The European War* 1, no. 5 (1915): 977–79.

Apel, Robert, and Daniel S. Nagin. "General Deterrence: A Review of Recent Evidence." In *Crime and Public Policy*, edited by James Q. Wilson and Joan Petersilia, 411–36. New York: Oxford University Press, 2011.

Arrigo, Bruce A., and Natalie Claussen. "Police Corruption and Psychological Testing: A Strategy for Preemployment Screening." *International Journal of Offender Therapy and Comparative Criminology* 47, no. 3 (2003): 272–90. https://doi.org/10.1177/0306624X03047003003.

Associated Press. "Pittsburgh Detectives Charged in After-Concert Brawl." *Philly.com*, August 22, 2007.

Athens, Lonnie H. "Violent Crime: A Symbolic Interactionist Study." *Symbolic Interaction* 1, no. 1 (1977): 56–70. https://doi.org/10.1525/si.1977.1.1.56.

Aultman, M. G. "A Social Psychological Approach to the Study of Police Corruption." *Journal of Criminal Justice* 4, no. 4 (1976): 323–32. https://doi.org/10.1016/0047-2352(76)90015-5.

Avila, Jim, Alison Lynn, and Lauren Pearle. "Police Sergeant Had Secret Life as Serial Rapist." *ABC News*, August 30, 2010.

Ayoob, Massad. *The Ayoob Files: The Book*. Concord, NH: Police Bookshelf, 2004.

Baak, Carlijn van, Brittany E. Hayes, Joshua D. Freilich, and Steven M. Chermak. "Honor Crimes in the United States and Offenders' Neutralization Techniques." *Deviant Behavior* 39, no. 2 (2018): 187–202. https://doi.org/10.1080/01639625.2016.1266870.

Bach, Amy. *Ordinary Injustice: How America Holds Court*. New York: Metropolitan Books, 2009.

Balko, Radley. *Rise of the Warrior Cop: The Militarization of America's Police Forces*. New York: PublicAffairs, 2014.

Barak, Gregg. "Crime, Criminology and Human Rights: Towards an Understanding of State Criminality." *Journal of Human Justice* 2, no. 1 (1990): 11–28. https://doi.org/10.1007/BF02637528.

———. "Doing Newsmaking Criminology from within the Academy." *Theoretical Criminology* 11, no. 2 (2007): 191–207. https://doi.org/10.1177/1362480607075847.

———. "Media, Society, and Criminology." In *Media, Process, and the Social Construction of Crime: Studies in Newsmaking Criminology*, 3–45. New York: Garland, 1995.

Barker, Thomas. "Peer Group Support for Police Occupational Deviance." *Criminology* 15, no. 3 (1977): 353–66. https://doi.org/10.1111/j.1745-9125.1977.tb00071.x.

Barker, Thomas, and David L. Carter. "Police Lies and Perjury: A Motivation-Based Taxonomy." In *Police Deviance*, 139–54. Cincinnati, OH: Anderson, 1994.

Barnes, J. C., Tony Dukes, Richard Tewksbury, and Timothy M. De Troye. "Analyzing the Impact of a Statewide Residence Restriction Law on South Carolina Sex Offenders." *Criminal Justice Policy Review* 20, no. 1 (2009): 21–43. https://doi.org/10.1177/0887403408320842.

Baron, Stephen W., and David R. Forde. "Street Youth Crime: A Test of Control Balance Theory." *Justice Quarterly* 24, no. 2 (2007): 335–55. https://doi.org/10.1080/07418820701294870.

Bartels, Elizabeth C., and Eli B. Silverman. "An Exploratory Study of the New York City Civilian Complaint Review Board Mediation Program." *Policing: An International Journal of Police Strategies and Management* 28, no. 4 (2005): 619–30. https://doi.org/10.1108/13639510510628703.

Bartol, Curt R. "Predictive Validation of the MMPI for Small-Town Police Officers Who Fail." *Professional Psychology: Research and Practice* 22, no. 2 (1991): 127–32. https://doi.org/10.1037/0735-7028.22.2.127.

Baughman, Penelope, Desta Fekedulegn, Luenda E. Charles, Ja. K. Gu, Claudia C. Ma, John M. Violanti, Michael Wirth, et al. "Shift Work and Health Consequences in Policing." In *Dying for the Job: Police Work Exposure and Health*, edited by John M. Violanti, 73–92. Springfield, IL: Charles C. Thomas, 2014.

Beccaria, Cesare. *On Crimes and Punishments*. Indianapolis: Hackett, 1986.

Bell, Derrick A. "Brown v. Board of Education and the Interest-Convergence Dilemma." *Harvard Law Review* 93, no. 3 (1980): 518. https://doi.org/10.2307/1340546.

Bentham, Jeremy. *An Introduction to the Principles of Morals and Legislation*. Chestnut Hill, MA: Elibron Classics, 2005.

Bernard, Thomas J. "Angry Aggression among the Truly Disadvantaged." *Criminology* 28, no. 1 (1990): 73–96. https://doi.org/10.1111/j.1745-9125.1990.tb01318.x.

Bharat, Krishna. "Google News Turns 10." *Google News Blog*, September 22, 2012.

Bishopp, Stephen A., Nicole Leeper Piquero, John L. Worrall, and Alex R. Piquero. "Negative Affective Responses to Stress among Urban Police Officers: A General Strain Theory Approach." *Deviant Behavior*, March 29, 2018, 1–20. https://doi.org/10.1080/01639625.2018.1438069.

Bittner, Egon. *The Functions of the Police in Modern Society: A Review of Background Factors, Current Practices, and Possible Role Models*. Reprint of the 1970 ed. published by National Institute of Mental Health, Center for Studies of Crime and Delinquency. Cambridge, MA: Oelgeschlager, Gunn & Hain, 1980.

Black, Donald J. *The Behavior of Law*. New York: Academic Press, 1976.

———. "The Boundaries of Legal Sociology." *Yale Law Journal* 81, no. 6 (1972): 1086–100.

———. *The Manners and Customs of the Police*. New York: Academic Press, 1980.

———. "The Social Organization of Arrest." *Stanford Law Review* 23, no. 6 (1971): 1087–111.

Blalock, Hubert M. *Conceptualization and Measurement in the Social Sciences*. Beverly Hills: Sage, 1982.

———. "The Presidential Address: Measurement and Conceptualization Problems: The Major Obstacle to Integrating Theory and Research." *American Sociological Review* 44, no. 6 (1979): 881–94.

———. *Social Statistics*. Boston: McGraw-Hill, 1979.

Blomberg, Thomas G. "David Matza—Criminologist: With New Reflections from David Matza." In *Delinquency and Drift Revisited: The Criminology of David Matza and Beyond*, edited by Thomas G. Blomberg, Francis T. Cullen, Christoffer Carlsson, and Cheryl Lero Jonson, 3–12. Advances in Criminological Theory 21. New York: Routledge, 2018.

Braga, Anthony A., Andrew V. Papachristos, and David M. Hureau. "The Effects of Hot Spots Policing on Crime: An Updated Systematic Review and Meta-analysis." *Justice Quarterly* 31, no. 4 (2014): 633–63. https://doi.org/10.1080/07418825.2012.673632.

Braga, Anthony A., Brandon C. Welsh, and Cory Schnell. "Can Policing Disorder Reduce Crime? A Systematic Review and Meta-analysis." *Journal of Research in Crime and Delinquency* 52, no. 4 (2015): 567–88. https://doi.org/10.1177/0022427815576576.

Braithwaite, John. "Building Legitimacy through Restorative Justice." In *Legitimacy and Criminal Justice: An International Perspective*, 146–62. New York: Russell Sage Foundation, 2007.

———. *Crime, Shame and Reintegration*. Cambridge: Cambridge University Press, 1989.

Brandl, Steven G., and Meghan S. Stroshine. "Toward an Understanding of the Physical Hazards of Police Work." *Police Quarterly* 6, no. 2 (2003): 172–91. https://doi.org/10.1177/1098611103006002003.

Brown v. Board of Education, 347 U.S. 483 (1954).

Buerger, Michael E., and Amy Farrell. "The Evidence of Racial Profiling: Interpreting Documented and Unofficial Sources." *Police Quarterly* 5, no. 3 (2002): 272–305. https://doi.org/10.1177/109861102129198165.

Burgess, Robert L., and Ronald L. Akers. "A Differential Association-Reinforcement Theory of Criminal Behavior." *Social Problems* 14, no. 2 (1966): 128–47. https://doi.org/10.2307/798612.

Burke, Peter. "BSO Sergeant Paid for Off-Duty Detail He Never Performed, Affidavit Says." *Local10.com*, September 23, 2016.

Burke, Ronald J. "Burnout in Police Work: Sources, Consequences, and Remedies." In *Stress in Policing: Sources, Consequences and Interventions*, edited by Ronald J. Burke, 153–69. New York: Routledge, 2017.

Burke, Ronald J., and Aslaug Mikkelsen. "Suicidal Ideation among Police Officers in Norway." *Policing: An International Journal of Police Strategies and Management* 30, no. 2 (2007): 228–36. https://doi.org/10.1108/13639510710753234.

Burnham, David. *The Role of the Media in Controlling Corruption.* New York: John Jay College of Criminal Justice, Criminal Justice Center, 1977.

Butler, Paul. "Stop and Frisk and Torture-Lite: Police Terror of Minority Communities." *Ohio State Journal of Criminal Law* 12, no. 1 (2014): 57–69.

Byers, Bryan, Benjamin W. Crider, and Greggory K. Biggers. "Bias Crimes Motivation: A Study of Hate Crimes and Offender Neutralization Techniques Used against the Amish." In *Crimes of Hate: Selected Readings*, 118–29. Thousand Oaks, CA: Sage, 2003.

Caillouet, Beth A., Marcus T. Boccaccini, Jorge G. Varela, Robert D. Davis, and Cary D. Rostow. "Predictive Validity of the MMPI-2 PSY-5 Scales and Facets for Law Enforcement Officer Employment Outcomes." *Criminal Justice and Behavior* 37, no. 2 (2010): 217–38. https://doi.org/10.1177/0093854809351948.

Caldero, Michael A., and John P. Crank. *Police Ethics: The Corruption of Noble Cause.* 2nd ed. Dayton, OH: Anderson/Lexis, 2004.

Cannizzo, Thomas A., and Peter Liu. "The Relationship between Levels of Perceived Burnout and Career Stage among Sworn Police Officers." *Police Studies* 18, no. 3 (1995): 53–68.

Cannon, Lou. *Official Negligence: How Rodney King and the Riots Changed Los Angeles and the LAPD.* Boulder, CO: Westview Press, 1999.

Capers, I. Bennett. "Critical Race Theory and Criminal Justice." *Ohio State Journal of Criminal Law* 12, no. 1 (2014): 1–7.

Carleo-Evangelist, Jordan. "Suspended Schenectady Police Officer Charged with Breaking Window in Jail Cell." *Times Union*, April 3, 2010.

Carlson, Matt. "Order versus Access: News Search Engines and the Challenge to Traditional Journalistic Roles." *Media, Culture and Society* 29, no. 6 (2007): 1014–30. https://doi.org/10.1177/0163443707084346.

Carlson, Tucker. "DC Blues: The Rap Sheet on the Washington Police." *Policy Review* 63 (1993): 26–33.

Cascio, Wayne F. "Formal Education and Police Officer Performance." *Journal of Police Science and Administration* 5, no. 1 (1977): 89–96.

Caspi, Avshalom, and Terrie E. Moffitt. "The Continuity of Maladaptive Behavior: From Description to Understanding in the Study of Antisocial Behavior." In *Developmental Psychopathology*, edited by Dante Cicchetti and Donald J. Cohen, 2:472–511. New York: Wiley, 1995.

Castaneda, Ruben. "DUI Arrest Is Officer's 4th This Year: Prince George's Lieutenant Allegedly Asleep behind the Wheel." *Washington Post*, December 17, 2008, sec. B.

Chajewski, Michael, and Cynthia Calkins Mercado. "An Evaluation of Sex Offender Residency Restriction Functioning in Town, County, and City-Wide Jurisdictions." *Criminal Justice Policy Review* 20, no. 1 (2009): 44–61. https://doi.org/10.1177/0887403408320845.

Chambliss, William J. "State-Organized Crime: The American Society of Criminology, 1988 Presidential Address." *Criminology* 27, no. 2 (1989): 183–208. https://doi.org/10.1111/j.1745-9125.1989.tb01028.x.

Chambliss, William J., and Robert B. Seidman. *Law, Order, and Power.* Reading, MA: Addison-Wesley, 1971.

Chappell, Allison T., and Alex R. Piquero. "Applying Social Learning Theory to Police Misconduct." *Deviant Behavior* 25, no. 2 (2004): 89–108. https://doi.org/10.1080/01639620490251642.

Charles, Luenda E., Cecil M. Burchfiel, Desta Fekedulegn, Bryan Vila, Tara A. Hartley, James Slaven, Anna Mnatsakanova, and John M. Violanti. "Shift Work and Sleep: The Buffalo Police Health Study." *Policing: An International Journal of Police Strategies and Management* 30, no. 2 (2007): 215–27. https://doi.org/10.1108/13639510710753225.

Cheh, Mary M. "Are Lawsuits an Answer to Police Brutality?" In *Police Violence: Understanding and Controlling Police Abuse of Force*, edited by William A. Geller and Hans Toch, 247–72. New Haven, CT: Yale University Press, 1996.

Chermak, Steven M., Edmund McGarrell, and Jeffrey Gruenewald. "Media Coverage of Police Misconduct and Attitudes toward Police." *Policing: An International Journal of Police Strategies and Management* 29, no. 2 (2006): 261–81. https://doi.org/10.1108/13639510610667664.

Christopher Commission. *Report of the Independent Commission on the Los Angeles Police Department.* Los Angeles: City of Los Angeles, 1991.

Clarke, Ronald V. "Introduction to the Transaction Edition." In *The Reasoning Criminal: Rational Choice Perspectives on Offending*, edited by Derek B. Cornish and Ronald V. Clarke, ix–xvi. New York: Transaction Publishers, 2014.

———. "Situational Crime Prevention: Theoretical Background and Current Practice." In *Handbook on Crime and Deviance*, edited by Marvin D. Krohn, Alan J. Lizotte, and Gina Penly Hall, 259–76. New York: Springer New York, 2009. www.springerlink.com/index/10.1007/978-1-4419-0245-0_14.

Clarke, Ronald V., and Derek B. Cornish. "Modeling Offenders' Decisions: A Framework for Research and Policy." *Crime and Justice* 6 (1985): 147–85. https://doi.org/10.1086/449106.

———. "Rational Choice." In *Explaining Criminals and Crime: Essays in Contemporary Criminological Theory*, edited by Raymond Paternoster and Ronet Bachman, 23–42. Los Angeles: Roxbury, 2001.

Clarke, Ronald V., and Marcus Felson, eds. *Routine Activity and Rational Choice.* Advances in Criminological Theory 5. New Brunswick, NJ: Transaction Publishers, 1993.

Clinard, Marshall, and Richard Quinney. "Crime by Government." In *Corporate and Governmental Deviance: Problems of Organizational Behaviour in Contemporary Society*, edited by R. David Ermann and Richard Lundmann, 137–50. New York: Oxford University Press, 1978.

Cochrane, Robert E., Robert P. Tett, and Leon Vandecreek. "Psychological Testing and the Selection of Police Officers: A National Survey." *Criminal Justice and Behavior* 30, no. 5 (2003): 511–37. https://doi.org/10.1177/0093854803257241.

Cohen, Lawrence E., and Marcus Felson. "Social Change and Crime Rate Trends: A Routine Activity Approach." *American Sociological Review* 44, no. 4 (1979): 588–608. https://doi.org/10.2307/2094589.

Collins, Allyson. *Shielded from Justice: Police Brutality and Accountability in the United States.* New York: Human Rights Watch, 1998.

Comey, James B. "The True Heart of American Law Enforcement." Paper presented at the International Association of Chiefs of Police Annual Conference, San Diego, CA, October 16, 2016. https://www.fbi.gov/news/speeches/the-true-heart-of-american-law-enforcement.

Commission on Accreditation for Law Enforcement Agencies. "Standard 31.5.7: Emotional Stability/Psychological Fitness Examinations." In *CALEA Standards for Law Enforcement*, 6th ed. Gainesville, VA: Commission on Accreditation for Law Enforcement Agencies, 2010.

———. "Standard 35.1.9: Personnel Early Intervention System." In *CALEA Standards for Law Enforcement Agencies*, 6th ed. Gainesville, VA: Commission on Accreditation for Law Enforcement Agencies, 2010.

Cook, Steven. "Former Schenectady Police Officer Found Dead." *Daily Gazette*, February 20, 2014.

———. "Schenectady Police Officer Arrested for Third Time." *Daily Gazette*, November 11, 2008.

Copple, James E., and Patricia M. Dunn. *Gender, Sexuality, and 21st Century Policing: Protecting the Rights of the LGBTQ+ Community*. Washington, DC: US Department of Justice, Office of Community Oriented Policing Services, 2017.

Cordner, Gary W. "Police Patrol Workload Studies: A Review and Critique." *Police Studies* 2, no. 4 (1979): 50–60.

Corey, David M., and Randy Borum. "Forensic Assessment for High-Risk Occupations." In *Handbook of Psychology*, edited by Irving Weiner, 2nd ed., 11:246–70. Hoboken, NJ: John Wiley and Sons, 2012. https://doi.org/10.1002/9781118133880.hop211011.

Crank, John P. *Understanding Police Culture*. 2nd ed. Dayton, OH: Anderson/LexisNexis, 2004.

Crank, John P., and Michael A. Caldero. *Police Ethics: The Corruption of Noble Cause*. 3rd ed. Cincinnati, OH: Anderson/Lexis, 2010.

Crank, John P., Dan Flaherty, and Andrew Giacomazzi. "The Noble Cause: An Empirical Assessment." *Journal of Criminal Justice* 35, no. 1 (2006): 103–16. https://doi.org/10.1016/j.jcrimjus.2006.11.019.

Crime of Official Deprivation of Civil Rights, N.J. Rev. Stat. § 2C:30–6 (2013).

Crowe, Kenneth C. "Suspended Schenectady Police Officer Charged with DWI." *Times Union*, January 24, 2010.

Cullen, Francis T., and Robert Agnew. *Criminological Theory Past to Present: Essential Readings*. 2nd ed. Roxbury Park, CA: Sage, 2003.

Curry, Theodore R. "Integrating Motivating and Constraining Forces in Deviance Causation: A Test of Causal Chain Hypotheses in Control Balance

Theory." *Deviant Behavior* 26, no. 6 (2005): 571–99. https://doi.org/10.1080
/01639620500218286.

Davidson, Barbara. "The Knapp Commission Didn't Know It Couldn't Be Done."
New York Times, January 9, 1972.

Davis, Angela J. *Arbitrary Justice: The Power of the American Prosecutor.* New York:
Oxford University Press, 2007.

Davis, Elizabeth, and Anthony Whyde. *Contacts between Police and the Public, 2015.*
Washington, DC: US Department of Justice, Office of Justice Programs, Bureau
of Justice Statistics, 2018.

Delattre, Edwin J. *Character and Cops: Ethics in Policing.* 6th ed. Washington, DC:
AEI Press, 2011.

Delgado, Richard, and Jean Stefancic. *Critical Race Theory: An Introduction.* 3rd ed.
New York: New York University Press, 2017.

Delisi, Matt, and Andrew Hochstetler. "An Exploratory Assessment of Tittle's Control Balance Theory: Results from the National Youth Survey." *Justice Professional*
15, no. 3 (2002): 261–72. https://doi.org/10.1080/08884310215666.

Demir, Mustafa, Robert Apel, Anthony A. Braga, Rod K. Brunson, and Barak Ariel.
"Body Worn Cameras, Procedural Justice, and Police Legitimacy: A Controlled
Experimental Evaluation of Traffic Stops." *Justice Quarterly*, 2018, 1–32. https://
doi.org/10.1080/07418825.2018.1495751.

Dershowitz, Alan M. *The Abuse Excuse: And Other Cop-Outs, Sob Stories, and Eva-
sions of Responsibility.* Boston: Back Bay Books, 1994.

———. "Controlling the Cops; Accomplices to Perjury." *New York Times*, May 2, 1994.

Dollinger, Arielle, and Marc Santora. "James Burke, Ex-Suffolk County Police
Chief, Pleads Guilty." *New York Times*, February 26, 2016.

Dominguez, Damian. "Ware Shoals Police Chief on Leave after Facing Gun
Charge." *Index Journal*, January 2, 2018.

Donnelly, Frank. "Charges Dropped against Cop: Wife Refuses to Cooperate."
Staten Island Advance, March 7, 2006.

Donner, Christopher M., Lorie A. Fridell, and Wesley G. Jennings. "The Relationship between Self-Control and Police Misconduct: A Multi-agency Study of First-
Line Police Supervisors." *Criminal Justice and Behavior* 43, no. 7 (2016): 841–62.
https://doi.org/10.1177/0093854815626751.

Donner, Christopher M., and Wesley G. Jennings. "Low Self-Control and Police
Deviance: Applying Gottfredson and Hirschi's General Theory to Officer
Misconduct." *Police Quarterly* 17, no. 3 (2014): 203–25. https://doi.org/10.1177
/1098611114535217.

Donner, Christopher, Jon Maskaly, and Lorie Fridell. "Social Bonds and Police
Misconduct: An Examination of Social Control Theory and Its Relationship to
Workplace Deviance among Police Supervisors." *Policing: An International Journal of Police Strategies and Management* 39, no. 2 (2016): 416–31. https://
doi.org/10.1108/PIJPSM-10-2015-0109.

Donner, Christopher M., Jon Maskaly, Alex R. Piquero, and Wesley G. Jennings.
"Quick on the Draw: Assessing the Relationship Between Low Self-Control and

Officer-Involved Police Shootings." *Police Quarterly* 20, no. 2 (2017): 213–34. https://doi.org/10.1177/1098611116688066.

Donner, Christopher M., Jon Maskaly, and Kanani N. Thompson. "Self-Control and the Police Code of Silence: Examining the Unwillingness to Report Fellow Officers' Misbehavior among a Multi-agency Sample of Police Recruits." *Journal of Criminal Justice* 56 (2018): 11–19. https://doi.org/10.1016/j.jcrimjus.2017.10 .002.

Drayton, M. "The Minnesota Multiphasic Personality Inventory-2 (MMPI-2)." *Occupational Medicine* 59, no. 2 (2009): 135–36. https://doi.org/10.1093/occmed /kqn182.

Durkheim, Émile. *The Division of Labor in Society.* 1st paperback ed. New York: Free Press, 1997.

———. *Suicide: A Study in Sociology.* New York: Free Press, 1997.

Durkin, Erin. "Councilman Pushing to Make It Explicitly Illegal for NYPD Cops to Have Sex with Someone in Custody." *New York Daily News*, October 24, 2017.

Eck, John E., and Emily B. Eck. "Crime Place and Pollution: Expanding Crime Reduction Options Through a Regulatory Approach." *Criminology and Public Policy* 11, no. 2 (2012): 281–316. https://doi.org/10.1111/j.1745-9133.2012.00809.x.

Edwards, Frank, Michael H. Esposito, and Hedwig Lee. "Risk of Police-Involved Death by Race/Ethnicity and Place, United States, 2012–2018." *American Journal of Public Health* 108, no. 9 (2018): 1241–48. https://doi.org/10.2105 /AJPH.2018.304559.

Elder, Glen Holl, ed. *Life Course Dynamics: Trajectories and Transitions, 1968–1980.* Ithaca, NY: Cornell University Press, 1985.

Elder, Glen Holl, Monica Kirkpatrick Johnson, and Robert Crosnoe. "The Emergence and Development of Life Course Theory." In *Handbook of the Life Course*, edited by Jeylan T. Mortimer and Michael J. Shanahan, 3–19. New York: Springer, 2004.

Elinson, Zusha. "Federal Count in Deadly Police Shootings Is Slow to Get Going." *Wall Street Journal*, March 31, 2018.

Epp, Charles R., Steven Maynard-Moody, and Donald P. Haider-Markel. *Pulled Over: How Police Stops Define Race and Citizenship.* Chicago: University of Chicago Press, 2014.

Farrington, David P., ed. *Integrated Developmental and Life-Course Theories of Offending.* New Brunswick, NJ: Transaction Publishers, 2005.

Fattah, Ezzat A. "The Rational Choice/Opportunity Perspectives as a Vehicle for Integrating Criminological and Victimological Theories." In *Routine Activity and Rational Choice*, edited by Ronald V. Clarke and Marcus Felson, 225–58. Advances in Criminological Theory 5. New Brunswick, NJ: Transaction Publishers, 1993.

Faulk, Kent. "Former Birmingham Police Officer Denies Setting Fires in Warrior and Western Birmingham." *Birmingham News*, June 12, 2013.

Felson, Marcus. "The Routine Activity Approach: A Very Versatile Theory of Crime." In *Explaining Criminals and Crime: Essays in Contemporary Criminological Theory*, edited by Raymond Paternoster and Ronet Bachman, 43–46. Los Angeles: Roxbury, 2001.

———. "Those Who Discourage Crime." In *Crime and Place*, edited by John E. Eck and David L. Weisburd, 53–66. Crime Prevention Studies 4. Monsey, NY: Willow Tree Press, 1995.

Felson, Marcus, and Lawrence E. Cohen. "Human Ecology and Crime: A Routine Activity Approach." *Human Ecology* 8, no. 4 (1980): 389–406. https://doi.org/10.1007/BF01561001.

Felson, Marcus, and Mary Eckert. *Crime and Everyday Life*. 5th ed. Los Angeles: Sage, 2016.

Ferrise, Adam. "Fired Trooper Gets His Job Back, New Post." *Tribune Chronicle*, January 6, 2012.

Fishman, Janet E. *Measuring Police Corruption*. New York: John Jay College of Criminal Justice, Criminal Justice Center, 1978.

Fletcher, Joseph. "The New Look in Christian Ethics: Six Propositions." *Harvard Divinity Bulletin* 24, no. 1 (1959): 7–18.

———. *Situation Ethics: The New Morality*. Louisville, KY: Westminster John Knox Press, 1966.

Foster, Gerald Pentland. "Police Administration and the Control of Police Criminality: A Case Study Approach." PhD dissertation, University of Southern California, 1966. https://search.proquest.com/docview/302224642.

Franklin, Benjamin. *The Papers of Benjamin Franklin: January 1, 1735, through December 31, 1744*. Edited by Leonard Woods Labaree. Vol. 2. New Haven, CT: Yale University Press, 1960.

Friedrichs, David O. "State Crime or Governmental Crime: Making Sense of the Conceptual Confusion." In *Controlling State Crime*, edited by Jeffrey Ian Ross, 2nd ed., 53–79. New Brunswick, NJ: Transaction, 2000.

Fyfe, James J. "Always Prepared: Police Off-Duty Guns." *Annals of the American Academy of Political and Social Science* 452 (1980): 72–81. https://doi.org/10.1177/000271628045200108.

———. "Good Judgment: Defending Police against Civil Suits." *Police Quarterly* 1, no. 1 (1998): 91–117.

Fyfe, James J., and Robert J. Kane. *Bad Cops: A Study of Career-Ending Misconduct among New York City Police Officers*. NCJ No. 215795. Washington, DC: US Department of Justice, National Institute of Justice, 2006.

Gabbidon, Shaun L. "Blackaphobia: What Is It? And Who Are Its Victims?" In *Black on Black Crime: Facing Facts—Challenging Fictions*, edited by P. Ray Kedia, 232–44. Bristol, IN: Wyndham Hall, 1994.

———. "Racial Profiling by Store Clerks and Security Personnel in Retail Establishments: An Exploration of 'Shopping While Black.'" *Journal of Contemporary Criminal Justice* 19, no. 3 (2003): 345–64. https://doi.org/10.1177/1043986203254531.

Garofalo, James. "Reassessing the Lifestyle Model of Criminal Victimization." In *Positive Criminology*, edited by Michael R. Gottfredson and Travis Hirschi, 23–42. Newbury Park, CA: Sage, 1987.

Garrity v. New Jersey, 385 U.S. 493 (1967).

Gaspar, Jose. "Investigative Reports: Ex-deputy Admits to Stealing Money." *BakersfieldNow.com*, February 3, 2011.

Gauntner, Mike. "Trooper Arrested in Austintown Pleads to Reduced Charge." *WFMJ.com*, July 18, 2013.

Gershon, Robyn. *Police Stress and Domestic Violence in Police Families in Baltimore, Maryland, 1997–1999*. ICPSR Study No. 2976. Ann Arbor, MI: Interuniversity Consortium for Political and Social Research, 2000. https://www.icpsr.umich.edu/icpsrweb/NACJD/studies/2976/version/1/export.

———. *Project Shields: Final Report*. Washington, DC: US Department of Justice, Office of Justice Programs, National Institute of Justice, 2000. https://www.ncjrs.gov/pdffiles1/nij/grants/185892.pdf.

Gershon, Robyn, Briana Barocas, Allison N. Canton, Xianbin Li, and David Vlahov. "Mental, Physical, and Behavioral Outcomes Associated with Perceived Work Stress in Police Officers." *Journal of Criminal Justice and Behavior* 36, no. 3 (2009): 275–89. https://doi.org/10.1177/0093854808330015.

Gibbs, Jack P. "Crime, Punishment, and Deterrence." *Southwestern Social Science Quarterly* 48, no. 4 (1968): 515–30.

———. "Punishment and Deterrence: Theory, Research, and Penal Policy." In *Law and the Social Sciences*, edited by Leon Lipson and Stanton Wheeler, 319–68. New York: Russell Sage Foundation, 1986.

Gibbs, John J., and Dennis Giever. "Self-Control and Its Manifestations among University Students: An Empirical Test of Gottfredson and Hirschi's General Theory of Crime." *Justice Quarterly* 12 (1995): 231–55. https://doi.org/10.1080/07418829500092661.

Gibson, Chris L., Marc L. Swatt, and Jason R. Jolicoeur. "Assessing the Generality of General Strain Theory: The Relationship among Occupational Stress Experienced by Male Police Officers and Domestic Forms of Violence." *Journal of Crime and Justice* 24, no. 2 (2001): 29–57.

Glover, Karen S. *Racial Profiling: Research, Racism, and Resistance*. Lanham, MD: Rowman & Littlefield, 2009.

Glueck, Sheldon. *Lives of Labor, Lives of Love: Fragments of Friendly Autobiographies*. Hicksville, NY: Exposition Press, 1977.

Glueck, Sheldon, and Eleanor Glueck. *Unraveling Juvenile Delinquency*. New York: Commonwealth Fund, 1950.

Goffman, Erving. *Interaction Ritual: Essays on Face-to-Face Behavior*. Garden City, NY: Anchor Books, 1967.

———. "The Moral Career of the Mental Patient." *Psychiatry* 22, no. 2 (1959): 123–42. https://doi.org/10.1080/00332747.1959.11023166.

———. *Strategic Interaction*. Philadelphia: University of Pennsylvania Press, 1969.

Goldstein, Herman. *Policing a Free Society*. Cambridge, MA: Ballinger, 1977.

Goldstein, Joseph. "'Testilying' by Police: A Stubborn Problem." *New York Times*, March 18, 2018, sec. NY / Region.

Goodman, Alan M. "A Model for Police Officer Burnout." *Journal of Business and Psychology* 5, no. 1 (1990): 85–99. https://doi.org/10.1007/BF01013947.

Goot, Michael. "Schenectady Police Officer Charged with DWI." *Daily Gazette*, December 29, 2008.

Gosling, Kristen. "Former Uplands Park Officer Leon Pullen Sentenced to 25 Years." *KSDK.com*, January 28, 2011.

Gottfredson, Michael R., and Travis Hirschi. *A General Theory of Crime*. Stanford, CA: Stanford University Press, 1990.

Gottschalk, Petter. "White-Collar Crime and Police Crime: Rotten Apples or Rotten Barrels?" *Critical Criminology* 20, no. 2 (2012): 169–82. https://doi.org/10.1007/s10612-011-9133-0.

Graham, Troy. "Two Philadelphia Police Charged with Crimes." *Philadelphia Inquirer*, January 29, 2011.

Graham v. Connor, 490 U.S. 386 (1989).

Griffin, Sean P., and Thomas J. Bernard. "Angry Aggression among Police Officers." *Police Quarterly* 6, no. 1 (2003): 3–21. https://doi.org/10.1177/1098611102250365.

Groopman, Jerome. "The Grief Industry: How Much Crisis Counselling Help—or Hurt?" *New Yorker*, January 26, 2004.

Guthrie, Doug. "Detroit Cop Charged with Felony Torture for Breakup Fracas." *Detroit News*, March 6, 2008.

Haller, Mark H. "Historical Roots of Police Behavior: Chicago, 1890–1925." *Law and Society Review* 10, no. 2 (1976): 303–23. https://doi.org/10.2307/3053102.

Hargrave, George E., Deirdre Hiatt, and Tim W. Gaffney. "F+4+9+Cn: An MMPI Measure of Aggression in Law Enforcement Officers and Applicants." *Journal of Police Science and Administration* 16, no. 4 (1988): 268–73.

Harlow v. Fitzgerald, 457 U.S. 800 (1982).

Harris, Christopher J. *Pathways of Police Misconduct: Problem Behavior Patterns and Trajectories from Two Cohorts*. Durham, NC: Carolina Academic Press, 2010.

———. "Problem Behaviors in Later Portions of Officers' Careers." *Policing: An International Journal of Police Strategies and Management* 34, no. 1 (2011): 135–52. https://doi.org/10.1108/13639511111106650.

———. "Towards a Career View of Police Misconduct." *Aggression and Violent Behavior* 31 (2016): 219–28. https://doi.org/10.1016/j.avb.2016.10.001.

Hawley, Amos H. *Human Ecology: A Theory of Community Structure*. New York: Ronald Press, 1950.

Henkel, James, and Eugene P. Sheehan. "Relation of Police Misconduct to Authoritarianism." *Journal of Behavior and Personality* 12, no. 2 (1997): 551–55.

Herbert, Steve. "Police Subculture Reconsidered." *Criminology* 36, no. 2 (1998): 343–69. https://doi.org/10.1111/j.1745-9125.1998.tb01251.x.

Hiatt, Deirdre, and George E. Hargrave. "MMPI Profiles of Problem Peace Officers." *Journal of Personality Assessment* 52, no. 4 (1988): 722–31. https://doi.org/10.1207/s15327752jpa5204_11.

Hickman, Matthew J. "On the Context of Police Cynicism and Problem Behavior." *Applied Psychology in Criminal Justice* 4, no. 1 (2008): 1–44.

Hickman, Matthew J., Alex R. Piquero, Brian A. Lawton, and Jack R. Greene. "Applying Tittle's Control Balance Theory to Police Deviance." *Policing: An*

International Journal of Police Strategies and Management 24, no. 4 (2001): 497–519. https://doi.org/10.1108/EUM0000000006497.

Hickman, Matthew J., and Jane E. Poore. "National Data on Citizen Complaints about Police Use of Force: Data Quality Concerns and the Potential (Mis)Use of Statistical Evidence to Address Police Agency Conduct." *Criminal Justice Policy Review* 27, no. 5 (2016): 455–79. https://doi.org/10.1177/0887403415594843.

Higginbotham, A. Leon. *Shades of Freedom: Racial Politics and Presumptions of the American Legal Process*. New York: Oxford University Press, 1998.

Higgins, George E., Christopher Lauterbach, and Richard Tewksbury. "Control Balance Theory and Violence: An Examination of Contingencies." *Sociological Focus* 38, no. 4 (2005): 241–60. https://doi.org/10.1080/00380237.2005.10571268.

Hindelang, Michael J., Michael R. Gottfredson, and James Garofalo. *Victims of Personal Crime: An Empirical Foundation for a Theory of Personal Victimization*. Cambridge, MA: Ballinger, 1978.

Hirschfeld Davis, Julie, and Maggie Haberman. "Trump Pardons Joe Arpaio, Who Became Face of Crackdown on Illegal Immigration." *New York Times*, August 25, 2017.

Hirschi, Travis. *Causes of Delinquency*. Berkeley: University of California Press, 1969.

———. *Causes of Delinquency*. New Brunswick, NJ: Transaction Publishers, 2002.

———. "Self-Control and Crime." In *Handbook of Self-Regulation: Research, Theory, and Applications*, edited by Roy F. Baumeister and Kathleen D. Vohs, 537–52. New York: Guilford Press, 2004.

Hobbes, Thomas. *The Elements of Law, Natural and Politic: Part I, Human Nature; Part II, De Corpore Politico with Three Lives*. New York: Oxford University Press, 1999.

Hopkins, Ernest Jerome. *Our Lawless Police: A Study of the Unlawful Enforcement of the Law*. New York: Viking, 1931.

Hunter, George. "Fallout Continues from Detroit Police Precinct Racial Scandal." *Detroit News*, March 19, 2019.

Hutchins, Renee McDonald. "Racial Profiling: The Law, the Policy, and the Practice." In *Policing the Black Man*, edited by Angela J. Davis, 95–134. New York: Pantheon Books, 2017.

Illinois v. Perkins, 496 U.S. 292 (1990).

Intravia, Jonathan, Kevin T. Wolff, and Alex R. Piquero. "Investigating the Effects of Media Consumption on Attitudes toward Police Legitimacy." *Deviant Behavior* 39, no. 8 (2018): 963–80. https://doi.org/10.1080/01639625.2017.1343038.

Jee-Lyn García, Jennifer, and Mienah Zulfacar Sharif. "Black Lives Matter: A Commentary on Racism and Public Health." *American Journal of Public Health* 105, no. 8 (2015): e27–e30. https://doi.org/10.2105/AJPH.2015.302706.

Jesilow, Paul, Henry N. Pontell, and Gilbert Geis. *Prescription for Profit: How Doctors Defraud Medicaid*. Berkeley: University of California Press, 1993.

Johnson, Leanor Boulin, Michael Todd, and Ganga Subramanian. "Violence in Police Families: Work-Family Spillover." *Journal of Family Violence* 20, no. 1 (2005): 3–12. https://doi.org/10.1007/s10896-005-1504-4.

Joker3249. *Cop Gets TASER Ride.* YouTube, 2007. www.youtube.com/watch?v=
xZvoEW3EVi8&feature=related.

Jones, James M. *Prejudice and Racism.* 2nd ed. McGraw-Hill Series in Social Psychology. New York: McGraw-Hill, 1997.

Jones-Brown, Delores, and Brian A. Maule. "Racially Biased Policing: A Review of
the Judicial and Legislative Literature." In *Race, Ethnicity, and Policing: New and
Essential Readings*, edited by Stephen K. Rice and Michael D. White, 140–73.
New York: New York University Press, 2010.

Kahneman, Daniel. "Maps of Bounded Rationality: Psychology for Behavioral
Economics." *American Economic Review* 93, no. 5 (2003): 1449–75. https://
doi.org/10.1257/000282803322655392.

———. "A Perspective on Judgment and Choice: Mapping Bounded Rationality."
American Psychologist 58, no. 9 (2003): 697–720. https://doi.org/10.1037
/0003-066X.58.9.697.

Kakar, Suman. "Self-Evaluations of Police Performance: An Analysis of the Relationship between Police Officers' Education Level and Job Performance." *Policing: An International Journal of Police Strategies and Management* 21, no. 4 (1998):
632–47. https://doi.org/10.1108/13639519810241665.

Kane, Robert J. "Collect and Release Data on Coercive Police Actions." *Criminology and Public Policy* 6, no. 4 (2007): 773–80. https://doi.org/10.1111/j.1745-9133
.2007.00485.x.

———. "The Social Ecology of Police Misconduct." *Criminology* 40, no. 4 (2002):
867–96. https://doi.org/10.1111/j.1745-9125.2002.tb00976.x.

Kane, Robert J., and Michael D. White. "Bad Cops: A Study of Career-Ending
Misconduct among New York City Police Officers." *Criminology and Public
Policy* 8, no. 4 (2009): 737–69. https://doi.org/10.1111/j.1745-9133.2009.00591.x.

———. *Jammed Up: Bad Cops, Police Misconduct, and the New York City Police
Department.* New York: New York University Press, 2013.

Kappeler, Victor E. *Critical Issues in Police Civil Liability.* Long Grove, IL: Waveland Press, 2006.

Kappeler, Victor E., and Peter B. Kraska. "Normalising Police Militarisation, Living
in Denial." *Policing and Society* 25, no. 3 (2015): 268–75. https://doi.org/10.1080
/10439463.2013.864655.

Kappeler, Victor E., Allen D. Sapp, and David L. Carter. "Police Officer Higher
Education, Citizen Complaints and Departmental Rule Violations." *American
Journal of Police* 11, no. 2 (1992): 37–54.

Kappeler, Victor E., Richard D. Sluder, and Geoffrey P. Alpert. *Forces of Deviance:
Understanding the Dark Side of Policing.* 2nd ed. Long Grove, IL: Waveland Press,
1998.

Kelley, Janet. "Girls: Cop Molested Us." *Lancaster New Era*, October 25, 2007.

Kelling, George L., and Mark H. Moore. *The Evolving Strategy of Policing.* Washington, DC: US Department of Justice, National Institute of Justice, 1988.

Key, V. O. "Police Graft." *American Journal of Sociology* 40, no. 5 (1935): 624–36.
https://doi.org/10.1086/216900.

Kibler, William. "APD Officer Pleads Guilty to Role in Concert Incident." *Altoona Mirror*, March 1, 2014.

Kimball, Michael. "Oklahoma City Police Officer Accused of Falsifying Time Cards." *Oklahoman*, March 24, 2011.

Kindy, Kimberly. "Some U.S. Police Departments Dump Body-Cameras amid High Costs." *Washington Post*, January 21, 2019.

Kindy, Kimberly, and Kimbriell Kelly. "Thousands Dead, Few Prosecuted." *Washington Post*, April 12, 2015.

Klinger, David A. "Negotiating Order in Patrol Work: An Ecological Theory of Police Response to Deviance." *Criminology* 35, no. 2 (1997): 277–306. https://doi.org/10.1111/j.1745–9125.1997.tb00877.x.

Klockars, Carl B. "Street Justice: Some Micro-moral Reservations: Comment on Sykes." *Justice Quarterly* 3, no. 4 (1986): 513–16. https://doi.org/10.1080/07418828600089091.

———. "A Theory of Excessive Force and Its Control." In *Police Violence: Understanding and Controlling Police Abuse of Force*, edited by William A. Geller and Hans Toch, 1–22. New Haven, CT: Yale University Press, 1996.

Knapp Commission. *Commission to Investigate Allegations of Police Corruption and the City's Anti-corruption Procedures: The Knapp Commission Report on Police Corruption*. New York: George Braziller, 1972.

Kohler-Hausmann, Issa. *Misdemeanorland: Criminal Courts and Social Control in an Age of Broken Windows Policing*. Princeton, NJ: Princeton University Press, 2018.

Kornhauser, Ruth. *Social Sources of Delinquency: An Appraisal of Analytic Models*. Chicago: University of Chicago Press, 1978.

Koslicki, Wendy M., David A. Makin, and Dale Willits. "When No One Is Watching: Evaluating the Impact of Body-Worn Cameras on Use of Force Incidents." *Policing and Society*, 2019, 1–14. https://doi.org/10.1080/10439463.2019.1576672.

Kraska, Peter B., and Victor E. Kappeler. "Militarizing American Police: The Rise and Normalization of Paramilitary Units." *Social Problems* 44, no. 1 (1997): 1–18. https://doi.org/10.2307/3096870.

Kubrin, Charis E., Thomas D. Stucky, and Marvin D. Krohn. *Researching Theories of Crime and Deviance*. New York: Oxford University Press, 2009.

Kunard, Laura, and Charlene Moe. *Procedural Justice for Law Enforcement: An Overview*. Washington, DC: US Department of Justice, Office of Community Oriented Policing Services, 2015.

Kurtz, Don L., Egbert Zavala, and Lisa A. Melander. "The Influence of Early Strain on Later Strain, Stress Responses, and Aggression by Police Officers." *Criminal Justice Review* 40, no. 2 (2015): 190–208. https://doi.org/10.1177/0734016814564696.

Kutnjak Ivkovic, Sanja. *Fallen Blue Knights: Controlling Police Corruption*. New York: Oxford University Press, 2005.

———. "To Serve and Collect: Measuring Police Corruption." *Journal of Criminal Law and Criminology* 93, nos. 2–3 (2003): 593–650.

LaFave, Wayne R. *Criminal Law*. 3rd ed. St. Paul, MN: West Group, 2000.

LaForgia, Michael. "Boynton Police Officer Allegedly Spouts Drunken Obscenities." *Palm Beach Post*, May 1, 2007.

Laguna, Louis, Ashley Linn, Kyle Ward, and Rasa Rupslaukyte. "An Examination of Authoritarian Personality Traits among Police Officers: The Role of Experience." *Journal of Police and Criminal Psychology* 25, no. 2 (2009): 99–104. https://doi.org/10.1007/s11896-009-9060-0.

Lamendola, Michael. "City Police Officer Innocent of Harassment in Domestic Dispute." *Daily Gazette*, June 24, 2008.

LaRenzie, Alyssa. "DeKalb Cop Arrested after Fight at Local McDonald's." *Forsyth News*, April 17, 2013.

LaRosa, Paul. *Tacoma Confidential*. New York: Signet, 2006.

Larson, Lynn D., John F. Schnelle, Robert Kirchner, Adam F. Carr, Michele Domash, and Todd R. Risley. "Reduction of Police Vehicle Accidents through Mechanically Aided Supervision." *Journal of Applied Behavior Analysis* 13, no. 4 (1980): 571–81. https://doi.org/10.1901/jaba.1980.13-571.

Laub, John H., and Robert J. Sampson. *Shared Beginnings, Divergent Lives: Delinquent Boys to Age 70*. Cambridge, MA: Harvard University Press, 2003.

———. "Turning Points in the Life Course: Why Change Matters to the Study of Crime." *Criminology* 31, no. 3 (1993): 301–25. https://doi.org/10.1111/j.1745-9125.1993.tb01132.x.

———. "Unraveling Families and Delinquency: A Reanalysis of the Glueck's Data." *Criminology* 26 (1988): 355–79. https://doi.org/10.1111/j.1745-9125.1988.tb00846.x.

Laub, John H., Robert J. Sampson, and Gary A. Sweeten. "Assessing Sampson and Laub's Life-Course Theory of Crime." In *Taking Stock: The Status of Criminological Theory*, edited by Francis T. Cullen, John Paul Wright, and Kristie R. Blevins, 313–33. Advances in Criminological Theory 15. New Brunswick, NJ: Transaction Publishers, 2008.

Lautenberg Amendment, Gun Ban for Individuals Convicted of a Misdemeanor Crime of Domestic Violence, Pub. L. No. 104–208, § 658, 18 U.S.C. § 922(g)(9) (1996).

Law Enforcement Officers Safety Act, Pub. L. No. 108–277, 18 U.S.C. § 926B (2004).

Leasure, Peter. "Neutralizations in Retail Banking: A Qualitative Analysis." *Deviant Behavior* 38, no. 4 (2017): 448–60. https://doi.org/10.1080/01639625.2016.1197018.

Lee, Anna. "Woman Sues Pickens PD, Officer in Laundromat Sex Assault." *Greenville News*. August 17, 2016.

Liederbach, John. "Controlling Suburban and Small-Town Hoods: An Examination of Police Encounters with Juveniles." *Youth Violence and Juvenile Justice* 5, no. 2 (2007): 107–24. https://doi.org/10.1177/1541204006295151.

Liederbach, John, and James Frank. "Policing Mayberry: The Work Routines of Small-Town and Rural Officers." *American Journal of Criminal Justice* 28, no. 1 (2003): 53–72. https://doi.org/10.1007/BF02885752.

———. "Policing the Big Beat: An Observational Study of County Level Patrol and Comparisons to Local Small Town and Rural Officers." *Journal of Crime and Justice* 29, no. 1 (2006): 21–44. https://doi.org/10.1080/0735648X.2006.9721216.

Liederbach, John, and Lawrence F. Travis. "Wilson Redux: Another Look at Varieties of Police Behavior." *Police Quarterly* 11, no. 4 (December 2008): 447–67. https://doi.org/10.1177/1098611108314567.

Lilly, J. Robert, Francis T. Cullen, and Richard A. Ball. *Criminological Theory: Context and Consequences.* 4th ed. Thousand Oaks, CA: Sage, 2007.

Lippman, Matthew Ross. *Contemporary Criminal Law: Concepts, Cases, and Controversies.* 5th ed. Thousand Oaks, CA: Sage, 2018.

Lowmaster, Sara E., and Leslie C. Morey. "Predicting Law Enforcement Officer Job Performance with the Personality Assessment Inventory." *Journal of Personality Assessment* 94, no. 3 (May 2012): 254–61. https://doi.org/10.1080/00223891.2011.648295.

Lundman, Richard J. *Police and Policing: An Introduction.* New York: Holt, Rinehart, and Winston, 1980.

Maguire, Edward R., and Stephen D. Mastrofski. "Patterns of Community Policing in the United States." *Police Quarterly* 3, no. 1 (2000): 4–45. https://doi.org/10.1177/1098611100003001001.

Maguire, Edward R., and Craig D. Uchida. "Measurement and Explanation in the Comparative Study of American Police Organizations." In *Measurement and Analysis of Crime and Justice*, 491–557. NCJ No. 182411. Washington, DC: US Department of Justice, National Institute of Justice, 2000. www.ncjrs.gov/criminal_justice2000/vol4/04j.pdf.

Manning, Peter K. "Lying, Secrecy and Social Control." In *Policing: A View from the Street*, edited by Peter K. Manning and John Van Maanen, 238–55. Santa Monica, CA: Goodyear, 1978.

Martin, John Levi. "The Authoritarian Personality, 50 Years Later: What Questions Are There for Political Psychology?" *Political Psychology* 22, no. 1 (2001): 1–26. https://doi.org/10.1111/0162-895X.00223.

Martin, Susan E. "Policing Career Criminals: An Examination of an Innovative Crime Control Program." *Journal of Criminal Law and Criminology* 77, no. 4 (1986): 1159–82. https://doi.org/10.2307/1143672.

Martin, Susan E., and Lawrence W. Sherman. "Catching Career Criminals: Proactive Policing and Selective Apprehension." *Justice Quarterly* 3, no. 2 (1986): 171–92. https://doi.org/10.1080/07418828600088881.

Martinez, Michael. "Officer Evaluations Are Based in Part on Their Ticket Totals." *Washington Post*, April 12, 1984.

Martinussen, Monica, Astrid M. Richardsen, and Ronald J. Burke. "Job Demands, Job Resources, and Burnout among Police Officers." *Journal of Criminal Justice* 35, no. 3 (2007): 239–49. https://doi.org/10.1016/j.jcrimjus.2007.03.001.

Maslach, Christina, and Susan E. Jackson. "The Measurement of Experienced Burnout." *Journal of Organizational Behavior* 2, no. 2 (1981): 99–113. https://doi.org/10.1002/job.4030020205.

Mastrofski, Stephen D., David Weisburd, and Anthony A. Braga. "Rethinking Policing: The Policy Implications of Hot Spots of Crime." In *Contemporary Issues in Criminal Justice Policy: Policy Proposals from the American Society of Criminology Conference*, edited by Natasha A. Frost, Joshua D. Freilich, and Todd R. Clear, 251–64. Belmont, CA: Wadsworth Cengage, 2010.

Mathias, Christopher. "NYC to Pay $280,000 over Cop Who Exposed City's Quota System." *Huffington Post*, December 7, 2015.

Matthews v. City of New York, et al., 779 F.3d 167 (2nd. Cir. 2015).

Mazerolle, Lorraine, Sarah Bennett, Jacqueline Davis, Elise Sargeant, and Matthew Manning. "Legitimacy in Policing: A Systematic Review." *Campbell Systematic Reviews* 2013, no. 1 (2013): 1–146. https://doi.org/10.4073/csr.2013.1.

McCarthy, Craig. "Ex-cop's 'Nightmarish Storyline' Deserves 20 Years in Prison, Judge Says." *NJ.com*, September 7, 2017.

Menzies, Ken. "State Crime by the Police and Its Control." In *Controlling State Crime*, edited by Jeffrey Ian Ross, 2nd ed., 141–62. New Brunswick, NJ: Transaction, 2000.

Merkel, Jim. "County Officer Charged with Pulling Gun." *South Side Journal*, April 3, 2008.

Merton, Robert K. "Social Structure and Anomie." *American Sociological Review* 3, no. 5 (1938): 672–82.

Messner, Steven, and Richard Rosenfeld. *Crime and the American Dream*. 4th ed. Belmont, CA: Thomson/Wadsworth, 2007.

Meyer, Ed. "Former Police Officers Get Probation: Two Men Plead Guilty to Assault at Blossom." *Akron Beacon Journal*, December 21, 2005.

Miller, Donna J. "State Trooper Accused of Drunken, Disorderly Conduct Destroys Holding Cell at Browns Stadium." *Cleveland.com*, January 4, 2011.

Miranda v. Arizona, 384 U.S. 436 (1966).

Mitchell, Jeffrey T. "When Disaster Strikes: The Critical Incident Stress Debriefing Process." *Journal of Emergency Medical Services* 8, no. 1 (1983): 36–39.

Moffitt, Terrie E. "Adolescent-Limited and Life-Course Persistent Antisocial Behavior: A Developmental Taxonomy." *Psychological Review* 100, no. 4 (1993): 674–701. https://doi.org/10.1037/0033-295X.100.4.674.

Moffitt, Terrie, Avshalom Caspi, Michael Rutter, and Phil A. Silva. *Sex Differences in Antisocial Behaviour: Conduct Disorder, Delinquency, and Violence in the Dunedin Longitudinal Study*. New York: Cambridge University Press, 2001.

Moffitt, Terrie E., Robert F. Krueger, Avshalom Caspi, and Jeff Fagan. "Partner Abuse and General Crime: How Are They the Same? How Are They Different?" *Criminology* 38, no. 1 (2000): 199–232. https://doi.org/10.1111/j.1745-9125.2000.tb00888.x.

Mollen Commission. *Commission to Investigate Allegations of Police Corruption and the Anti-corruption Procedures of the Police Department: Commission Report; Anatomy of Failure, a Path for Success*. New York: City of New York, 1994.

Monell v. Department of Social Services, 436 U.S. 658 (1978).

Monroe v. Pape, 365 U.S. 167 (1961).

Mulford, Carrie F., Ronald E. Wilson, and Angela Moore Parmley. "Geographic Aspects of Sex Offender Residency Restrictions: Policy and Research." *Criminal Justice Policy Review* 20, no. 1 (2009): 3–12. https://doi.org/10.1177/0887403408327683.

Mullins, Wayman C., and Michael J. McMains. "Impact of Traumatic Stress on Domestic Violence in Policing." In *Domestic Violence by Police Officers: A Compilation of Papers Submitted to the Domestic Violence by Police Officers Conference at the FBI Academy, Quantico, VA*, 257–68. Washington, DC: US Government Printing Office, 2000.

Murphy, Sean. "Ex-Oklahoma City Police Officer Convicted of Rape; Victimized Black Women on Beat." *Washington Times*, December 10, 2015.

National Advisory Commission on Criminal Justice Standards and Goals. *Task Force Report on Police*. Washington, DC: US Government Printing Office, 1973.

Neidig, Peter H., Harold E. Russell, and Albert F. Seng. "Interspousal Aggression in Law Enforcement Families: A Preliminary Investigation." *Police Studies: The International Review of Police Development* 15, no. 1 (1992): 30–38.

Nelson, Jill, ed. *Police Brutality: An Anthology*. New York: W. W. Norton, 2000.

Nelson, Paul. "Schenectady Cop Fired in 2010 Dies." *Times Union*, February 20, 2014.

New Hampshire Police Standards and Training Council. "Full-Time Police Officer Academy." 2015. https://www.pstc.nh.gov/academy.htm.

Niederhoffer, Arthur. *Behind the Shield: The Police in Urban Society*. Garden City, NY: Anchor Books, 1967.

Nix, Justin, Scott E. Wolfe, and Bradley A. Campbell. "Command-Level Police Officers' Perceptions of the 'War on Cops' and De-policing." *Justice Quarterly* 35, no. 1 (2018): 33–54. https://doi.org/10.1080/07418825.2017.1338743.

Nye, F. Ivan. *Family Relationships and Delinquent Behavior*. New York: Wiley, 1958.

Oglesby, T. "Use of Emotional Screening in the Selection of Police Applicants." *Public Personnel Review* 18 (1957): 228–31, 235.

Oliver, Willard M. *August Vollmer: The Father of American Policing*. Durham, NC: Carolina Academic Press, 2017.

———. *Depolicing: When Police Officers Disengage*. Boulder, CO: Lynne Rienner, 2019.

Packer, Herbert L. *The Limits of the Criminal Sanction*. Stanford, CA: Stanford University Press, 1968.

Panzarella, Robert, and Joanna Funk. "Police Deception Tactics and Public Consent in the United States and Great Britain." *Criminal Justice Policy Review* 2, no. 2 (1987): 133–49. https://doi.org/10.1177/088740348700200203.

Paoline, Eugene A., and William Terrill. "Police Education, Experience, and the Use of Force." *Criminal Justice and Behavior* 34, no. 2 (2007): 179–96. https://doi.org/10.1177/0093854806290239.

Park, Robert E., Ernest W. Burgess, and Roderick D. McKenzie. *The City*. Chicago: University of Chicago Press, 1925.

Parks, Roger B., Stephen D. Mastrofski, Christina DeJong, and M. Kevin Gray. "How Officers Spend Their Time with the Community." *Justice Quarterly* 16, no. 3 (1999): 483–518. https://doi.org/10.1080/07418829900094241.

Paternoster, Raymond. "The Deterrent Effect of the Perceived Certainty and Severity of Punishment: A Review of the Evidence and Issues." *Justice Quarterly* 42, no. 2 (1987): 173–217. https://doi.org/10.1080/07418828700089271.

Paternoster, Raymond, Robert Brame, and David P. Farrington. "On the Relationship between Adolescent and Adult Conviction Frequencies." *Journal of Quantitative Criminology* 17, no. 3 (2001): 201–25. https://doi.org/10.1023/A:1011007016387.

Paternoster, Raymond, and Alex R. Piquero. "Reconceptualizing Deterrence: An Empirical Test of Personal and Vicarious Experiences." *Journal of Research in Crime and Delinquency* 32, no. 3 (1995): 251–86. https://doi.org/10.1177/0022427895032003001.

Payne, Brian K. *White-Collar Crime: The Essentials.* Thousand Oaks, CA: Sage, 2013.

Payne, Brian K., Bruce L. Berg, and Ivan Y. Sun. "Policing in Small Town America: Dogs, Drunks, Disorder, and Dysfunction." *Journal of Criminal Justice* 33, no. 1 (2005): 31–41. https://doi.org/10.1016/j.jcrimjus.2004.10.006.

Payton, George T. *Patrol Procedure.* Los Angeles: Legal Book, 1966.

Pearce, Matt. "Timeline: The Rise and Fall of Arizona Sheriff Joe Arpaio." *Los Angeles Times,* August 1, 2017.

Pepinsky, Harold E. "Better Living through Police Discretion." *Law and Contemporary Problems* 47, no. 4 (1984): 249–67. https://doi.org/10.2307/1191692.

Perry, Kimball. "Cop Admits Promoting Prostitution, Misusing Database." *Cincinnati Enquirer,* January 9, 2014.

———. "Crooked Cop Helped Suspected Robbers." *Cincinnati Enquirer,* April 1, 2014.

Petersilia, Joan. "Keynote Address: Looking Back to See the Future of Prison Downsizing in America." Presented at the National Institute of Justice Conference, Arlington, VA, June 19, 2012. https://www.hsdl.org/?view&did=721626.

Pew Research Center. "Demographics of Mobile Device Ownership and Adoption in the United States." Pew Research Center: Internet and Technology, February 5, 2018. www.pewinternet.org/fact-sheet/mobile.

Phillips, Scott W. "Police Discretion and Boredom: What Officers Do When There Is Nothing to Do." *Journal of Contemporary Ethnography* 45, no. 5 (2016): 580–601. https://doi.org/10.1177/0891241615587385.

Phippen, J. Weston. "One Day in 1970 That Changed Policing in the U.S." *Atlantic,* July 15, 2016.

Piquero, Alex R., Robert Brame, and Terrie E. Moffitt. "Extending the Study of Continuity and Change: Gender Differences in the Linkage Between Adolescent and Adult Offending." *Journal of Quantitative Criminology* 21, no. 2 (2005): 219–43. https://doi.org/10.1007/s10940-005-2494-3.

Piquero, Alex R., and Matthew J. Hickman. "An Empirical Test of Tittle's Control Balance Theory." *Criminology* 37, no. 2 (1999): 319–40. https://doi.org/10.1111 /j.1745–9125.1999.tb00488.x.

Piquero, Nicole Leeper, and Alex R. Piquero. "Control Balance and Exploitative Corporate Crime." *Criminology* 44, no. 2 (2006): 397–430. https://doi.org/10 .1111/j.1745–9125.2006.00053.x.

Pollak, Jessica M., and Charis E. Kubrin. "Crime in the News: How Crimes, Offenders and Victims Are Portrayed in the Media." *Journal of Criminal Justice and Popular Culture* 14, no. 1 (2007): 59–83.

Pool, Bob. "The Ambush Killings of 4 CHP Officers That Changed California Policing in 1970." *Los Angeles Times*, July 9, 2016.

Pratt, Travis C., and Jillian J. Turanovic. "Lifestyle and Routine Activity Theories Revisited: The Importance of 'Risk' to the Study of Victimization." *Victims and Offenders* 11, no. 3 (2016): 335–54. https://doi.org/10.1080/15564886.2015.1057351.

President's Commission on Law Enforcement and Administration of Justice. *The Challenge of Crime in a Free Society: A Report.* Washington, DC: US Government Printing Office, 1967.

President's Task Force on 21st Century Policing. *Final Report of the President's Task Force on 21st Century Policing.* Washington, DC: US Department of Justice, Office of Community Oriented Policing Services, 2015. https://www.ncjrs.gov /App/Publications/Abstract.aspx?ID=271066.

Puente, Mark. "Some Baltimore Police Officers Face Repeated Misconduct Lawsuits." *Baltimore Sun*, October 4, 2014.

Punch, Maurice. "Police Corruption and Its Prevention." *European Journal on Criminal Policy and Research* 8, no. 3 (2000): 301–24. https://doi.org/10.1023 /A:1008777013115.

Pyrooz, David C., Scott H. Decker, Scott E. Wolfe, and John A. Shjarback. "Was There a Ferguson Effect on Crime Rates in Large U.S. Cities?" *Journal of Criminal Justice* 46 (2016): 1–8. https://doi.org/10.1016/j.jcrimjus.2016.01.001.

Queiros, Cristina, Mariana Kaiseler, and Antonio Leitao Da Silva. "Burnout as a Predictor of Aggressivity among Police Officers." *European Journal of Police Studies* 1, no. 2 (2013): 110–35.

Quinn, Mary Joy, and Susan K. Tomita. *Elder Abuse and Neglect: Causes, Diagnosis, and Intervention Strategies.* New York: Springer, 1997.

Quinney, Richard. *Class, State, and Crime: On the Theory and Practice of Criminal Justice.* New York: Longman, 1978.

———. *The Social Reality of Crime.* Boston: Little Brown, 1970.

Rabe-Hemp, Cara E., and Jeremy Braithwaite. "An Exploration of Recidivism and the Officer Shuffle in Police Sexual Violence." *Police Quarterly* 16, no. 2 (2013): 127–47. https://doi.org/10.1177/1098611112464964.

Radnofsky, Louise, Zusha Elinson, John R. Emshwiller, and Gary Fields. "Why Some Problem Cops Don't Lose Their Badges." *Wall Street Journal*, December 30, 2016.

Rafky, David M. "Police Cynicism Reconsidered: An Application of Smallest Space Analysis." *Criminology* 13, no. 2 (1975): 168–92. https://doi.org/10.1111/j.1745-9125.1975.tb00664.x.

Rahr, Sue, and Stephen K. Rice. *From Warriors to Guardians: Recommitting American Police Culture to Democratic Ideals.* New Perspectives in Policing Bulletin. NCJ 248654. Washington, DC: US Department of Justice, National Institute of Justice, 2015.

Rankin, Bill. "Ex-officer Avoids Murder Charge." *Atlanta Journal Constitution*, April 2, 2011.

Rayburn, Michael T. "Shooting Outside of the Box." *Police Magazine*, October 2009.

Ready, Justin, Michael D. White, and Christopher Fisher. "Shock Value: A Comparative Analysis of News Reports and Official Records on TASER Deployments." *Policing: An International Journal of Police Strategies and Management* 31, no. 1 (2008): 148–70. https://doi.org/10.1108/13639510810852620.

Reckless, Walter C. "A New Theory of Delinquency and Crime." *Federal Probation* 25 (1961): 42–46.

Redmond, Lisa. "New Trial Date for Lowell Officer in Rape Case." *Lowell Sun*, November 8, 2012.

Regoli, Robert, Robert G. Culbertson, John P. Crank, and James R. Powell. "Career Stage and Cynicism among Police Chiefs." *Justice Quarterly* 7, no. 3 (1990): 593–614. https://doi.org/10.1080/07418829000090741.

Reiss, Albert J. "Delinquency as the Failure of Personal and Social Controls." *American Sociological Review* 16, no. 2 (1951): 196–207.

———. *The Police and the Public.* New Haven, CT: Yale University Press, 1971.

———. "Police Brutality—Answers to Key Questions." *Trans-Action* 5, no. 8 (1968): 10–19. https://doi.org/10.1007/BF02804717.

———. "Systematic Observation of Natural Social Phenomena." *Sociological Methodology* 3 (1971): 3–33.

———. "Unraveling Juvenile Delinquency: II. An Appraisal of the Research Methods." *American Journal of Sociology* 57, no. 2 (1951): 115–20. https://doi.org/10.1086/220911.

———. "Why Are Communities Important in Understanding Crime?" In *Communities and Crime*, 8:1–33. Crime and Justice. Chicago: University of Chicago Press, 1986. www.jstor.org/stable/1147423.

Reynald, Danielle M. "Informal Guardians and Offender Decision Making." In *The Oxford Handbook of Offender Decision Making*, 361–72. Oxford Handbooks in Criminology and Criminal Justice 6. New York: Oxford University Press, 2017.

Rhodes, Dusty. "Perversion of Justice." *Illinois Times*, August 14, 2008.

Ritchie, Andrea J. *Invisible No More: Police Violence against Black Women and Women of Color.* Boston: Beacon Press, 2017.

Robinson, Sean. "The Brame Files." *Tacoma News Tribune*, October 23, 2005.

Rose, Sontaya. "Ex-deputy William Nulick to Stand Trial for Sexual Assault." *ABC30.com*, May 29, 2014.

Rosecrance, John. "Adapting to Failure: The Case of Horse Race Gamblers." *Journal of Gambling Studies* 2, no. 2 (1986): 81–94. https://doi.org/10.1007/BF01019627.

Ross, Jeffrey Ian. "Controlling State Crime: Toward an Integrated Structural Model." In *Controlling State Crime*, edited by Jeffrey Ian Ross, 2nd ed., 3–33. New Brunswick, NJ: Transaction, 2000.

———. *Making News of Police Violence: A Comparative Study of Toronto and New York City*. Westport, CT: Praeger, 2000.

———. *Policing Issues: Challenges and Controversies*. Sudbury, MA: Jones & Bartlett Learning, 2012.

Sampson, Robert J. *Great American City: Chicago and the Enduring Neighborhood Effect*. Chicago: University of Chicago Press, 2012.

Sampson, Robert J., and John H. Laub. *Crime in the Making: Pathways and Turning Points through Life*. Cambridge, MA: Harvard University Press, 1993.

Samuels, Tanyainka, Tony Scalafani, and Robert F. Moore. "Make a (Death) Wish! Cop Accused of Threatening Wife at His Birthday Bash." *New York Daily News*, November 23, 2005.

Sanders, Beth A. "Using Personality Traits to Predict Police Officer Performance." *Policing: An International Journal of Police Strategies and Management* 31, no. 1 (2008): 129–47. https://doi.org/10.1108/13639510810852611.

Saucier v. Katz, 533 U.S. 194 (2001).

Schaible, Lonnie M., Joseph De Angelis, Brian Wolf, and Richard Rosenthal. "Denver's Citizen/Police Complaint Mediation Program: Officer and Complainant Satisfaction." *Criminal Justice Policy Review* 24, no. 5 (2013): 626–50. https://doi.org/10.1177/0887403412455327.

Scharr, Cindy. "Marcus Hook Cop Allegedly Strikes Wrestling Coach." *Delaware County Times*, February 4, 2007.

Schenectady Mayor's Office. "Stratton Fires Police Officer John Lewis." Press release, April 12, 2010.

Schladebeck, Jessica. "Former Minneapolis Officer Charged with Fatally Shooting Australian Woman Sparked Concern from Psychiatrists, Training Officers." *New York Daily News*, September 6, 2018.

Schraer, Mark. "Setting the Record Straight on the Newhall Incident." *PoliceOne News*, May 9, 2012.

Schwab, Kyle. "Jurors View Video of Accused Former OKC Police Officer's Interrogation." *Oklahoman*, November 5, 2015.

Schwartz, Adina. "Just Take Away Their Guns: The Hidden Racism of Terry v. Ohio." *Fordham Urban Law Review* 23, no. 2 (1996): 317–75.

Schwartz, Martin A., and Kathryn R. Urbonya. *Section 1983 Litigation*. 2nd ed. Washington, DC: Federal Judicial Center, 2008.

Scott, Dylan. "Exclusive: New Data Show Police Rarely Arrested for Killings on the Job." *Talking Points Memo*, August 20, 2014.

Sellbom, Martin, Gary L Fischler, and Yossef S. Ben-Porath. "Identifying MMPI-2 Predictors of Police Officer Integrity and Misconduct." *Criminal Justice and Behavior* 34, no. 8 (2007): 985–1004. https://doi.org/10.1177/0093854807301224.

Sellin, Thorsten. *The Death Penalty: A Report for the Model Penal Code Project of the American Law Institute*. Philadelphia: American Law Institute, 1959.

Seltzer, Richard, Sucre Alonè, and Gwendolyn Howard. "Police Satisfaction with Their Jobs: Arresting Officers in the District of Columbia." *Police Studies* 19, no. 4 (1996): 25–37. https://doi.org/10.1108/13639519610151865.

Shakespeare, William. *The Taming of the Shrew*. New York: Signet, 1998.

Sharps, Michael J. *Processing under Pressure: Stress, Memory and Decision-Making in Law Enforcement*. Flushing, NY: Looseleaf Law Publications, 2010.

Shaw, Clifford R., and Henry D. McKay. *Juvenile Delinquency and Urban Areas: A Study of Rates of Delinquency in Relation to Differential Characteristics of Local Communities in American Cities*. Revised. Chicago: University of Chicago Press, 1969.

Sherman, Lawrence W. "Causes of Police Behavior: The Current State of Quantitative Research." *Journal of Research in Crime and Delinquency* 17, no. 1 (1980): 69–100. https://doi.org/10.1177/002242788001700106.

———. "The Police." In *Crime*, edited by James Q. Wilson and Joan Petersilia, 327–48. San Francisco: ICS Press, 1995.

———. *Police Corruption: A Sociological Perspective*. Garden City, NY: Anchor Books, 1974.

Sherman, Lawrence W., Patrick R. Gartin, and Michael E. Buerger. "Hot Spots of Predatory Crime: Routine Activities and the Criminology of Place." *Criminology* 27, no. 1 (1989): 27–56. https://doi.org/10.1111/j.1745-9125.1989.tb00862.x.

Sherman, Lawrence W., and Robert H. Langworthy. "Measuring Homicide by Police Officers." *Journal of Criminal Law and Criminology* 70, no. 4 (1979): 546–60. https://doi.org/10.2307/1142641.

Sherman, Lawrence W., and Dennis P. Rogan. "Effects of Gun Seizures on Gun Violence: 'Hot Spots' Patrol in Kansas City." *Justice Quarterly* 12, no. 4 (1995): 673–93. https://doi.org/10.1080/07418829500096241.

Shjarback, John A., David C. Pyrooz, Scott E. Wolfe, and Scott H. Decker. "Depolicing and Crime in the Wake of Ferguson: Racialized Changes in the Quantity and Quality of Policing among Missouri Police Departments." *Journal of Criminal Justice* 50 (2017): 42–52. https://doi.org/10.1016/j.jcrimjus.2017.04.003.

Siacon, Alenna. "Police: Off-Duty Officer Arrested after Altercation with Girlfriend Involved Gun." *Detroit Free Press*, April 22, 2018.

Silva, Phil A., and Warren R. Stanton, eds. *From Child to Adult: The Dunedin Multidisciplinary Health and Development Study*. Auckland: Oxford University Press, 1996.

Silver, Isidore. *Police Civil Liability*. New York: Matthew Bender, 2010.

Silverstein, Jason. "Oklahoma City Police Ignored Early Sexual Assault Complaint about Officer Daniel Holtzclaw, Lawsuit Says." *New York Daily News*, March 8, 2016.

Simons, Randy. "Schenectady Police Officer John Lewis Acquitted on Three Counts." *CBS6Albany.com*, February 17, 2010.

Skogan, Wesley, and Kathleen Frydl. *Fairness and Effectiveness in Policing: The Evidence*. Washington, DC: National Academies Press, 2004.

Skolnick, Jerome H. *Justice without Trial: Law Enforcement in Democratic Society.* New York: Macmillan, 1994.

Skolnick, Jerome H., and James J. Fyfe. *Above the Law: Police and the Excessive Use of Force.* New York: Free Press, 1993.

Smith, Aaron. "Record Shares of Americans Now Own Smartphones." Pew Research Center, January 12, 2017. www.pewresearch.org/fact-tank/2017/01/12/evolution-of-technology.

Smith, Brad W., Kenneth J. Novak, and James Frank. "Community Policing and the Work Routines of Street-Level Officers." *Criminal Justice Review* 26, no. 1 (2001): 17–37. https://doi.org/10.1177/073401680102600103.

Smith, Douglas A. "The Neighborhood Context of Police Behavior." In *Communities and Crime*, 8:313–41. Crime and Justice. Chicago: University of Chicago Press, 1986. www.jstor.org/stable/1147431.

Stafford, Mark C., and Mark Warr. "A Reconceptualization of General and Specific Deterrence." *Journal of Research in Crime and Delinquency* 30, no. 2 (1993): 123–35. https://doi.org/10.1177/0022427893030002001.

State v. Thompson. 702 S.E.2d 198 (Ga. 2010).

Stinson, Philip M. "The Henry A. Wallace Police Crime Database." Bowling Green State University, 2019. https://policecrime.bgsu.edu.

———. *The Impact of Police Crime on LGBTQ+ People.* Criminal Justice Faculty Publications. Bowling Green, OH: Bowling Green State University, 2016. https://scholarworks.bgsu.edu/crim_just_pub/70.

———. "Police Crime: A Newsmaking Criminology Study of Sworn Law Enforcement Officers Arrested, 2005–2007." PhD dissertation, Indiana University of Pennsylvania, 2009. https://knowledge.library.iup.edu/etd/709.

Stinson, Philip M., and Steven L. Brewer. "Federal Civil Rights Litigation Pursuant to 42 U.S.C. § 1983 as a Correlate of Police Crime." *Criminal Justice Policy Review*, 2016. https://doi.org/10.1177/0887403416664115.

Stinson, Philip M., Steven L. Brewer, Brooke E. Mathna, John Liederbach, and Christine M. Englebrecht. "Police Sexual Misconduct: Arrested Officers and Their Victims." *Victims and Offenders* 10 (2014): 117–51. https://doi.org/10.1080/15564886.2014.939798.

Stinson, Philip M., Jennifer L. Huck, and Jason D. Spraitz. "A Content Analysis of Criminal Justice Policy Review, 1986–2008." *Criminal Justice Policy Review* 21, no. 2 (2010): 239–60. https://doi.org/10.1177/0887403409353165.

Stinson, Philip M., and John Liederbach. "Fox in the Henhouse: A Study of Police Officers Arrested for Crimes Associated with Domestic and/or Family Violence." *Criminal Justice Policy Review* 24 (2013): 601–25. https://doi.org/10.1177/0887403412453837.

Stinson, Philip M., John Liederbach, Steven L. Brewer, and Brooke E. Mathna. "Police Sexual Misconduct: A National Scale Study of Arrested Officers." *Criminal Justice Policy Review* 26 (2014): 665–90. https://doi.org/10.1177/0887403414526231.

Stinson, Philip M., John Liederbach, Steven L. Brewer, Hans D. Schmalzried, Brooke E. Mathna, and Krista L. Long. "A Study of Drug-Related Police Corruption Arrests." *Policing: An International Journal of Police Strategies and Management* 36, no. 3 (2013): 491–511. https://doi.org/10.1108/PIJPSM-06-2012-0051.

Stinson, Philip M., John Liederbach, Steven L. Brewer, and Natalie Erin Todak. "Drink, Drive, Go to Jail? A Study of Police Officers Arrested for Drunk Driving." *Journal of Crime and Justice* 37, no. 3 (2014): 356–76. https://doi.org/10.1080/0735648X.2013.805158.

Stinson, Philip M., John Liederbach, Michael Buerger, and Steven L. Brewer. "To Protect and Collect: A Nationwide Study of Profit-Motivated Police Crime." *Criminal Justice Studies* 31, no. 3 (2018): 310–31. https://doi.org/10.1080/1478601X.2018.1492919.

Stinson, Philip M., John Liederbach, and Tina L. Freiburger. "Exit Strategy: An Exploration of Late-Stage Police Crime." *Police Quarterly* 13, no. 4 (2010): 413–35. https://doi.org/10.1177/1098611110384086.

Stinson, Philip M., John Liederbach, Steven P. Lab, and Steven L. Brewer. *Police Integrity Lost: A Study of Law Enforcement Officers Arrested.* Washington, DC: US Department of Justice, Office of Justice Programs, National Institute of Justice, 2016. https://www.ncjrs.gov/App/publications/abstract.aspx?ID=272010.

Stinson, Philip M., Bradford W. Reyns, and John Liederbach. "Police Crime and Less-than-Lethal Coercive Force: A Description of the Criminal Misuse of TASERs." *International Journal of Police Science and Management* 14, no. 1 (2012): 1–19. https://doi.org/10.1350/ijps.2012.14.1.237.

Stinson, Philip M., Natalie Erin Todak, and Mary Dodge. "An Exploration of Crime by Policewomen." *Police Practice and Research* 16, no. 1 (2015): 79–93. https://doi.org/10.1080/15614263.2013.846222.

Stinson, Philip M., and Adam M. Watkins. "The Nature of Crime by School Resource Officers: Implications for SRO Programs." *Sage Open* 4, no. 1 (2014): 1–10. https://doi.org/10.1177/2158244014521821.

Stinson, Philip M., Chloe A. Wentzlof, and Megan L. Swinehart. "On-Duty Police Shootings: Officers Charged with Murder or Manslaughter 2005–2018." *BGSU Criminal Justice Faculty Publications* 98 (2019). https://scholarworks.bgsu.edu/crim_just_pub/98.

Stoddard, Ellwyn R. "The Informal Code of Police Deviancy: A Group Approach to Blue-Coat Crime." *Journal of Criminal Law, Criminology and Police Science* 59, no. 2 (1968): 201–13. https://doi.org/10.2307/1141940.

Stokols, Daniel. *Social Ecology in the Digital Age: Solving Complex Problems in a Globalized World.* London: Academic Press, 2018.

Strong, Jared. "Police Chief Was Slow to Address 'Problem Officer.'" *Daily Times Herald*, May 25, 2018.

Sullivan, John, Zane Anthony, Julie Tate, and Jennifer Jenkins. "Nationwide, Police Shot and Killed Nearly 1,000 People in 2017." *Washington Post*, January 5, 2018.

Sullivan, Joseph F. "New Jersey Police Are Accused of Minority Arrest Campaign." *New York Times*, February 19, 1990.

Sunshine, Jason, and Tom R. Tyler. "The Role of Procedural Justice and Legitimacy in Shaping Public Support for Policing." *Law and Society Review* 37, no. 3 (2003): 513–48. https://doi.org/10.1111/1540-5893.3703002.

Sutherland, Edwin H. *Principles of Criminology*. 4th ed. Chicago: J. B. Lippincott, 1947.

Swatt, Marc L., Chris L. Gibson, and Nicole Leeper Piquero. "Exploring the Utility of General Strain Theory in Explaining Problematic Alcohol Consumption by Police Officers." *Journal of Criminal Justice* 35 (2007): 596–611. https://doi.org/10.1016/j.jcrimjus.2007.09.005.

Sykes, Gary W. "Street Justice: A Moral Defense of Order Maintenance Policing." *Justice Quarterly* 3, no. 4 (1986): 497–512. https://doi.org/10.1080/07418828600089081.

Sykes, Gresham M., and David Matza. "Techniques of Neutralization: A Theory of Delinquency." *American Sociological Review* 22, no. 6 (1957): 664–70. https://doi.org/10.2307/2089195.

Tarescavage, Anthony M., David M. Corey, and Yossef S. Ben-Porath. "Minnesota Multiphasic Personality Inventory–2–Restructured Form (MMPI-2-RF) Predictors of Police Officer Problem Behavior." *Assessment* 22, no. 1 (2015): 116–32. https://doi.org/10.1177/1073191114534885.

Taylor, Ralph. *Breaking Away from Broken Windows: Baltimore Neighborhoods and the Nationwide Fight against Crime, Grime, Fear, and Decline*. Boulder, CO: Westview Press, 2001.

Tennessee v. Garner, 471 U.S. 1 (1985).

Tepper, Rachel. "Arlington County Police Denies Quota System, Rescinds Memo." *Huffington Post*, March 20, 2012.

Terman, Lewis M., Arthur S. Otis, Virgil Dickson, O. S. Hubbard, J. K. Norton, Lowry Howard, J. K. Flanders, and C. C. Cassingham. "A Trial of Mental and Pedagogical Tests in a Civil Service Examination for Policemen and Firemen." *Journal of Applied Psychology* 1, no. 1 (1917): 17–29. https://doi.org/10.1037/h0073841.

Terrill, William. "Police Use of Force and Suspect Resistance: The Micro Process of the Police-Suspect Encounter." *Police Quarterly* 6, no. 1 (2003): 51–83. https://doi.org/10.1177/1098611102250584.

Terry v. Ohio, 392 U.S. 1 (1968).

Tittle, Charles R. *Control Balance: Toward a General Theory of Deviance*. Boulder, CO: Westview Press, 1995.

———. "Crime Rates and Legal Sanctions." *Social Problems* 16, no. 4 (1969): 409–23. https://doi.org/10.2307/799950.

———. "Refining Control Balance Theory." *Theoretical Criminology* 8, no. 4 (2004): 395–428. https://doi.org/10.1177/1362480604046657.

Toch, Hans. *Stress in Policing*. Washington, DC: American Psychological Association, 2002.

Tyler, Tom R., and Jeffrey Fagan. "Legitimacy and Cooperation: Why Do People Help the Police Fight Crime in Their Communities?" *Ohio State Journal of Criminal Justice* 6, no. 1 (2008): 231–75.

Tyler, Tom R., and Yuen J. Huo. *Trust in the Law: Encouraging Public Cooperation with the Police and Courts.* New York: Russell Sage Foundation, 2002.

Tyler, Tom R., and Cheryl J. Wakslak. "Profiling and Police Legitimacy: Procedural Justice, Attributions of Motive, and Acceptance of Police Authority." *Criminology* 42, no. 2 (2004): 253–82. https://doi.org/10.1111/j.1745–9125.2004.tb00520.x.

United States v. Hayes, 555 U.S. 415 (2009).

US Commission on Civil Rights. *Revisiting "Who Is Guarding the Guardians?": A Report on Police Practices and Civil Rights in America.* Washington, DC: US Commission on Civil Rights, 2000. http://permanent.access.gpo.gov/lps13614 /www.usccr.gov/pubs/guard/main.htm.

———. *Who Is Guarding the Guardians? A Report on Police Practices.* Washington, DC: US Commission on Civil Rights, 1981.

US Department of Justice. *Census of State and Local Enforcement Agencies (CSL-LEA), 2008: ICPSR27681-v1 Data Set.* Ann Arbor, MI: Interuniversity Consortium for Political and Social Research, 2008. https://doi.org/10.3886 /ICPSR27681.v1.

———. *Principles for Promoting Police Integrity: Examples of Promising Police Practices and Policies.* Washington, DC: US Department of Justice, 2001.

US Department of Justice, Civil Rights Division. *Investigation of the Ferguson Police Department.* Washington, DC: US Department of Justice, Civil Rights Division, March 4, 2015. https://www.justice.gov/sites/default/files/opa/press-releases /attachments/2015/03/04/ferguson_police_department_report_1.pdf.

Van Cleve, Nicole Gonzalez. *Crook County: Racism and Injustice in America's Largest Criminal Court.* Stanford, CA: Stanford Law Books, 2016.

Van Derbeken, Jaxon. "Ex-Fremont Cop Guilty of Post-concert Assault." *San Francisco Chronicle*, April 8, 2009.

Van Maanen, John. "The Asshole." In *Policing: A View from the Street*, edited by Peter K. Manning and John Van Maanen, 221–38. Santa Monica, CA: Goodyear, 1978.

———. "Observations on the Making of Policemen." *Human Organization* 32 (1973): 407–18. https://doi.org/10.17730/humo.32.4.13h7x81187mh8km8.

———. *Tales of the Field: On Writing Ethnography.* Chicago Guides to Writing, Editing, and Publishing. Chicago: University of Chicago Press, 1988.

———. *Working the Street: A Developmental View of Police Behavior.* MIT Working Paper No. 681–73. Cambridge: Massachusetts Institute of Technology, 1973. https://dspace.mit.edu/handle/1721.1/1873.

Van Ness, Daniel, and Karen Heetderks Strong. *Restoring Justice.* 2nd ed. Cincinnati, OH: Anderson, 2002.

Vaughn, Michael S. "Parameters of Trickery as an Acceptable Police Practice." *American Journal of Police* 11, no. 4 (1992): 71–96.

Vila, Bryan. "Tired Cops: Probable Connections between Fatigue and the Performance, Health and Safety of Patrol Officers." *American Journal of Police* 15, no. 2 (1996): 51–92. https://doi.org/10.1108/07358549610122485.

Vila, Bryan, Gregory B. Morrison, and Dennis J. Kenney. "Improving Shift Schedule and Work-Hour Policies and Practices to Increase Police Officer Performance, Health, and Safety." *Police Quarterly* 5, no. 1 (2002): 4–24. https://doi.org/10.1177/109861102129197995.

Violanti, John M., ed. *Dying for the Job: Police Work Exposure and Health*. Springfield, IL: Charles C. Thomas, 2014.

———. *Police Retirement: The Impact of Change*. Springfield, IL: Charles C. Thomas, 1992.

———. *Police Suicide: Epidemic in Blue*. 2nd ed. Springfield, IL: Charles C. Thomas, 2007.

———. "Police Work May Be Hazardous to Your Health: An Examination of Harmful Physical Work Exposures." In *Dying for the Job: Police Work Exposure and Health*, edited by John M. Violanti, 3–20. Springfield, IL: Charles C. Thomas, 2014.

———. "Predictors of Police Suicide Ideation." *Suicide and Life-Threatening Behavior* 34, no. 3 (2004): 277–83. https://doi.org/10.1521/suli.34.3.277.42775.

Violanti, John M., Cecil M. Burchfiel, Tara A. Hartley, Anna Mnatsakanova, Desta Fekedulegn, Michael E. Andrew, Luenda E. Charles, and Bryan J. Vila. "Atypical Work Hours and Metabolic Syndrome among Police Officers." *Archives of Environmental and Occupational Health* 64, no. 3 (2009): 194–201. https://doi.org/10.1080/19338240903241259.

Violanti, John M., Claudia C. Ma, Ja K. Gu, Desta Fekedulegn, Anna Mnatsakanova, and Michael E. Andrew. "Social Avoidance in Policing: Associations with Cardiovascular Disease and the Role of Social Support." *Policing: An International Journal* 41, no. 5 (2018): 539–49. https://doi.org/10.1108/PIJPSM-02–2017–0017.

Violent Crime Control and Law Enforcement Act of 1994, Pub. L. No. 10–322, 42 U.S.C. § 14142 (1994).

Vold, George B. *Theoretical Criminology*. New York: Oxford University Press, 1958.

Vold, George, Thomas J. Bernard, and Jeffrey B. Snipes. *Theoretical Criminology*. 5th ed. New York: Oxford University Press, 2002.

Walker, Samuel, Geoffrey P. Alpert, and Dennis J. Kenney. *Early Warning Systems: Responding to the Problem Police Officer*. Washington, DC: US Department of Justice, Office of Justice Programs, National Institute of Justice, 2001.

Walker, Samuel, and Dawn Irlbeck. *Driving While Female: A National Problem in Police Misconduct*. Omaha: University of Nebraska at Omaha, Department of Criminal Justice, Police Professionalism Initiative, 2002. http://samuelwalker.net/wp-content/uploads/2010/06/dwf2002.pdf.

———. *Police Sexual Abuse of Teenage Girls: A 2003 Update on Driving While Female*. Omaha: University of Nebraska at Omaha, Department of Criminal Justice, Police Professionalism Initiative, 2003. http://samuelwalker.net/wp-content/uploads/2010/06/dwf2003.pdf.

Web staff. "Schenectady Police Officer Charged with Criminal Mischief." *Capital-News9.com*, January 12, 2009.

Weisburd, David. *Place Matters: Criminology for the Twenty-First Century.* New York: Cambridge University Press, 2016.

Weiss, William U., Peter A. Weiss, Scharee Cain, and Brittney Manley. "Impression Management in Police Officer Candidacy on the MMPI-2." *Journal of Police and Criminal Psychology* 24, no. 2 (2009): 120–25. https://doi.org/10.1007/s11896-009-9044-0.

WESH.com. "Cop Accused of Having Sex with Prostitute in Patrol Car Pleads Guilty." February 15, 2013.

Westley, William A. "Secrecy and the Police." *Social Forces* 34, no. 3 (1956): 254–57. https://doi.org/10.2307/2574048.

———. *Violence and the Police: A Sociological Study of Law, Custom, and Morality.* Cambridge, MA: MIT Press, 1970.

White, Chris. "Former Schenectady Officer Charged Again." *CBS6Albany.com,* June 12, 2010.

White, Michael D., and Robert J. Kane. "Pathways to Career-Ending Police Misconduct: An Examination of Patterns, Timing, and Organizational Responses to Officer Malfeasance in the NYPD." *Criminal Justice and Behavior* 40, no. 11 (2013): 1301–25. https://doi.org/10.1177/0093854813486269.

White, Michael D., and Justin Ready. "Examining Fatal and Nonfatal Incidents Involving the TASER: Identifying Predictors of Suspect Death Reported in the Media." *Criminology and Public Policy* 8, no. 4 (2009): 865–91. https://doi.org/10.1111/j.1745-9133.2009.00600.x.

Whren v. United States, 517 U.S. 806 (1996).

Wickersham Commission. *United States National Committee on Law Observance and Enforcement: Report on the Police.* Washington, DC: US Government Printing Office, 1931.

Williams, Franklin P., III, and Marilyn McShane. *Criminological Theory.* 4th ed. Upper Saddle River, NJ: Pearson Education, 2004.

Wilson, James Q. *Varieties of Police Behavior: The Management of Law and Order in Eight Communities.* Cambridge, MA: Harvard University Press, 1978.

Wilson, James Q., and George L. Kelling. "The Police and Neighborhood Safety: Broken Windows." *Atlantic Monthly,* March 1982, 29–38.

Wilson, Scott. "California Considers Nation's Strictest Police Use-of-Force Standard after Stephon Clark Shooting." *Washington Post.* April 2, 2019.

Wilson, William Julius. *The Truly Disadvantaged: The Inner City, the Underclass, and Public Policy.* 2nd ed. Chicago: University of Chicago Press, 2012.

Wootson, Cleve R. "Officer Charged with Assaulting Softball Coach." *Charlotte Observer,* April 21, 2009.

Worden, Robert E., and Sarah J. McLean. *Mirage of Police Reform: Procedural Justice and Police Legitimacy.* Oakland: University of California Press, 2017.

Zandbergen, Paul A., and Timothy C. Hart. "Geocoding Accuracy Considerations in Determining Residency Restrictions for Sex Offenders." *Criminal Justice Policy Review* 20, no. 1 (2009): 62–90. https://doi.org/10.1177/0887403408323690.

Zavala, Egbert, and Don L. Kurtz. "Using Gottfredson and Hirschi's General Theory of Crime to Explain Problematic Alcohol Consumption by Police Officers: A Test of Self-Control as Self-Regulation." *Journal of Drug Issues* 47, no. 3 (2017): 505–22. https://doi.org/10.1177/0022042617706893.

Zgoba, Kristen M., Jill Levenson, and Tracy McKee. "Examining the Impact of Sex Offender Residence Restrictions on Housing Availability." *Criminal Justice Policy Review* 20, no. 1 (2009): 91–110. https://doi.org/10.1177/0887403408322119.

Zhao, Jihong, Quint Thurman, and Ni He. "Sources of Job Satisfaction among Police Officers: A Test of Demographic and Work Environment Models." *Justice Quarterly* 16, no. 1 (1999): 153–73. https://doi.org/10.1080/07418829900094091.

Zimbardo, Philip. "Diary of a Vandalized Car." *Time*, February 28, 1969, 68.

Zimring, Franklin E. *Perspectives on Deterrence*. Crime and Delinquency Issues: A Monograph Series. Chevy Chase, MD: US Department of Health, Education, and Welfare, National Institutes of Health, National Institute of Mental Health, Center for Studies of Crime and Delinquency, 1971.

———. *When Police Kill*. Cambridge, MA: Harvard University Press, 2017.

Zimring, Franklin E., and Gordon J. Hawkins. *Deterrence: The Legal Threat in Crime Control*. Chicago: University of Chicago Press, 1973.

INDEX

homophobia, 105
Horan, Michael, 4
hostile environment, 127
hot spots, 42, 46–47
Houston, Texas, 29
Huck, Jennifer, 46
Hudson, Ohio, 5
human ecology, 45, 73
Human Rights Watch, 29–30
Hylton, Roberto, 4

imitation, 93
immigration, 74, 128; illegal, 110
immunity, 26, 53, 152n13
independent commissions, 25–26, 28, 30, 33
Indianapolis, Indiana, 29, 32
indirect experience, 40
Industrial Revolution, 97
inner containment, 98
innocence, 80, 106
institutional racism, 114, 120–22
integrated theory, 130
internal affairs, 17–18, 65, 85
International Association of Chiefs of Police, 96
interventions, 42, 48–49, 126
intoxication, 5–6
Irlbeck, Dawn, 11, 57

Jackson, Susan, 72
jaundiced viewpoint, 106
Jolicoeur, Jason, 88
Judson, Crystal, 9
juries, 14, 51
justice: obstruction of, 5; procedural, 51, 126–27; restorative, 114, 117, 124–25; street, 19, 28, 78–81; vigilante, 27; without trial, 78
justifications, 102, 105
juveniles, 74, 101, 136. See also delinquency

Kahneman, Daniel, 44
Kane, Robert: New York City, 32–33, 36, 47; rotten apple theory, 65; social disorganization, 74–75; social process theories, 89, 94–96, 101
Kappeler, Victor, 102–3, 106, 108

Keith, Toby, 6
Kelling, George, 41
Key, V.O., 75
kidnapping, 57
Kindy, Kimberly, 31
King, Rodney, 25, 29, 81, 114, 128
Klinger, David, 36, 46, 75
Klockars, Carl, 78
Knapp Commission, 26, 65
Ku Klux Klan, 53
Kurtz, Don, 88

labeling, 130
labor strikes, 41
larceny, 54, 101–2
late-stage police crime, 140–41
Latinos, 75, 110, 122
Laub, John, 100, 136–39
law and social control, definition, 89
lawsuits, 23, 53, 88, 109
lead exposure, 85
legal guilt, 80, 108, 111
legitimacy, 75, 78, 113–14, 125–27
leniency, 89
Levinson, Daniel, 66
Lewis, Howard, 7
Lewis, John, 4, 64–65
Lexow Commission, 26
LGBTQ+, 105
Liederbach, John, 36, 69, 79, 140–41
life-course criminology, 130, 133, 139–42
life-course persistent theory, 133
lifestyle, 19, 39, 44, 54–56
litigation, 23, 53, 88, 109
Loeb, Christopher, 8
Los Angeles, 25, 29, 81, 114
loyalty, 102, 110
Lundman, Richard, 59
lying, 4, 12, 76, 110–12, 152n13

Magielski, Kenneth, 6
Maguire, Edward, 34
Manheim Township, Pennsylvania, 10
manslaughter: deadly force, 23–24; Ferguson, 30; on-duty shootings, 15, 18, 31, 51, 63, 123; race, 123–24
Marcus Hook, Pennsylvania, 7
Maricopa County, Arizona, 109–110

theories, 91–93; life, 74, 90; media, 12, 129; pathways, 137; process theories, 73, 91, 92–97

socialization, 59, 75–77, 91, 97, 99

sodomy, 10, 57

South Carolina, 50, 52, 81, 108, 129

sporting events, 5–7

spouses, 79, 139

Spraitz, Jason, 46

Stafford, Mark, 40

stalking, 1–2, 4–5, 7

state crimes, 118

Steele, Gary, 12-13

Stefancic, Jean, 119

St. Elizabeth's Hospital, 96

Stokols, Daniel, 35

stop-and-frisk, 87, 121–22

St. Petersburg, Florida, 32

Stradley, William, 7

strain theories: general strain theory, 81–83; strain in policing, 83–88; strain research, 88–89

strangers, 90

street encounters: police misconduct, 14, 18, 21–22, 28, 33; race, 120–22; stop-and-frisk, 87; street justice, 19, 28, 78–81

stress: aggression theory, 68; policing, 69–72; preemployment screening, 63; strain theory, 82, 84–87; strain research, 88; Tasers, 104

stun guns, 3, 52, 56, 78–80, 103–4

subculture: aggression, 68; code of secrecy, 91; cynicism, 67; differential association, 94–95; neutralization, 102–4, 110; falsification, 111, 113; misconduct, 2, 3, 28; psychological aspects, 59; racism, 120–22; social learning, 96–97; social structure theory, 75–78; street justice, 78; strain, 83, 89; Tasers, 80; us-versus-them mentality, 118, 127

Suffolk County, New York, 8

Sun, Ivan, 69

Supreme Court, 9, 15, 18, 23, 53, 119, 121

suspensions, 5, 12, 60, 64. See also disciplinary sanctions

Sutherland, Edwin, 92–93, 101

Swatt, Marc, 88

Sykes, Gary, 78

Sykes, Gresham, 101, 103–6, 110

symbolic interaction, 92–93

Systematic Social Observation (SSO) methods, 31

tachograph, 49–50

Tacoma, Washington, 62

Talking Points Memo, 30

Taser, 3, 52, 56, 78–80, 103–4

Taylor, James, 5

techniques of neutralization, 101–110. See also neutralization

technological advancements, 128

television, 81, 87, 117

Tennessee v. Garner, 23–24

termination, 4, 15, 60–61

Terry, John, 121

Terry v. Ohio, 121

testilying, 14, 112

third degree tactics, 128

Tittle, Charles, 40, 130–32

Toch, Hans, 83–84

Toledo, Ohio, 60

tolerance, 27, 33, 84, 98, 112

traffic stops, 10–11, 50, 57, 71, 86, 110, 129

training: academy, 59, 67, 76–77, 84, 104, 127; interventions, 49; lack of downtime, 70; police corruption, 1; social process theories, 99; SSO methods, 31; Taser, 80, 103–4

trajectories, 100, 133, 137–38, 141

transgender persons, 105

transitions, 100, 133, 137, 139–41

transparency, 51

Trump, Donald, 110

trust, 51, 125, 127

turning points, 100, 133, 137–39, 141

Tyler, Tom, 125

Uchida, Craig, 34

University of Chicago, 73–74

US Commission on Civil Rights, 29, 48

US Department of Justice, 25, 33–34, 42, 49, 105, 129

US Supreme Court, 9, 15, 18, 23, 53, 119, 121

us-versus-them mentality, 76, 91, 118, 126–27

vandalism, 6, 41
Van Maanen, John, 76–78
vehicle tracking devices, 50
victimization, 39, 42, 54–55, 104, 122, 132
video recordings, 14, 25, 51, 81, 112–14
vigilante justice, 27
Violanti, John, 126, 140
vocational activities, 55
Vold, George, 116
Vollmer, August, 75
vulnerability, 10–11, 58, 68, 105, 122

Walker, Robert, 5
Walker, Samuel, 11, 57
walkie-talkies, 128
Wall Street Journal, 12
war model, 128
war on drugs, 122, 128
Warr, Mark, 40
warrior mentality, 127

Washington, DC, 16, 29–30, 32, 36, 70, 86, 89, 96, 105, 109, 117, 123.
Washington Post, 4, 31, 123
Weisburd, David, 46
Westley, William, 21, 75, 78
whistleblower lawsuit, 87
white-collar crime, 63
White, Michael, 33, 35, 65, 89, 94, 101, 117
Whren v. United States, 121
Wickersham Commission, 75
Wilmington, Delaware, 60
Wilson, Darren, 31
Wilson, James, 41
women of color, 10, 105, 122
Worden, Robert, 126
World War II, 101, 138
Wright, Claudia, 12

Zavala, Egbert, 88–89
Zeamer, Dave, 1
Zimbardo, Philip, 41–42

Founded in 1893,
UNIVERSITY OF CALIFORNIA PRESS
publishes bold, progressive books and journals
on topics in the arts, humanities, social sciences,
and natural sciences—with a focus on social
justice issues—that inspire thought and action
among readers worldwide.

The UC PRESS FOUNDATION
raises funds to uphold the press's vital role
as an independent, nonprofit publisher, and
receives philanthropic support from a wide
range of individuals and institutions—and from
committed readers like you. To learn more, visit
ucpress.edu/supportus.